Enjoy ~
Happy heart healthy cooking,
Olive you!
Gemma S. Sciabica

Table of Contents

2003 2nd Printing Revised
Copyright© 1998 by Gemma Sanita Sciabica
2150 Yosemite Blvd., Modesto, CA 95354

Well here I go again with the continuation of Dolci and Biscotti book.

One of the last things I thought I would do is put out a book of recipes. And now am doing so once again.

By popular demand I put these recipes for cooking together.

The reason for the Dolci and Biscotti book was to have it be known how good olive oil is in baking cakes, cookies, pie crusts, etc. (sweets).

Many liked the book but kept saying they would like one with cooking recipes also.

I was pleased I got the biscotti recipes out for everyone, especially the children. It is healthy to give them cookies without animal fat.

Using a small amount of olive oil makes them much lower in calories and cholesterol too, if you use only egg whites.

We talked to many people who said they do not cook; either they don't like to or they work out and do not have the time.

It doesn't take too much time or work to have a balanced diet for one's dear family. The following are a few fast and easy meals.

Salad greens in the markets are washed, chopped and bagged, ready to go. Just add a tomato, avocado, olive oil, lemon juice or vinegar, toss gently. Don't forget olives!

Pasta is another thing that is easy and fast. Just saute frozen mixed vegetables in a little olive oil until crisp tender, season. Spoon over cooked pasta, a sprinkle of Romano cheese grated or Gorganzola cheese crumbled and there you go.

Drizzle a little olive oil on toast, delicious! If you like, add a slice of roast beef (from deli) ham, cheese, canned water packed tuna, sardines, slice of tomato, avocado, pickles etc., yum.

Scrub potato, place in microwave, cook 5 to 10 minutes (depending on size) until tender. Cut in half lengthwise, drizzle with olive oil, sprinkle with Romano cheese and pepper, great!

Top a 10 or 12 inch store bought ready baked pizza dough crust with mozzarella, provolone, sliced tomatoes and/or onions, basil leaves, oregano, pepper or any topping desired. Drizzle with olive oil. Bake in a 375 degrees oven for about 15 minutes or until bubbly.

For dessert: In this country we are blessed with beautiful fresh fruits all year round. They are easy to prepare and take a little time and work. Serve with angel food cake and vanilla frozen yogurt (low fat). Happy healthy eating!

Dedication

Once again I would like to dedicate this book to Joseph's and my parents.

Our Moms were so loving, caring, unselfish and always ready to put everyone else in the family first.

At meal time they were always last to sit at the table and first to get up.

Never complaining about cooking, cleaning, baby sitting, etc. Always soft spoken.

Made everything by hand, never had the conveniences of our modern kitchens.

Our fathers were also special. No matter how hard they worked for the family, they always had a sense of humor.

Had a garden every summer so the family always enjoyed fresh fruits and vegetables.

Never would they start their meal unless the whole family was at the table together.

Growing up in those days we had no radio, television or any other entertainment to speak of, thus quiet days without excitement or tension.

They really were beautiful, sweet days, though we didn't realize it at the time.

Many of these recipes are nostalgic, beautiful memories of the past, mingling and reaching out to the future.

Hope you will find in these pages a special recipe that will become a family favorite.

Happy cooking!

Gemma

Awards from:

California State Fair and Exposition - 1959 - 1960 - 1961
Chefs in America - 8 Gold Medals.
Chefs in America - 2 Gold Medals for Best of Show.
American Tasting Institute - 6 Gold Medals.
American Tasting Institute - 1 Gold Medal for Best of Show.
Los Angeles County Fair - 1 Gold Medal - 2000
Los Angeles County Fair - 1 Gold Medal for Best of Class - 2000
Los Angeles County Fair - 1 Bronze Medal - 2000
Los Angeles County Fair - 3 Gold Medals - 2001
Los Angeles County Fair - 1 Gold Medal for Best of Show - 2001
Los Angeles County Fair - 2 Gold Medals - 2002
American Tasting Institute Award of Excellence - 2002
for Manzanillo, Sevillano and Basil Olive Oil

First COOC Pioneer Award 1999 for
Joseph Sciabica of Nick Sciabica and Sons

Los Angeles County Fair 2003
Gold Medal - For Jalapeño
Best of Show
Best of Class
Silver Medal For Sciabica's Arbequina
Silver Medal For Sciabica's Garlic Olive Oil
Bronze Medal for Sciabica's Fall Harvest Sevillano

The following is an excerpt from an article in the April 30, 1997 issue of Wine Spectator: In November 1995, at the World Olive Oil Day competition in Lucca, Italy, California-made Sciabica Sevillano Fall Harvest Olive Oil received scores of 7.5 and 7 (no oil got the high score of 8) from two of Italy's most prominent tasters. Perhaps more importantly, one judge asked if he could take the Sciabica home.

I want to thank...

Joseph, my best cheerleader for his enormous help and continual support of this project even when I wanted to throw in the towel.

A debt of gratitude to Angie Bugarin who is so very talented and a joy to work with. She has been so patient with all the changes, retyping many recipes. Could not have done this book without her invaluable help.

Proofreading, Terese Marie Sciabica, my daughter-in-law. We had a good time going through the recipes and getting hungry.

My daughter-in-law Genevieve and my granddaughter Christa, for their fantastic sales of the Dolci book.

Nicholas and Daniel for their interest and good ideas, taking time from their very busy schedules.

In appreciation once again to Frank Parks, Mike Nielsen and all the staff of Parks Printing and Lithography of Modesto for their expertise.

Special recognition to all who shared their recipes.

Food photographs by Angie Bugarin.

Andrea Wallace who helped market our books and typing the new recipes.

Diane Bostwick who is so kind, dependable and for proof reading this second printing.

"First" magazine for women for permission to reprint health benefits of food.

4

California Olive Oil History

The olive tree, cultivated in Phoenicia, Syria and Palestine around 3,000 B.C., was brought to southern France, Italy and Sardinia by the Greeks. The Romans are credited with bringing the tree from Africa, where it grew before their arrival, then extending the olive tree's cultivation throughout their empire.

In the 16th century the Spanish brought the olive into south America and in the early 1700s Spanish Jesuits brought the olive into Mexico and Baja California as they established their missions. In 1769 Franciscan padres, under the leadership of Father Junipero Serra, journeyed north into present-day California and established Mission San Diego de Alcala.

Within two decades olive trees were flourishing at the Mission. As the Franciscans Continued to establish new missions to the north, olives were planted at each of them. It was at these missions that today's Mission Variety Olive was developed. Although its origins are from Spain this olive developed differently in the New World and became a unique cultivar and variety unto its own.

The first organized production of oil from California olives is documented to have taken place on February 21, 1803 at Mission San Diego de Alcala. The olives, after being crushed, were placed in cloth bags which were stacked in a wooden press. The olive mash was then compressed cold by hand. Although heating it would have led to the extraction of more oil from the crushed olives, such oil would have been of inferior quality. The completely natural method of cold pressing the olives supplied the California missions with an excellent oil, used in all aspects of mission life.

"Early explorers, such as George Vancouver in 1792 and Edwin Bryant and John Fremont in 1846, wrote of seeing olive trees in California. Bryant noticed olives trees growing at Mission San Luis Obispo, and Fremont wrote that olives and other fruits grew luxuriantly together in spring-fed valley gardens among the hills south of San Diego.

In 1834, secularization of the missions led to the decline of most of the mission orchards and gardens. Olives in the mission orchards survived neglect, drought and browsing cattle for several decades until early American pioneers between 1855 and 1875 began to propagate new trees using cuttings from the old mission orchards.

Statistics from the California State Agricultural Society indicate that by 1855, 503 olive trees were growing in the state. A renewed interest in olive oil production led to significant expansion of the industry between 1870 and 1890. In 1872, Frank and Warren Kimball secured olive cuttings from among the 347 trees remaining at Mission San Diego de Alcala and planted an orchard at their ranch in national City in San Diego County. Ellwood Cooper of Santa Barbara planted six olive orchards in different locations, the first near Goleta in 1870. Edward E. Goodrich had an 80

Continued next page

5

acre orchard at his El Quito ranch near Los Gatos in Santa Clara County. All these early pioneers were involved in the production of olive oil. Aside from the early efforts in the missions, the first commercially produced olive oil in California probably came from the Camulos oil mill established in 1871 in Ventura County.

Between 1850 and 1900, numerous olive cultivars from Mediterranean countries were introduced in California, primarily for the purpose of improving oil production. The cultivars other than Mission that are important in the contemporary olive industry were all introduced into California during the boom period between 1875 and 1900.

By 1885, California growers had learned to produce olive oil equal to the best imported oil. With this success in oil production, the number of trees planted in the state went from 5,603 in 1876 to 539,568 in 1901. Though the heavy increase in production that followed led to lower prices, growers found that they could not compete with the less expensive European olive oil."[1]

Quality therefore became the emphasis for growth of the industry in the state rather than price.

Today the crop (all varieties) averages between 100,000 and 150,000 tons per year with as much as 15,000 to 20,000 tons being produced into olive oil. In addition to the Mission Variety, which is still widely planted, California has a wonderful selection of additional varieties all producing world-class olive oils. Among them are the Manzanillo Variety, Sevillano Variety, Picholine Variety, Nevadillo Variety, Ascolano Variety, Barouni Variety and the Lucque Variety.

Although Europe and the rest of the olive producing countries classify their olive oils by region in California we have fine-tuned olive oil production to its separation by variety. All of the established California varieties produce delicious Extra Virgin olive oils. One can experience a wide range of flavor and aroma profiles with California Extra Virgin Olive Oils. These wonderful olive oils can be easily used in every area of food preparation.

In the following recipes we have chosen to use our Marsala Brand 100% Extra Virgin California Olive Oil. We call Marsala Olive Fruit Oil because it is the oil of a fruit and not that of a vegetable. It is very high in mono-unsaturated fats and has no cholesterol. Marsala Olive Fruit Oil is a varietal combination of medium intensity with great versatility which our family has been producing since 1936. Other varietals, which our family produces under the Sciabica Brand, can be substituted in many of the recipes and we encourage you to enjoy using all of them in good health!

Nick Sciabica & Sons

---

[1] Louise Ferguson, G. Steven Sibbett, and George C. Martin.
1994. Olive Production Manual. University of California,
Division of Agriculture and Natural Resources, Oakland, CA.

Daniel, Grandson Jonathan and Joseph at Carnegie Hall in New York City. 1992 was the first year of three they were invited there to receive a gold medal for Nick Sciabica and Sons olive oil.

Source of health benefits from

First

(magazine for women)

Researchers at the University of Illinois in Chicago have identified more than 30 disease-preventing substances in **basil**.

Several studies have proven that **garlic** fights off both viral and bacterial infections. And adding garlic to your daily diet may also help lower "bad" LDL cholesterol levels, and helps prevent blood clots.

Almonds, like most nuts are seeds, are rich in vitamin E, an antioxidant that may prevent heart disease. Nuts are also good sources of fiber, which lowers cholesterol.

Lemons are very rich in limonene, a type of phytochemical that researchers believe stimulates the immune system. Lemon peel - as opposed to juice - contains the highest concentration of limonene.

Olive oil is one of the healthiest oils you can use because it contains mostly mono-unsaturated fat which won't clog arteries and may even help reduce cholesterol. Oil is needed for healthy hair, nails, skin and energy; it contains vitamin E.

Broccoli is one of the richest sources of three disease fighting phytochemicals: indoles, monoterpenes and sulforaphane.

Tomatoes are rich in lycopene, a potent disease fighter. To get the most lycopene from tomatoes, it's necessary to cook them. Even a 3 minute sauté makes more of this compound available.

Cocoa contains phenylethylamine, which helps boost serotonin, the brain's "feel good" chemical.

Oranges are full of folic acid (17% of the RDA), a B vitamin that may help prevent heart disease.

In a recent study, **blueberries** beat 30 other fruits and veggies for the highest antioxidant capacity.

Rhubarb is packed with potassium, which stabilizes blood pressure.

Broccoli sprouts offer a consistently high percentage of sulforaphane which studies continue to suggest may prevent diseases.

For high blood sugar, sprinkle **cinnamon** in your food. It can triple insulin activity for more efficient processing of sugars.

Just 3 **apricots** provide 65% of the RDA for vitamin A, a valuable nutrient for eyes, skin and healthy teeth.

Consuming hot spices like ground **ginger** and **cayenne pepper** can help soothe indigestion, say researchers.

Continued next page

Scientists have identified a compound in **onions**, sulforaphane, that lowers the risk of many diseases'.

Salmon contains beneficial omega-3 fatty acids, which are known to cut the risk of heart disease.

A serving of **beets** provides 52% of the RDA for folic acid, a B vitamin.

Parsley is rich in beta carotene and vitamin C.

Green and wax beans are both high in fiber, which can help lower cholesterol and prevent digestive disorders.

Spinach is an impressive source of vitamin A, which the body converts into the disease fighting compound beta carotene.

One cup of **beans** supplies 25% of the RDA of iron. To increase absorption of this fatigue fighting mineral, eat beans with foods containing vitamin C, such as red and green peppers and tomatoes.

Cherries contain potassium which can help to maintain normal blood pressure.

Eggs are high in protein, which is a primary component of muscles, hair, nails, skin, eyes and internal organs - especially the heart and brain.

Dried fruits are rich in antioxidants. They're also a great source of fatigue fighting iron.

Figs are rich in bone-building calcium. In fact dried figs contain 17% more calcium than skim milk.

California **avocados** contain appreciable amounts of 11 vitamins, 14 basic minerals and emulsified, easily digested fruit oils which are largely unsaturated.

Red **peppers** are a great source of vitamin C which boosts iron absorption.

Sweet potatoes and other orange fruits and veggies, like cantaloupe and carrots, contain beta-carotene, which helps lower cholesterol.

By eating **cod**, you can get more omega-3 fatty acids than from eating most other species of fish.

A medium **apple** supplies 17% of your daily requirement of fiber, most of it from pectin, which is very effective in lowering cholesterol.

If you are following a low cholesterol diet, include lean **pork**; it can help keep cholesterol levels low as effectively as lean poultry.

Potatoes are rich in potassium, a mineral that's instrumental in keeping blood pressure stable.

Beta-carotene, abundant in **carrots** help reduce risk of heart disease.

Raspberries and <u>most</u> other berries contain ellagic acid, a chemical which studies show can help prevent diseases.

Reprinted by permission.

Chit Chat

Many have told me they liked the little stories in the Dolci book. The following are a few of my memories and reflections around the table.

I have tried to include recipes that are easy, quick and flavorful, always trying to include fresh fruits and vegetables for daily diets.

The reason I chose to have a spiral bound book is because the pages lie flat. It is difficult to read recipes when the pages start flipping.

When I was little, I disliked helping to cook but Mom insisted I did. She would say "Learn, because when you marry you will be glad you know how." I answered, "I'm not going to marry an Italian." Well, not only did I marry an Italian but he is even more so than my parents were. He loves everything Italian, especially meals. Now I am so glad I learned what Mom taught me. I am the happiest when the children and grandchildren have a balanced diet.

We have a relative who loves lentils so much that one day he said, "If Louise leaves, who is going to make me my lentils and pasta?" We were all amused.

During the summer, growing up we would look forward to go gather wild mushrooms and blueberries with my Dad in the woods, a short way from our home. The flavors were special. Mom made pies and muffins with the blueberries. My brother would run to the store for vanilla ice cream; that is a favorite way he likes wild blueberries served.

Many years ago, like many children of immigrant parents, we were raised on homemade bread. Whenever we had store bought sliced bread, we thought it was cake.

A teacher asked a little neighbor boy, "Sammy, you look nice and healthy with your rosy cheeks; what kind of cereal do you have for breakfast?" He answered, "A chunk of bread in a bowl of milk."

A relative said when she moved, she tossed out all her recipe books because they were outdated, containing too much animal fat. I told her all she may have done is substituted (in many recipes) olive oil, sometimes half or one fourth of what the recipe calls for.

A recipe is a guide, may be changed to your liking. I, whenever possible, use fresh fruits and vegetables, without drowning them in sauces made with animal fat.

I very seldom deep fry food. The few things I do are around the Christmas holidays, like Cannoli Shells, Sicilian Sfinghi and a couple of other foods.

Continued next page

We call our olive oil, fruit oil, because olives are a fruit. The recipes in this book have ingredients that are easy to find. Feel free to use truffles or any exotic ingredient desired; they will all go very well with Marsala or Sciabica olive oil.

It's sad that cooking and eating at home is fast fading from our lives.

A Mom or Dad may give their family good nutrition of a priceless gift of serving a well balanced meal. Dinner is one of the happiest times the family has together.

After many years of cooking or baking sometimes I still have a recipe that doesn't come out the way I expected (a flop). Do not get discouraged if that happens, just try again.

I like aluminum foil (Reynolds release) to line cookie sheets. I could hardly believe how quick the cookies were removed from the foil without greasing it.

Olive oil has been used for over 3000 years.

It takes approximately 5000 olives for 2 quarts of olive oil.

A chef on a TV show put a whole chicken on a rack in a roasting pan. I said to myself "good all the fat will drain off the chicken".

But then he placed the cooked chicken onto a serving platter and poured all the drippings of animal fat over it. Not only that, he added more fat to "thicken the sauce", he said.

Cooking at home one may control the amount of grease, salt and sugar found in many processed foods, that are **higher than necessary**.

I use little or no salt in most foods when I cook. When making pasta with gravy I omit the salt in the hand made pasta. I omit the salt in the water when cooking pasta and no salt in the gravy.

When I make meatballs I do not use salt because the cheese I use has enough salt to flavor them.

When serving pasta with gravy we each sprinkle a little Ramono grated cheese over it. We do not miss all the extra salt otherwise.

For many years Joseph went east to sell olive oil and carloads of grapes that they grew in California. The boys and I would go also.

I had my Mom, Dad and family there, so it was a nice few months of visiting.

We would go by car, train or plane. Going by car I remember how after so many days on the road to Connecticut, I couldn't wait to have Mom's home made chicken soup with hand made noodles.

The food on the way had all the same flavor, loaded with grease and salt.

Then coming back to California I couldn't wait to have a dish of "minestra" greens, any kind that Joseph's Mom made. She steamed them with olive oil and garlic. What a treat!

Continued next page

There really isn't very much that is new in cooking. It is the combination of fresh and flavorful ingredients and the way dishes are presented.

We have a friend that when her husband comes home from work, looks at what she is cooking for supper. When she sees him reaching for a banana, she knows instantly that he does not care too much for what she is going to serve for that evening.

After cooking pasta I drained it and placed it in a serving bowl. I usually sprinkle it with black pepper before I spoon on the pesto sauce. Well instead of shaking the pepper on, I unscrewed the top of the bottle and shook the whole thing on the pasta. It was a good thing the company was in the living room. I panicked, but right away I washed it off and continued with the fixings. While having supper I could taste the strong flavor of the pepper. No one said anything so it was a disaster averted!

Serving pizza to company one day our friend said he hadn't had pizza like it since he left Italy. He said what he has been having tasted like crackers with ketchup on it.

We had a relative who only used her china dishes when she had company. I say, "Who is better company than your own family?"

A recipe that isn't shared with others will soon be forgotten, but when it's shared, it will be enjoyed by future generations.

I always try to turn "ho hum" foods into dishes with different ingredients — like adding a handful of dried cherries into baked beans — cinnamon or honey to taste into coleslaw — 1 tablespoon cocoa or poppy seeds to stews, etc.

Joseph met a customer who has the Dolci book. He told Joseph, "Oh I am so happy I can have desserts again, especially apple pie, being the crust is made without animal fat."

Extra virgin olive oil, like every food is always best when used fresh.

Cooking can be fun. It is even more fun when you know you are cooking well balanced meals for your loved ones.

Enjoy what you are doing, happy healthy cooking and baking!

Notes

Many times I try to use one herb at a time, so one herb does not clash with another.

I usually use unbleached flour.

To keep peeled potatoes from browning, cover with cold water until ready to use.

To whip cream quickly, add a drop or two of lemon juice and chill before whipping.

To remove bones from fish fillets use a small plier or tweezer.

A cake is done when it shrinks slightly from sides of pan, springs back when lightly pressed in center with finger or when cake tester comes out clean from center of cake.

To toast coconut, spread thinly in shallow baking pan. Place in a 350 degrees oven for about 10 minutes, until light golden brown. Stir often to toast evenly.

It is helpful to have an instant read thermometer, especially to check meat.

When using dried mushrooms, soak in warm water for about 30 minutes. Lift out with slotted spoon, any dirt will remain.

When recipes call for mushrooms, olives or nuts, use whatever variety desired.

Before starting to put a recipe together it is important to wash fruits and vegetables thoroughly. Including melons such as cantaloupe, watermelon, honeydew, etc., to avoid debris entering fruit as it is cut.

A good idea is to keep 2 little brushes by the sink, one to scrub fruits and vegetables and the other to scrub hands and nails, especially when curling cavatelli.

Check canned pitted cherries, prunes or olives before serving for any pit left behind.

Olives, olive oil, avocados and nuts are all good sources of mono-unsaturated fats - the "right type of fat".

Ovens bake differently, watch carefully, check before given time when cooking or baking.

To get the most flavor from fresh herbs add to food last few minutes of cooking

Olives are a fruit.

Continued next page

When cooking it is best to taste, taste, and taste.

When recipes call for pasta or macaroni, use any shape or variety desired, such as spinach, whole wheat, multi colored, store bought or hand made, etc.

For an herb brush, tie stem ends of several sprigs of rosemary, basil, sage, mint or thyme together. Dip in a bowl of olive oil and minced garlic; brush over meats and vegetables while grilling or baking.

Turkey, chickens, cornish hens (poultry) must be washed thoroughly to avoid salmonella. Wash with cold water, drain well, pat dry with paper towels.

Keep raw meat and poultry separated from other foods. Wash working surface (including cutting boards) utensils and hands after touching raw meat or poultry.

Excess moisture dilutes the salad dressing. To dry washed greens, place on a clean towel and gently pat dry. Or use a salad spinner; it is easier, quicker and thorough.

Toss salads with dressing just before serving; use only enough to lightly coat the leaves.

If honey has crystallized, place jar in a pan of simmering water, and stir occasionally until crystals dissolve.

To prevent tearing, peel onions under cold running water.

When recipes call for vinegar, use whatever desired: red or white wine vinegar, balsamic, rice vinegar, apple cider vinegar, etc.

To keep juice from spilling out of a fruit pie, place a small metal funnel in center of top crust. Juice will bubble into funnel.

For creamy vegetable soups, puree soup in jar of blender, food processor or food mill. Soup may have to be pureed in batches.

To remove pomegranate seeds, peel and place in a large deep bowl of cold water. Gently separate seeds from pulp under water. Seeds will sink to the bottom. Remove pieces of pulp, drain.

To make taco seasoning mix, put 1/4 cup chili powder, 2 tablespoons oregano and 2 tablespoons ground cumin in a jar, mix. Keep in a covered container.

Nuts are easier to chop if warm. Heat in microwave on high for 1 or 2 minutes or in a 325 degrees oven for about 5 minutes.

When measuring honey or molasses, lightly oil measuring spoon

Continued next page

or cup before pouring honey in.

Five large California ripe olives actually contain only about 25 calories, 2 grams of fat and like all plant foods - no cholesterol at all.

Many times corrections are made in magazines, books, newspapers etc. For example: if a cake recipe states 1 cup salt, common sense tells us it may be 1 teaspoon salt.

Prepared meatballs may be frozen on waxed paper lined cookie sheet. When completely frozen, place in plastic freezer ziplock bags. Defrost as needed.

To make 12 to 16 – 2-inch chocolate mint leaves, melt 1/3 cup chocolate chips. With pastry brush, paint washed and dried fresh mint leaves with melted chocolate. Place on waxed paper lined tray in refrigerator until firm.

After all pickles have been used up, slice cucumbers in jar with remaining juice to marinate for a couple of days. Keep refrigerated.

To thicken soups, stir in 1/4 to 1/3 cup semolina; cook several more minutes.

For almond paste, combine 1-1/2 cups ground almonds, 1-1/2 cups confectioners' sugar, 2 egg whites, 1 teaspoon almond extract and 1/4 teaspoon salt in mixing bowl. Knead to make a stiff paste, store in covered container, refrigerate.

To retain the delicate flavor of fresh basil (my favorite herb) add just a few minutes before ending of cooking time.

To check if cookies are loaded with grease (animal fat) place several cookies on a brown paper bag overnight.

A meal may be made only with an array of appetizers. For company, when we first went into housekeeping, I would have a tray of antipasti (before the meal). Everyone would fill up on it and the main meal was always left over. Now I either serve antipasti or a regular meal.

For a full delicious flavor of olive oil, drizzle a little over prepared food in serving dish.

Add to any standard recipe, 1/2 to 1 cup glazed chestnuts, chopped, such as sweet breads, panettone or cookies.

Glazed chestnuts may be purchased from Italian speciality stores.

The following letters are a few that we have received. Thought of sharing the kind words that have been said about our olive oil and recipe books using it.

Dear Mrs. Sciabica, (Gemma),

After our wonderful afternoon in your home, I served sliced, fresh tomatoes with olive oil to my family for dinner! Thank you for allowing us, as strangers, to step into your day and talk about "olive oil."

Since that time, I have expounded on the attributes of olive oil for producing beautiful skin. I also have enjoyed your cook book and fins myself throwing out all butter and margarine. We love our time. We hope to repay your kindness someday.

Sincerely,

Elizabeth

E Mail from Connecticut

Hello from Connecticut,

This is Mario Jannetty's granddaughter who is a great friend of Joe's. I was just viewing the website and wanted to tell you how great it looks. I keep telling myself I will go out to Calif. to visit and see how this GREAT Olive Oil is created into such a master piece.

Love and Peace from Back in CT,

Kathleen Moran

Dear Mrs. Sciabica,

It is always a pleasure to hear from you. You and Mr. Sciabica have become very dear to us. Your friendship, your kindness and thoughtfulness make us feel good. It all began many yours ago (at least 30) when we first arrived in California and tried many brands of olive oil, the man at the grocery store seeing our dissatisfaction said: "I think I know which olive oil you will like", and he handed us a gallon of MARSALA extra virgin olive oil. It was so good that we wanted more and in larger quantities than one gallon at a time. We only use olive oil in all our cooking. So we got in touch with you, and ever since, your excellent oil has become indispensable to our cooking. I also eliminated using butter in baking. Your oil makes my cookies and cakes not only taste better, but much lighter and healthier for us.

We consume many gallons a year, and we make sure to tell our friends to do the same! We feel that we got a double bonus because through this delicious oil of yours, we met you and your husband.

I hope you are fine. We can't complain, except for all the gardening I have to do!

Sincerely,

Beatrice Tornabene

Dear Gemma,
& all the Sciabica's,

1st your *"Dolci & Biscotti"* is just a real **jewel** of a cook book!

I can barely wait to bake & share from it!

It tells a lot about you Gemma, you really love your family!

Just a few year's ago, I discovered California had other olive oils and I found yours – Wonderful – but not "Marsala", so I'm waiting to bake.

Please write books for your other brands (which I've just discovered).

How lovely for all your children to have this heritage!

Push it!

We need this & more families like yours in the good ol USA!

Thank You,
& May God Bless,

Joeleen Martin

Wonderful Book! Lovely Olive Oil!

Dear Mrs. Sciabica,

Your two recipe books, the Treasured Family Recipes and the Dolci and Biscotti Recipes books, are a very welcome addition to my kitchen. Reading cookbooks has long been an interest of mine, and yours I also cook from! I am especially fond of your pie and pastry recipes – and my husband is very appreciative, as well.

Although I grew up in a home where no week went by without home-made pies being served, as a middle-aged adult I had all but given up pie baking to cut down on unhealthy fats. However, I find your pastry crusts made with your light, buttery olive oil to be delicious and rejoice in the fact that olive oil is heart-healthy. Also, these recipes seem to be never-fail ones even for someone who had not made a pie crust for more than 10 years. Although my hands had long ago lost the skill for making a flakey pie crust, my palate never lost the ability to tell when too much flour or an inferior shortening had been used in a crust. I often leave pie crust on the plate when I eat pie in restaurants because of this. It is so lovely to be able to make a flakey, delicious pie crust using your recipes. I am deeply in your dept.

Thank you so much for writing these two books. I especially like the variations you suggest as I often use recipes as inspiration rather than as blueprints to be followed exactly, and your suggestions are a wonderful nudge for my own imagination. Last night I made a peach and nectarine free form pie following your Free Form Cherry Pie recipe, but having far too much ripe fruit for a single pie, used the single crust on the bottom of a deep dish, and put a crumb crust on top as you did in your Pear Tart recipe. Needless to say, my husband was delighted.

Sincerely,

Susan Bovee

Susan Bovee

Dear Gemma & Joseph,
Your cookbooks are a blessing in the Mazzo's house.

Happy Holidays,

Grace & Bill

Dear "Mom" Sciabica,

 With fondness I remember my Wednesday afternoon with you! Thank you so much for your gracious hospitality and the delightful lunch! I still talk about your pasta and pesto sauce! I **love** your cook book, I read through enjoying the little bits of information on favorite family recipes and about your parents, adds such a special touch to your cook book. I have marked about 20 recipes that I'd like for our Food Services to use very, very soon!!!

 Thank you for the lovely cook book, the green long crocheted "socks" and for your homemade biscottis!!! Your biscottis <u>are</u> the best!!! Far better than the ones sold at Starbucks!!! It was great spending my afternoon with you. Thank you.

Sister Jane

Dear Mrs. Sciabica,

 I talked with your fine husband about a month ago at the farmers market in Pleasanton, I bought some oil and recipe books. I was really impressed by the fact that there is no cholesterol in olive oil. Since I have been using the oils and trying to change my way of cooking. I grew up eating cream, butter and grease. And always thought that if it was good, it had to have at least 1 of the previous ingredients in it.

 My Father sat down in a chair and died when he was 45 years old. As also my husband's Father died at an early age. The cause of both of their deaths was cholesterol. Their diet was not the entire reason for the problem, but it was a huge factor. I am excited about the things that I am learning! I have been reading about nutrition and what sorts of foods are good and bad for you.

 Your husband really touched my heart in that he sort of reminded me of my Grandfather who has been dead about 2 years now. I guess it was the fact that he and his sons are working a company that was passed on to him by his Father. As was the same in my family.

 My Grandparents were just like my Parents. Also, how I knew that he believed everything that he told me that day. I just love older wiser people, we have so much to learn from them, or you. If we will just take the time to listen. I wished that I would have listened more to my Grandparents, because what I did listen to has taught me much.

 Also one more similarity that you have with my Grandparents is in looking at your picture, you look like you are about the same height as my Grandmother, and your husband looks like he is about the same height as my Grandfather. My Grandmother always said that dynamite came in small packages, and I know that she was right.

Thanks again,
Bonnie

E-mail sent to Gemma from Betty Wilson Wynne of the Dave Wilson Nursery:

Yesterday I bought Gemma Sanita Sciabica's 296 page, easy-opening heavy spiral cook book, signed and initialed by Joseph Nicholas Sciabica. I like the book so much that I gave copies of the book with olive oil gifts for Christmas and wedding presents to ensure healthful long life for my loved ones. Gemma S. Sciabica has given permission to print here a few recipes from her book and share some secrets of healthful long life.

Gemma Sanita Sciabica's new 2001 book **"Cooking with California Olive Oil, Popular Recipes"** is an inspiration and a joy to read. She even has a recipe for Fido Doggie Biscuits – lucky Fido!

On Gemma's dedication page of her new cookbook, "Dedication To Joseph (The Worker)," she wrote:

"We are a small family company producing extra virgin Olive Oil for over 65 years. Our Olive Oil is unrefined, so the natural flavor of the olive comes through. No chemicals or caustics are used.

"In the fall the olives are green, the oil has a little tang. It is like biting into a fresh olive right from the tree. As the olives get darker, the oil comes deep golden. Later in the season the olives are black, and the oil comes light golden.

"Olive Oil has no more calories per tablespoon than any other type of vegetable oil, butter, margarine, mayonnaise, lard, and peanut butter. Olive Oil is completely cholesterol free. Marsala Brand and many of our Sciabica Brand Varietal Olive Oils work well in these recipes."

Gemma says, "The Olive is a fruit. ...Olive You!

Gemma's vegetable salads with variations and dressings are imaginative and tantalizing. Her recipe for Tomato Pasta Salad from page 44 has this "health tip" at the bottom of the page:

"Mushrooms boost your immunity: Mushrooms are loaded with zinc, a mineral that strengthens the immune system, helping it fight off the bacteria and viruses that cause infection and disease." "Olive You!"

Here is a sample of her recipes:
"Olive Oil and Honey Toast" page 282;
"Olive Oil Pie Crust" page 272;
"'Mom's Free Form Apricot Pie" page 270;
"Gemma's Tomato Pasta Salad";
"Pasta with Popular Pesto Sauce";
"Fido Doggie Biscuits" page 287.

Almost every page of Gemma S. Sciabica's new book (2001), **"Cooking with California Olive Oil, Popular Recipes,"** includes a health tip, such as the one on page 282: "It's so good for you: Studies show that cinnamaldehyde, a compound found in cinnamon, has tranquilizing properties that help alleviate anxiety."

Some of the gold medals received for olive oil by Nick Sciabica & Sons.
Photo by Nicholas A. Sciabica

Chef, Joseph and Nicholas at Carnegie Hall in New York City. 1993
was the second year of three they were invited to receive another gold
medal for Nick Sciabica and Sons olive oil.

Antipasto

1   **head bibb, Boston lettuce or lettuce of your choice**
         lime, lemon juice or white wine vinegar to taste
         Marsala Olive Fruit Oil to taste
         salt and white pepper
         fresh basil chopped

Line a large platter with 6 or 8 large lettuce leaves, shred remaining lettuce, arrange over leaves.

Choose as many from the following list as desired. Arrange colors and flavors over lettuce.

Drizzle with lemon juice or vinegar, and olive oil. Sprinkle with salt, pepper and basil over all, to taste.

mozzarella or dried ricotta, cut in strips
garbanzo or fava beans, cooked
fennel bulb, sliced thin (finocchio)
red, yellow or green bell pepper, julienne
artichoke hearts, sliced
prosciutto, salami or coppa, sliced thin
Italian sausage, cooked, well drained, sliced thin
tuna, crab, shrimp or smoked salmon, sliced thin
sardines or anchovies, rinsed
mushrooms grilled or olives of your choice
yellow or red cherry tomatoes
radishes or scallions
celery, julienned or 1/2 small cauliflower, cooked crisp tender
provolone, Monterey Jack, sliced, cut into strips
peppercini or roasted pepper slices
zucchini or carrots, julienne
turkey, chicken or ham, cooked, sliced, rolled
fresh tarragon, mint, parsley, chives or sage
avocado, sliced
jicama, julienned or broccoli flowerets, cooked crisp tender
sweet or hot cherry vinegar peppers
roasted onion slices or roasted garlic
apple, pear (or fruit of your choice) wedges
green onions
Romano cheese shavings
fontina cheese slices, or cheese of your choice
green beans, cooked crisp tender

Antipasto means, before the meal.

Bagna Cauda
6 cups Vegetables

1-1/4   **cups Marsala Olive Fruit Oil**
6   **garlic cloves (or to taste) minced**
           salt and white pepper to taste
           Italian or French bread sliced thin
4 to 6 **anchovies, rinsed and chopped small**

Cut vegetables into bite size pieces or into spears.

In a serving bowl combine olive oil, garlic, anchovies, salt and pepper.

Arrange vegetables on serving platter and set bowl of bagna cauda in center.

Dip vegetables into sauce, using bread to catch drippings.

Variation:

Add 2 tablespoons Marsala pesto sauce to bagna cauda, stir until blended.

Assorted fresh vegetables such as:

small or large mushrooms, sliced
celery stalks
cauliflower flowerets, cooked crisp tender
broccoli flowerets, cooked crisp tender
carrot sticks
cucumber spears
green onions
tomatoes in wedges
cherry tomatoes
radishes with leaves (leaves are used to hold for dipping)
zucchini spears, cooked crisp tender
asparagus, cooked crisp tender
artichoke hearts, sliced
fennel bulb sliced
green beans, cooked crisp tender
olives of your choice
jicama spears
red bell peppers, roasted, sliced
chayote, cooked, sliced into spears
Belgian endive leaves, separated
romaine lettuce, center tender leaves
cardoons, cut into 2 inch pieces, trimmed, cooked crisp tender
vegetables may be grilled if desired

> Crunch on cucumbers for clear, smooth skin.
>
> These cool salad veggies are a good source of silicon, a mineral that hydrates and helps diminish fine lines.

Bruschetta

Serves 6 to 8

1-1/2	pounds yellow or red tomatoes, chopped
	salt and white pepper to taste
1/3	cup Marsala Olive Fruit Oil
6	garlic cloves, or to taste, minced
1/2	cup fresh basil, chopped fine
1/3	cup green onions, chopped small
6 to 8	Italian bread sliced about 1 inch thick
1/4	cup lemon juice

Toast bread in oven toaster or on hot grill until golden on both sides.

Lightly brush each slice with olive oil. Combine tomatoes, salt, pepper, remaining oil, garlic, onions and basil.

Spoon tomato mixture over warm toast, arrange on serving platter.

Bruschetta is especially good with thin slices of prosciutto, smoked salmon, ham, goat cheese, mozzarella, Monterey Jack, Gorgonzola and fontina cheese.

Variation:

	Romano or provolone cheese, shaved
1	cup fennel bulb or celery sliced thin
1 or 2	avocados or figs diced
1	cup crab, cooked, picked over
1	cup shrimp or scallops cut in half if large, cooked
1	cup olives, plain or stuffed
1	cup fresh mushrooms, sauteed in 1 tablespoon olive oil
2	anchovies or sardines, rinsed, chopped
2	bell peppers, roasted, peeled, sliced
2	tablespoon capers or walnuts
1/2	cup ricotta or goat cheese
1/2	teaspoon tarragon, rosemary or sage

Tomato Bruschetta

Serves 4 to 6

In grooved non stick skillet, roast 4 to 6 tomatoes on medium heat until skins are chard and tomatoes are soft.

Place grilled tomatoes in shallow serving plate, mash.

Add 1/4 cup olive oil, 1/4 cup fresh basil, chopped, salt, pepper and hot red pepper flakes to taste, mix.

Place 6 slices of grilled bread on serving plate, spread with tomato mixture evenly.

Bruschetta With Mushrooms

Serves 8

1	pound fresh mushrooms (shiitake, chanterelle, portobello)
2	tablespoons fresh sage or tarragon, chopped
1	cup green onions sliced thin (white part)
4 to 6	garlic cloves, minced
	salt, pepper and paprika to taste
1/2	cup fresh basil, parsley or mint, chopped
1/4	cup cognac or cream sherry
1/2	pound mozzarella, fontina or Brie, sliced
8 to 10	slices Italian bread toasted
1/3	cup Marsala Olive Fruit Oil
1/4	cup lemon juice or white wine vinegar

Brush mushrooms on both sides with olive oil, grill until golden, cool, slice.

Place in salad bowl, add remaining ingredients, toss gently.

Spoon topping on toasted bread. Arrange on serving platter, garnish with sprigs of fresh basil, rosemary, sage, mint or tarragon.

Variation:

1/4 pound liver, cubed, grilled

> ### Health benefit
> Recent research has shown that mushrooms contain vitamin B12, an essential vitamin found in meat and dairy products, which boosts your immunity to disease.

Meatball Sandwich

Yields 6

2	cups mini meatball gravy
6	rolls cut in half lengthwise
2	bell peppers, roasted, sliced
6	1 ounce Swiss cheese or mozzarella, sliced
2	cups shredded lettuce of your choice

Preheat oven to 350 degrees. Spoon meatballs with a little gravy in equal amounts in each roll.

Top meatballs with cheese. Place rolls on baking sheets, bake about 5 minutes or until cheese melts a little.

Remove from oven, spread with a slice of pepper and lettuce.

Serve immediately with olives and pickles if desired.

Cheese Filled Celery

Makes about 18

Award Winning Recipe at Riverbank Cheese and Wine Exposition.

1	3 ounce package cream cheese (low fat)
1/4	cup chunky peanut butter
6	celery stalks
1/2	cup pineapple, crushed or mandarin oranges, drained, chopped
1/4	cup pure maple syrup
1/4	cup coconut, toasted
1/4	cup hazelnuts, chopped small

Cut celery into bite size pieces, soak in ice water about 2 hours.

Blend cheese, peanut butter, pineapple, syrup and coconut.

Fill centers of celery with cheese mixture, sprinkle with hazelnuts.

Health benefit

Keep colds at bay with onions and garlic. Allium compounds in these foods fight viral infections such as colds.

Olive Topping

Makes about 3 Cups

1-1/2	cups olives of your choice, pitted, chopped
2	anchovy fillets, rinsed, chopped
2	tablespoons capers
1/4	cup lemon juice
1/3	cup Marsala Olive Fruit Oil
4	tomatoes, plum, peeled, chopped
1/2	cup fresh basil, parsley or cilantro, chopped
2	garlic cloves, minced
1/2	cup artichokes, chopped
	white pepper to taste
1	jalapeno pepper, minced

Place all ingredients in mixing bowl, stir to mix. Keep refrigerated until ready to serve.

Olive topping may be spread on slices of toasted Italian bread cut into 3/4 inch thick.

Serve with grilled meats or fish.

Crostini

Serves 6 to 8

8	slices Italian bread, 1 inch thick
4	tablespoons Marsala Olive Fruit Oil
4	garlic cloves, minced
4	tablespoons provolone, shredded
1/4	cup fresh basil, chopped fine
4	tablespoons sweet red wine, Vermouth or sherry

Place bread slices on baking sheet, drizzle evenly with olive oil. Sprinkle on garlic, cheese and basil. Pour wine over top on each slice evenly.

Toast in oven at 350 degrees for 8 to 10 minutes or until golden.

Variation:

Substitute gorgonzola, crumbled or Romano cheese shavings for provolone.

1-1/2 cups steamed spinach, well drained, chopped

Crostini may be spread with caponata.

Crostini With Figs

6	slices Italian bread 1 inch thick, toasted
6 to 8	fresh figs, sliced
6	tablespoons honey or pure maple syrup
1/2	cup feta, goat or Gorgonzola, crumbled

Spread toasted bread with cheese, place on figs and drizzle with honey.

Variation:

Substitute dried figs, sliced, for fresh figs.

Fava beans, cooked tender crisp, mashed (or garbanzo)

mushrooms sautéed in a little olive oil

Genevieve's Garlic Bread

Serves 6 to 8

1	loaf Italian or French bread, cut in half lengthwise
1/3	cup Marsala Olive Fruit Oil
2	garlic cloves (or to taste)
	salt, pepper and paprika to taste
1/4	cup Romano cheese, grated
1	small tomato
1/2	cup fresh basil leaves
1/2	teaspoon oregano

In jar of blender add all ingredients (except bread) and blend.

Drizzle sauce over bread on cut sides.

Wrap bread in foil, bake in a 400 degrees oven for 12 to 15 minutes.

Cut slices or break as desired.

Health benefit

Heal faster with shrimp. These shellfish are a good source of zinc, a mineral that helps skin repair damage quickly.

Shrimp Cocktail

Serves 4 to 6

2	green onions (white part) sliced thin
2	garlic cloves, minced
1/4	cup lime or lemon juice
	salt and white pepper to taste
1	avocado, diced
1	cup olives, sliced (or pineapple, crushed)
2 or 3	cups fresh tomatoes, diced
2	chile peppers, minced
1	pound shrimp, cooked
1/2	cup fresh basil, parsley or cilantro, chopped
1/2	cup Marsala Olive Fruit Oil
2	tablespoons ketchup or sweet pickle relish
1/4	cup almonds, sliced

In large mixing bowl, combine all ingredients together.

Spoon mixture into a serving bowl or stemmed glasses, sprinkle with almonds.

Hang shrimp over edge of bowl or individual glasses.

Serve with tortilla chips.

Prosciutto Con Melon
(Prosciutto With Melon)

12   slices cantaloupe, honeydew or fresh figs
12   slices prosciutto paper thin

Cut chilled melon in thin wedges. If using figs, leave whole or slice in half lengthwise.

Place melon wedges on serving platter or individual plates (1 or 2 on each). Drape prosciutto over wedges.

Serve with fork and knife, cutting a piece of melon, then a piece of prosciutto, combining the two flavors.

Variation:

apricots, nectarines, peaches, pears or fruit of your choice, cut into wedges

Variation for serving:

In small bowl stir together 1 cup ricotta cheese, 1/4 cup pure maple syrup or honey.

Place on serving platter with fruit and prosciutto. Garnish with mint leaves.

> ### Tame tension with salmon
> This popular fish contains omega-3 fatty acids, which have been shown to reduce stress.

Avocado Prosciutto/Smoked Salmon
Makes 16 servings

2   avocados, cut into 8 slices lengthwise
8   slices smoked salmon, sliced thin
8   prosciutto slices, sliced thin
      lime or lemon wedges
1/2   cup macadamia nuts, chopped small or almond slices

Wrap each avocado slice with prosciutto or salmon slices diagonally.

Arrange wraps on serving platter, garnish with lime or lemon wedges.

Sprinkle with nuts.

Sausage and Pepper Sandwich

Serves 6

6	Italian rolls cut in half lengthwise
1/4	cup red wine
1-1/2	pounds hot or sweet Italian sausage
1/3	cup Marsala Olive Fruit Oil
3	onions, sliced
4	red, yellow or green bell peppers, cut into strips
4 to 6	garlic cloves, chopped
	salt, pepper and cayenne to taste
1/2	cup fresh basil, chopped
4 to 6	plum tomatoes, chopped
1	cup water
2	tablespoons lemon juice

In skillet add water and sausage, cook on all sides until browned. Lift out with slotted spoon, discard fat. Drain sausage on paper towels.

In another skillet add oil, onion, peppers and garlic, cook covered until crisp tender.

Add tomatoes, basil, wine, lemon juice, salt, pepper and cayenne.

Cut sausage into 6 pieces. Fill each roll with sausage and vegetable mixture.

Figs With Mascarpone

Serves 4 to 6

Award Winning Recipe at Riverbank Cheese and Wine Exposition.

1/4	pound mascarpone cheese (uncured cheese similar to ricotta cheese)
OR	
4	ounces cream cheese, low fat with 3 tablespoons plain yogurt
1/4	cup fresh mint leaves
2	tablespoons hazelnuts, ground
2	tablespoons creme de menthe liqueur
8 to 12	fresh figs
1/2	cup whipped cream

> **Health benefit**
>
> Figs are rich in bone-building calcium. In fact, dried figs contain 17% more calcium than skim milk.

Slice figs lengthwise almost to bottom.

In mixing bowl combine cheese, whipped cream, creme de menthe and hazelnuts.

Pipe cheese rosettes in center, decorate with mint leaves.

Grilled Goat Cheese and Ham Sandwich

Serves 4

6	ounces goat cheese (or fontina)
1	tablespoons basil, cilantro or tarragon chopped
4	tablespoons Marsala or Sciabica olive oil
8	slices (1/2 inch thick) brioche, challah or Italian bread
2	tablespoons Dijon mustard
1/4	pound ham (4 slices)
1/4	cup olives, minced

In small bowl combine cheese, olives, mustard and basil. Brush bread slices with olive oil on one side only.

Spread bread with mustard and cheese mixture evenly, cover with ham slices and second slice of bread with olive oil side out.

Heat a large nonstick pan (or one with groves) over medium high heat. Place sandwiches in pan, grill without crowding. Cover, cook until cheese melts and bread is deep golden on each side.

Cut sandwiches in half, serve warm with green salad if desired.

Variation:

smoked salmon, sliced or fish of your choice
grilled chicken, turkey or meats of your choice
mozzarella, basil, turkey ham, tomatoes
brie or camembert cheese, roasted bell peppers
grilled portabello, eggplant or zucchini slices, pesto mayonnaise
make up your favorite combinations

Four Surprise Diet Foods

These foods have a calorie-laden reputation, but can actually be great choices when you want to eat light:
1. Parmesan cheese. A mere teaspoon of grated Parmesan (or Romano) adds real flavor punch but contains only 8 calories. Sprinkle it on pasta, steamed vegetables, or your favorite green salad. **2. Canned Gravy.** A smooth solution when lean meats and plain rice or potatoes seem dry, tasteless, and boring. A couple of tablespoons of most brands will add only 10 to 15 calories and less than a gram of fat. (Check labels.) **3. Whipped cream in a can.** Go ahead, top off a low-fat hot cocoa or an espresso with a little squirt of real (pressurized) whipped cream. At 11 calories a tablespoon, it's a tiny indulgence compared to a typical rich dessert. **4. Jelly/jam/fruit spread.** At about 15 fat-free calories per teaspoon, these sweets have half the calories of butter or margarine. Brush warm jam or preserves on waffles or French toast, or stir a teaspoonful into in a cup of hot tea.

Avocado Open Face Sandwich

Serves 4

4   **slices sourdough, whole wheat pumpernickel or bread of your choice**
2   **avocados, sliced**
4   **slices ham or prosciutto**
1/4   **cup Marsala Olive Oil or Marsala basil mayonnaise**
2   **tomatoes, sliced**
4   **thin slices provolone, Monterey Jack or Swiss cheese**
       white pepper to taste

Drizzle 1 tablespoon olive oil on each slice of bread. Top with ham, avocado, cheese and tomato.

Sprinkle with pepper.

Variation:

     turkey, roast beef or chicken, cooked, sliced
     sweet onion, sliced thin
     olives, sliced
     shredded lettuce
     canned tuna or salmon, water packed
     Gorgonzola or blue cheese, crumbled
     roasted bell pepper slices

Substitute 2 large French rolls for sliced bread.

> ## Pop an olive for cool relief
>
> The black variety is rich in vitamin E, an antioxidant that may help reduce the frequency and intensity of hot flashes.

Olive Stuffed Meatballs

Makes 12 to 16

1/4   **cup Marsala Olive Oil**
1   **recipe for Italian meatballs**
12 to 16 olives, pitted (or pimiento stuffed)
1   **egg white lightly beaten**
1   **cup bread crumbs**

When forming meatballs, insert one olive in each meatball, cover completely with meat mixture.

Roll meatballs in egg white, then in bread crumbs all around.

In non stick skillet, over medium heat, brown meatballs in olive oil all around until well done.

Garnish with fresh basil, mint, or rosemary sprigs.

Serve with cranberry, raisin or plum sauce and green salad.

May be added to gravies, soups, stews, meat pies, etc.

Stuffed Figs

Makes 1 Pound

1	pound white or dark dried moist figs
1	cup almonds, macadamia or hazelnuts, lightly toasted
2	tablespoons anise or fennel seeds
1/2	cup confectioners' sugar
6	bay leaves
1/3	cup rum, anisette, Galliano or Strega liqueur

Trim off stems, cut figs open down on one side lengthwise. Place 1 or 2 almonds in each fig, press them shut again.

In container, place a layer of stuffed figs. Sprinkle with some sugar, anise seeds, liqueur and place 2 bay leaves on top.

Continue layering figs, seeds, sugar, liqueur and bay leaves. Cover with foil, keep refrigerated.

Keep for months, longer in a freezer.

Variation

Substitute instant sweet ground chocolate for confectioners' sugar.

Melt 2 ounces of milk chocolate, drizzle over figs evenly.

Sift 2 tablespoons cocoa with 1/2 cup confectioners' sugar together, sprinkle on tops.

1/3	cup candied orange peel
1/2	teaspoon cinnamon

Peaches and Wine

Serves 4 to 6

3 or 4 peaches, sliced (or strawberries)
3 or 4 cups wine of your choice

In a large pitcher add peaches, pour in wine, enough to cover them. Refrigerate until ready to serve.

Variation:

garnish with mint sprigs

This was one of my Dad's favorite ways
to serve peaches in summer.

Torta Rustica

Serves 10

Pastry

1/4	cup Marsala Olive Fruit Oil
2-1/2	cups flour
1-1/2	teaspoons baking powder
1/2	teaspoon salt
3	eggs (or 1 egg and 4 egg whites)
1/2	teaspoon caraway, anise or fennel seeds
2	tablespoons white wine or water

In mixing bowl combine dry ingredients, make well in center. Stir in remaining ingredients until dough holds together.

On lightly floured board, knead dough lightly, cut into two pieces, one slightly larger than the other. Roll into balls, cover, let rest about 20 minutes.

Roll out larger ball, ease to fit in a lightly greased 10 inch spring form pan.

Filling

1/2	cup olives, sliced
1/2	pound Italian sausage, cooked, well drained
1-1/2	cups ricotta (low fat)
3	eggs and 1 egg white
1-1/2	cup mozzarella, shredded
1/2	cup Romano cheese, grated
1/2	cup prosciutto or ham, chopped
1/2	cup fresh basil or parsley, chopped
	white pepper to taste
1	cup artichokes (water packed) quartered
4	garlic cloves, minced
1/2	cup fresh mushrooms, chopped (or peas)
6	small eggs
1	tablespoon fresh rosemary or sage
2	green onions, chopped
1	roasted bell pepper, chopped
1	tablespoon water (to brush top)
1	egg white (to brush top)

In mixing bowl combine filling ingredients (except 6 small eggs, egg white and water). Pour into prepared pan.

Make 6 indentations with tablespoon. Break eggs one at a time in saucer, slip egg into indentation, careful not to break yolk. Stir together egg white and water.

Cover with second rolled out pastry. Moisten edges, seal to bottom crust and flute. Roll out trimmings to 1/8 inch thick, cut 6 or 8 leaves with cookie cutter.

Make slits in center top of crust for steam vents. Arrange pastry leaves on top, brush with egg white and water mixture.

Bake at 375 degrees about 45 to 50 minutes. Cover with foil loosely if browning too quickly.

Wrapped Sandwich

Serves 4 to 6

1	lahvosh, soft Armenian flatbread
1	red bell pepper, roasted, sliced
1/2	cup feta, goat or gorgongola cheese, crumbled
2	green onions (white part) sliced thin
1/4	cup fresh basil or parsley, chopped
2	tablespoons Marsala Olive Fruit Oil
	pepper to taste
1	cup spinach or arugula leaves (or greens of your choice)
2	garlic cloves, minced

Arrange topping evenly on bread leaving 1 inch border all around. Drizzle with olive oil.

Roll up bread with filling, not too tightly. Trim dry ends of roll.

Using a serrated knife, cut roll straight across or on the diagonal to desired thickness.

Variation for fillings:

1 or 2	portobello mushrooms, grilled, sliced
1/2	cup mozzarella or provolone, shredded
1/2	onion, sweet red, minced
2	tablespoons Marsala pesto or mayonnaise
4	slices turkey, ham, chicken or cold cuts (lean)
1	tablespoon Dijon mustard
1	avocado, sliced
1	egg made into omelet, chopped
	roast beef slices
1/2	cup olives, chopped
2	tablespoons capers
1/4	cup dried tomatoes, chopped
1/4	cup tuna (water packed)
	fruits and vegetables of your choice
	nuts of your choice

> ### Health benefit
> Beta carotene-rich arugula, part of the cruciferous family of vegetables, contains indoles, which help protect you from several cancers.

Variation for bread:

large flour tortillas
Afghan snowshoe naan (oval shape) bread
pita, pocketless, rolled into a cone and filled

Olive You!

Egg Rolls

Makes 12

12   egg roll wrappers (7"x7")
      cheese, crab, beef or filling of your choice
      Marsala olive oil for brushing rolls

Place 1 egg wrapper on working surface, with 1 corner toward you. Spoon about 1/4 cup filling in center.

Place corner under filling. Fold left and right corners over filling, overlapping at center.

Brush last corner with water, roll egg roll away from you onto moistened corner.

Brush rolls on all sides with olive oil. Place on a foil lined greased baking sheet.

Bake in a 325 degrees oven for 10 to 15 minutes or until golden. Serve with sauce of your choice.

Beef Filling

1	small sweet onion, minced
1	ounce cellophane noodles
1/4	pound crab meat (picked over) cooked
4	green onions
4	garlic cloves minced
1	cup bean sprouts fresh
2	tablespoons fish sauce
1	egg
1/2	teaspoon black pepper
1/4	pound beef, lean, ground

> **It's _so_ good for you**
> Hot pepper sauce contains capsaicin, a natural anti-inflammatory that's been shown to relieve painful cluster headaches.

Soak noodles in warm water for 30 minutes, drain. Cut into about 1 inch lengths. Add remaining ingredients, blend well.

Crab Filling

1/2	pound crab (picked over) cooked
3/4	pound sole, salmon fillets or shrimp, cooked
3/4	cup water chestnuts, chopped
1/2	cup sun chokes chopped
2	green onions, finely chopped
2	tablespoons catchup
1	tablespoon soy sauce
1	tablespoon lime or lemon juice
1	egg
2	garlic cloves, minced

Continued next page

Chop sole and crab until minced, place in mixing bowl. Add remaining. Use about 1/4 cup filling for each egg roll

Fish Sauce

1	**tablespoon ginger, grated**
1/2	**cup peanuts, ground**
1	**cup mint or cilantro, chopped**
1	**small chili, minced**
2	**tablespoons honey or brown sugar**
2	**tablespoons lime juice**
1/4	**cup lemon juice**
2	**garlic cloves, minced**
1/3	**cup Marsala Olive Oil**
1	**carrot shredded**
1/3	**cup pineapple, crushed**

Combine all ingredients in serving bowl except carrot. Stir, float shredded carrot on sauce.

Serve with a side of salsa or guacamole, if desired.

Variation for egg rolls:

chili powder to taste
cumin or coriander
hot pepper sauce
oregano or rosemary
basil, mint, parsley, thyme or cilantro
bell pepper, red, diced
corn kernels
jalapeno pepper, minced
fennel bulbs, shredded
cabbage, shredded
olives, sliced
goat or feta cheese, crumbled
filo dough may also be substituted for egg roll wrappers.
duck in 1x1/4 inch strips or meat of your choice
2 ounces kumquats in syrup (about 4) thinly sliced

> ### Avocados prevent heart disease
> Avocados are rich in the mono-unsaturated fat oleic acid, which has been shown to lower the risk of heart disease by inhibiting the buildup of plaque on artery walls.

Note:

For vegetarian egg rolls, omit meat

Cactus Salad

Serves 6 to 8

2 or 3	cactus pears, peeled and sliced
1/2	pound spinach leaves
1/2	pound fresh trimmed cactus pads (nopalitos)
2	green onions, sliced thin
	salt and pepper to taste
1/2	teaspoon chili powder or paprika
2	yellow or red tomatoes, cut into wedges
3/4	cup goat, feta, farmer or Gorgonzola cheese, crumbled
1	cucumber, sliced thin
1/3	cup Marsala Olive Fruit Oil
1/3	cup lime of lemon juice (or white wine vinegar)
1/3	cup fresh basil or cilantro, chopped
2	mild yellow chiles, minced
4	garlic cloves, minced

Remove any thorns or spines from cactus pads. Cut into about 2 x 1/2 inch strips.

In saucepan add water, bring to a boil. Blanch nopalitos for 3 minutes. Do not overcook or they will turn grayish green. Drain well, set aside.

Line serving platter with spinach leaves. In mixing bowl combine remaining ingredients except cheese, tomatoes and cactus pears.

Arrange cactus mixture over spinach evenly. Garnish with tomatoes and cactus pear slices.

Sprinkle with crumbled cheese.

Variation:

1	cup olives, sliced
2	avocados, sliced
1	teaspoon fresh coriander, chopped
1/8	teaspoon hot pepper sauce
1	tablespoon poppy seeds
1	small red onion cut into rings
1	cup beets, cooked, julienned
1	shrimp, mussels or crab, cooked
1	cup mushrooms, sauted in olive oil
1/3	cup fresh parsley or mint, chopped
1	cup dried cherries, cranberries or blueberries
1	jicama, small, shredded
1	red orange in segments

Olive You!

Tomato & Mozzarella Salad Pg 55 ~ Jumbo Popovers Pg 149 ~ Cactus Salad, Cactus Fruit Pg 38

Endive Boat Salad Pg 60

Caesar Salad

Serves 4 to 6

1/4	cup hazelnuts, chopped fine
1	head romaine lettuce, bite size pieces
1/2	small head radicchio, bite size pieces
1	mango, papaya or persimmon, sliced
1	medium cucumber, sliced thin
1/2	cup Romano or fontina cheese, shaved
2	cups croutons, homemade

Dressing

4	anchovy fillets, rinsed
1/4	cup lime or lemon juice
2	teaspoons Dijon mustard
4	garlic cloves (or to taste)
1/2	cup Marsala Olive Fruit Oil
	salt, pepper and paprika to taste
1	egg white
1/4	cup fresh basil, chives, mint or parsley

In jar of blender add dressing ingredients, whirl until blended.

In large shallow serving salad bowl combine lettuce, radicchio and cucumber. Pour dressing over salad, toss gently to coat.

Add croutons, arrange mango slices over top, sprinkle with cheese and nuts.

Croutons

4	cups Italian or French bread, cut into 1/2 inch cubes
1/4	cup Marsala Olive Fruit Oil
2	tablespoons Romano cheese, grated

In mixing bowl add bread cubes, drizzle with olive oil, toss to coat evenly.

Place in baking sheet in a 400 degrees oven for 10 to 12 minutes or until golden. Watch carefully.

Sprinkle with cheese.

Variation:

	Oysters, shrimp or crab cooked
1	cup strawberries, blackberries or berries of your choice
1	cup olives, pimiento, stuffed
1	cup broccoli sprouts
8	ounces swordfish, lobster, salmon or catfish cooked, cubed

Corn Salad

Serves 4 to 6

1	cup celery, sliced thin
1/2	cup green onions (white part) sliced thin
2-1/2	cups fresh corn, cooked or canned
1/3	cup each red, yellow and green bell peppers, chopped small
1	avocado, diced
1/4	cup Marsala Olive Fruit Oil
1	large tomato, chopped
	salt, pepper and cayenne to taste
1/2	cup Gorgonzola or blue cheese, crumbled
1	teaspoon Dijon mustard
1	cup olives, sliced
3 to 4	small sweet pickles, chopped
1/4	cup lime or lemon juice
1-1/2	cups jicama, shredded

In mixing bowl add all ingredients, toss gently. Keep refrigerated until ready to serve.

Serve with grilled chicken, meats or fish of your choice.

Variation:

1	cup brown and wild rice mix, cooked
1	apple, golden delicious, diced
1-1/2	cups dried beans, cooked (or garbanzo)
2	cups iceberg lettuce, shredded
1/2	cup golden raisins
1/4	cup peanuts, chopped or almonds, sliced
1/3	cup fresh basil or parsley, minced
1	small cucumber, diced
1/2	cup feta cheese, crumbled (or cheese of your choice)
1/4	cup ham, cooked cubed (or prosciutto, chopped)
1	tablespoon soy sauce
1/2	teaspoon cumin, papriks or chili powder
1	cup barley, cooked
1/2	cup goat cheese
2	ounces jar pimiento stuffed olives
1	cup couscous, cooked

Health benefit

Cucumbers contain protease inhibitors, which can slow the growth of cancerous cells and help them return to a healthy state.

Fruit Salad

Serves 6

4	apricots, sliced
1	cup pimiento stuffed olives, sliced
1	tablespoon poppy seeds
1	avocado, diced
2	peaches or nectarines in bite size pieces
1/2	pound sweet cherries, pitted
1	cup dates, chopped
1	cup mozzarella or Swiss cheese, cubed
1/4	cup pecans, pistachios or pine nuts
1/2	cantaloupe or honeydew, balls or cubed
4	plums, sliced
1	cup blueberries or berries of your choice
1	cup pineapple tidbits
1	apple or pear diced (or grapes seedless)
4	fresh or dried figs, sliced
6 or 8	radicchio, red leaf or Boston lettuce leaves
1	cup miniature marshmallows

Line large shallow salad bowl with lettuce leaves.

Combine all salad ingredients, spoon dressing on, toss gently.

Arrange ingredients over lettuce. Garnish with sprigs of rose scented geranium, unsprayed.

Dressing

> ### Health benefit
> Both cantaloupe and orange give your body a blast of beta-carotene. Beta-carotene may reduce the risk of Alzheimer's and dementia.

	salt to taste
1/2	cup orange or pineapple juice
1/4	cup pure maple syrup, honey or corn syrup
1/3	cup Marsala Olive Fruit Oil
2	tablespoons lemon juice
1	teaspoon vanilla
1/2	teaspoon lavender, unsprayed

Whirl in jar of blender until well blended.

Variation:

2	oranges, diced (or grapefruit)
1	cup pumpkin seeds, toasted
4	kiwi fruit, sliced (or star fruite)
1	mango or papaya, diced
1/4	cup coconut
1/2	cup cashew, chopped or pistachios
1	cup pomegranate seeds
1/4	cup crystallized ginger, chopped

Greek Salad

Serves 6 to 8

6	radishes, sliced thin
1	cup celery, sliced thin
6	cups curly endive or spinach leaves
2	cups iceberg lettuce, shredded or mixed greens
2	cups lamb or beef cooked, cut into strips
2	tomatoes, chopped
1/2	cup feta or Gorgonzola, crumbled
1/2	cup olives, sliced
1	medium cucumber, sliced thin
4	fresh or dried figs, sliced
2	anchovies, rinsed, minced
2	tablespoons capers
12	pepperoncini
1/2	cup green beans, cooked, chopped

Dressing

1/2	teaspoon ginger
1	teaspoon Dijon mustard
4	garlic cloves (or to taste)
	salt, pepper and paprika to taste
1	teaspoon oregano
1/2	cup Marsala Olive Fruit Oil
1/3	cup lemon juice or vinegar
1	egg white

Blend together dressing ingredients in jar of blender.

Add remaining ingredients in large shallow serving bowl.

Pour dressing over salad, toss gently.

Variation:

1	red bell pepper, roasted, sliced
4	green onions (white part) sliced thin
1	onion, small, sweet, cut into rings
1/2	cup fresh basil or mint
2	tablespoons pesto sauce
1/4	cup fresh tarragon, chopped
6 to 8	yellow or red cherry tomatoes
1/4	cup pecans, walnuts or nuts of your choice
2	cups radicchio, chopped (or dandelion)
1	cup tuna, water packed, crumbled
1/2	cup goat cheese, crumbled
1	cup potatoes or beets, cooked, diced
1	cup sardines, canned, crumbled

> **It's _so_ good for you**
> Tarragon is loaded with eugenol, a natural antiseptic that helps provide relief from oral pain, such as minor toothaches.

Italian Potato Salad
Serves 6

6   potatoes, cooked, peeled
4 to 6 garlic cloves (or to taste) chopped
1/3   cup fresh basil, parsley or mint, chopped
         salt, pepper and cayenne to taste
1/3   cup Marsala Olive Fruit Oil
1/4   cup lemon juice or white vinegar
1 to 2 tablespoons pesto sauce
1/2   cup olives, minced
1/4   cup capers
1/2   cup green onions, sliced thin
4   anchovy fillets, rinsed and chopped
1/2   cup Romano cheese shavings (or mozzarella)

> **Protect wrists with potatoes**
> This side-dish favorite is high in B_6, a vitamin shown to reduce symptoms of carpal tunnel syndrome.

Slice potatoes and arrange overlapping on serving platter.

Combine garlic, basil, salt, pepper, cayenne, olive oil, lemon juice and pesto; stir, pour over potatoes evenly.

Sprinkle with remaining ingredients.

Variation:
Add 2 cups cooked mussels, clams or shrimp
1   cup artichoke hearts, sliced or green beans, chopped
1   cup fennel bulb or celery, sliced thin
1   cup yellow or red cherry tomatoes
1/2   cup green onions (white part) sliced thin
1/3   cup fontina or provolone cheese, shaved
1/3   cup goat cheese, Gorgonzola or feta cheese, crumbled
1   cup fresh or frozen peas
1   cup beets, sliced or broccoli sprouts
1/4   pound Italian sausage cooked, well drained, sliced thin
6   garlic cloves, roasted
1   cup bow tie pasta, spinach or plain
1   cup brussels sprouts, cooked, quartered
1   pear diced
1/2   cup walnuts
1/2   cup Gouda cheese, shredded
2   cups cauliflowerets, cooked crisp tender
2   cups cooked fava beans - remove skins on each bean
2   yams, diced, roasted
2   cups grilled chicken or turkey, cubed

Jerusalem Artichoke Salad
(sun choke)

Serves 4

4	slices Canadian bacon, chopped
1	cucumber, sliced thin
1	cup green onions, sliced thin
1	cup green beans, cooked crisp tender
1/2	pound Jerusalem artichoke, cooked crisp tender, sliced
1	avocado, sliced
1/2	pound fresh mushrooms, grilled, sliced
1/2	cup fresh basil, parsley or cilantro, chopped
1	head romaine, Boston, bibb or lettuce of your choice
1-1/2	cups shrimp or crab, cooked
1	cup yellow or red cherry tomatoes
1-1/2	cups watercress, chopped
1/4	pound grilled steak, sliced thin, chopped

Shred lettuce, place in serving shallow bowl evenly. Combine remaining ingredients, toss gently with dressing.

Dressing

1	teaspoon Dijon mustard
1/3	cup Marsala Olive Fruit Oil
1/4	cup lime or lemon juice or vinegar
2	garlic cloves (or to taste)
1	teaspoon paprika
	salt and pepper to taste
1	egg white
1/3	cup walnuts
1/2	teaspoon curry powder
1/2	avocado

> ### Nuts may stop Alzheimer's
> Recent research shows that regular consumption of the type of vitamin E in almonds may reduce the risk of developing Alzheimer's disease.

Place dressing ingredients in jar of blender, whirl until well blended.

Variation:

long green beans cut into 2 inch pieces (1 to 2 feet long) cooked crisp tender

Lentil Salad

Serves 4 to 6

2	cups lentils, cooked
2	tomatoes, chopped
2	cups broccoli flowerets, cooked crisp tender
1	cup orzo pasta, cooked, cooled
2	green onions (white part) sliced thin
1/2	cup raisins or dates, chopped
1	teaspoon fresh ginger, grated
2	garlic cloves, minced
1-1/2	cups chicken, rabbit or turkey, cooked, cubed
1	cup fresh mushrooms, cooked, quartered
1	cup carrots, shredded
1	cup peas, green beans or corn, cooked crisp tender
1	cup feta cheese, crumbled

Dressing

1/3	cup Marsala Olive Fruit Oil
1/3	cup orange juice
1/4	cup lime or lemon juice
2	tablespoons fresh tarragon or cilantro, chopped
1/3	cup fresh basil or mint, chopped
1/4	cup honey
1	tablespoon peanut butter

Combine dressing ingredients, blend.

Add all salad ingredients in large shallow serving bowl.

Pour on dressing, toss gently.

Variation:

Substitute tubetti for orzo pasta
Substitute broccoli slaw for flowerets

1/2	cup barley, cooked
1	cup rice, cooked
2	tablespoons chives, fresh
1/2	pound deli roast beef cut into 1/2 by 1/4 inch strips

Health benefit

Studies have shown that barley, which is high in soluble fiber, is just as effective as oats in reducing cholesterol levels and lowering heart attack risk.

Lola's Ensaladilla Rusa
(Russian Salad)

Serves 4 to 6

1	pound potatoes
	salt and pepper to taste
1/2	pound carrots, cubed
1-1/2	cups peas, fresh or frozen
3/4	pound shrimp, medium
3/4	cup Marsala mayonnaise
1/4	cup milk low fat
1/4	cup fresh basil or parsley, minced

Boil potatoes in water until tender. Cool, peel and cube.

Cook carrots crisp tender, cool, cube.

Cook shrimp in boiling water for about 1 minute. Drain, cool, peel and remove dark veins, if any.

In large shallow serving bowl add potatoes, carrots, peas, shrimp, salt and pepper.

Thin mayonnaise with milk, pour over salad, toss gently.

Refrigerate until ready to serve.

Variation:

Substitute clams, mussels, crab, tuna, salmon, scallops or lobster, diced, for shrimp.

4	hard cooked eggs, chopped, yolks removed if desired.
1	beet cooked, diced
1	cup green beans, cooked crisp tender, chopped
1	cup pimiento stuffed olives or mushrooms
1	cup artichoke hearts, sliced

Health benefit
A serving of beets provides 52% of the RDA for folic acid, a B vitamin that can lower the risk of birth defects during pregnancy.

Meatball Salad

Serves 4 to 6

2	cups mini meatballs, cooked
1-1/2	cups green beans, cooked, chopped
1	cup lima beans, cooked (or canned, drained)
1-1/2	cups garbanzo beans, cooked or canned
1	sweet small onion, cut into thin rings
1	cup olives, sliced
1	cup celery, sliced thin
1	bell pepper, roasted, chopped
2	tomatoes, chopped
1/3	cup fresh basil, parsley, mint or cilantro, chopped
1	head escarole (about 1 pound) or greens of your choice
1	cup asparagus tips, cooked crisp tender

Dressing

1/2	cup Marsala Olive Fruit Oil
	salt and pepper to taste
1/3	cup lemon juice
1/2	teaspoon oregano or rosemary
4	garlic cloves or to taste
1	teaspoon paprika
1	teaspoon Dijon mustard
1	egg white
1/2	cup Romano cheese shavings for garnish
1	jalapeno pepper

Health benefit

Slice cancer risk with tomatoes. These bursts of flavor are full of lycopene, a carotenoid that has been shown to lower the threat of breast cancer.

Place all dressing ingredients, except cheese, into jar of blender. Blend until well combined.

Remove 6 large outer leaves from escarole, reserve for garnish.

Coarsely chop remaining lettuce. In large bowl combine all salad ingredients with lettuce.

Toss with dressing to coat well. Arrange large reserved leaves on serving platter.

Spoon meatball and bean mixture over top of escarole leaves evenly. Garnish with Romano cheese shavings.

Variation:

1	carrot, shredded
4	green onions (white part) sliced
1-1/2	cups sugar snap peas, cooked crisp tender
1-1/2	cups fava beans, cooked, fine skins removed

Olga's Broccoli Salad

Serves 4 to 6

3	cups broccoli flowerets, cooked crisp tender
3/4	cup raisins, golden (or grapes, seedless)
1	cup celery, sliced thin
3/4	cup onions, sweet, red, sliced thin
1/4	pound Canadian or turkey bacon, lean, cooked, crumbled
1/2	cup Marsala mayonnaise (or to taste)
1/4	cup orange juice
	glazed pecans

Combine above ingredients in large shallow serving bowl.

Toss gently, refrigerate until ready to serve.

Variation:

Substitute 1/2 cup olive oil, 1/4 cup lemon juice and 2 tablespoons sugar, blended together, for mayonnaise.

Avocado and Orange Salad

Serves 4

2	mint sprigs
3	oranges, peeled, sliced about 1/4 inch thick
2	avocados, peeled, sliced
1	onion, small, sweet, sliced in thin rings
1	cup olives
	salt, pepper and paprika to taste
1/4	cup Marsala Olive Fruit Oil

> **Health benefit**
>
> One serving of beets packs a full day's supply of folic acid. This B vitamin lowers homocysteine levels, preventing heart disease.

Arrange oranges, avocados and onions overlapping on serving dish.

Scatter olives over, sprinkle with salt, pepper and paprika.

Drizzle with olive oil evenly. Garnish with mint or basil sprigs.

Variation:

2 to 4	tablespoons lime or lemon juice
1	cup edible flowers, unsprayed
1	cup beets, sliced
1	medium cucumber, sliced thin
1	cup strawberries or raspberries
1	tablespoon sesame seeds, toasted
1/2	pound lobster meat, cooked, cut into bite size pieces
1	cup shrimp-cooked
1	grapefruit, peeled and segmented

Orange and Beet Salad

Serves 6

2	cups beets, cooked, cut julienne or sliced
2	oranges in segments
1	onion, sliced thin into rings
1	cup olives, sliced
1	bunch watercress (about 6 ounces) or arugula
1	mango or papaya, diced
2	cups turkey, grilled or baked, cubed
1	cup canned whole cranberry sauce, cubed
4	cups mixed baby lettuce with edible flowers
1/4	cup pine nuts or nuts of your choice
1	cup pomegranate seeds

Dressing

1	teaspoon Dijon mustard
1	tablespoon honey
	salt and pepper to taste
1/3	cup Marsala Olive Fruit Oil
1/4	cup lemon juice or vinegar
1/4	cup orange juice and/or pomegranate juice
2	garlic cloves, minced

Combine salad ingredients in large shallow serving bowl.

Stir dressing ingredients together in mixing bowl.

Pour dressing over salad, toss gently. Refrigerate until ready to serve.

Variation:

1	red orange or red grapefruit segments
1/2	cup dates, quartered
4 to 6	radishes, sliced thin
1	cucumber, sliced thin
1/4	cup parsley or cilantro, chopped
1	tablespoon fresh ginger, grated
2	asian pears, chopped
2	tomatillos, chopped

Health benefit

The mono-unsaturated fat found in olives and olive oil increases blood levels of HDL (good) cholesterol, which helps reduce the levels of artery-clogging LDL (bad) cholesterol in the body.

Panzanella

(Bread Salad with Vegetables)

Serves 6 to 8

1/2	pound Italian bread several days old
1/2	cup Marsala Olive Fruit Oil
1/3	cup lemon juice or wine vinegar
	salt, pepper and paprika to taste
1	cucumber sliced thin
6	green onions (white part) chopped
1/2	cup fresh basil or parsley, chopped
6	tomatoes, chopped (red or yellow)
1	cup green beans or asparagus cooked crisp tender
1	cup olives (for top)
2	tablespoons capers
4	garlic cloves (or to taste) minced
2	bell peppers, roasted, diced
1 or 2	avocados sliced (for top)
1	teaspoon Dijon mustard
1	cup cherry tomatoes (for top)
	oregano to taste

Soak bread in cold water about 5 minutes. Squeeze to remove excess water. Place in a large shallow serving bowl.

In jar of blender, whirl together vinegar, lemon juice, oregano, olive oil, mustard, onions, garlic, paprika, salt, pepper and basil.

To bread add tomatoes, capers, peppers, cucumber and beans. Pour oil mixture over ingredients, toss gently.

Arrange avocado, olives and cherry tomatoes on top to garnish.

Variation:

1	cup mozzarella, Swiss, provolone or fontina, cubed 1/2 inch
2	hard cooked eggs, chopped or sliced (yolks removed if desired)
1 or 2	jalapeno peppers, minced
1/2	fennel bulb sliced thin
2	anchovies, rinsed, chopped (or sardines)
1/2	cup pistachios, pecans or nuts of your choice
1	cup celery sliced thin
1	cup jicama, shredded
1	6 ounce can water packed tuna, shrimp or crab
2	cups escarole, radicchio or arugula, chopped
2	cups watercress or dandelion

Bread salad is a very good way to use up Italian or French bread that has gotten too hard.

To make homemade bread crumbs use a food processor or blender.

Rice Salad

Serves 4

1/2   pound chicken baked or grilled, chopped
1   avocado, diced
2   cups rice, long grain, cooked
1/3   cup fresh basil, parsley or cilantro, chopped
1   medium cucumber, diced
4   yellow or red tomatoes, chopped
1   cup corn kernels or green beans, cooked
1   red, yellow or green bell pepper, minced
1   cup fresh mushrooms, sliced, sauteed in a little oil
1   cup peas or dried beans, cooked
1   cup water chestnuts, sliced
2   cups strawberries or berries of your choice
1   orange or tangerine segments
4   cups mixed baby lettuce or spinach

Dressing

1   teaspoon Dijon mustard
      salt, pepper and paprika to taste
1/3   cup Marsala Olive Fruit Oil
1/4   cup lime or lemon juice (or vinegar)
2   tablespoons soy sauce
1/3   cup cream Sherry
1/4   cup black or regular sesame seeds
1/4   teaspoon ginger
1/3   cup sweet pickle relish

Mix salad ingredients in a large bowl.

Line a large shallow serving salad bowl or platter with lettuce.

In bowl whisk together dressing ingredients, pour over salad, toss gently.

Spoon onto lettuce lined plate.

Variation:

1   cup roasted peppers, chopped
2   tablespoons fresh mint, chopped
1   cup yellow or red cherry tomatoes
4   green onions (white part) sliced thin
      Substitute brown and wild rice mix cooked, for white rice.
1   cup shrimp, cooked or canned salmon flaked
1/2   cup raisins, golden
1   apple or pear, chopped
1   cup pimiento stuffed olives

Seafood and Spinach Salad

Serves 4 to 6

1	cup squid, cut into rings, cooked
1/2	cup walnuts, chopped
1	pound spinach or mixed baby lettuce
1	small sweet or torpedo onion, cut into rings
1	small cucumber, sliced thin
1	cup red or yellow cherry tomatoes
1	cup shrimp or sea scallops, cooked
1	cup crab cooked, flaked
1	cup jicama, julienned or shredded
1	avocado, diced
1/2	teaspoon oregano
1/2	cup radishes, sliced thin
1	cup olives, sliced
1/2	cup Marsala Olive Fruit Oil
1	teaspoon Dijon mustard
	salt, pepper and paprika to taste
4	garlic cloves, minced
1/2	cup lime or lemon juice or vinegar
1/2	cup sesame seeds, black or regular
	fresh tarragon sprigs for garnish

> **It's _so_ good for you**
> Seafood is an excellent source of omega-3 fatty acids, which act as anti-inflammatories, helping to ease joint problems.

In small bowl add oil, lime juice, salt, pepper, paprika, oregano, garlic and mustard, stir.

In large salad serving bowl combine remaining ingredients, pour dressing over, toss gently.

Sprinkle with sesame seeds, garnish with tarragon sprigs.

Variation:

1/2	cup dried tomatoes, cut into thin strips
1	cup artichoke hearts, sliced
1	bunch watercress, chopped
1-1/2	cups fresh mushrooms, sauteed in a little olive oil
1/3	cup fresh basil or parsley, chopped
2	cups arugula, chopped
2	cups curly endive

> **Spinach protects eyesight**
> Spinach is loaded with lutein and zeaxanthin, two naturally occurring compounds that have been shown to counteract age-related diseases, such as macular degeneration.

Sunshine Coleslaw

Serves 6

1/4	cup honey or pure maple syrup
1/2	pound red or green cabbage, shredded
2	cups pineapple tidbits (or crushed)
4	carrots, shredded
1/2	cup walnuts, chopped (or pecans)
1/2	Marsala mayonnaise
1/4	cup lime or lemon juice
1/4	cup pineapple or orange juice
	salt, pepper and paprika to taste
1	cup grapes, seedless and/or 6 loquats, peeled, seeded
1	papaya or mango, diced
1	avocado, sliced
2	garlic cloves (or to taste) minced

In mixing bowl combine juices, garlic, honey, salt, pepper, paprika and mayonnaise.

In serving salad bowl add remaining ingredients, pour dressing over salad mixture, toss gently.

Variation:

1	teaspoon Dijon mustard
1	teaspoon oregano, cumin or chili
1-1/2	cups turkey, shrimp or crab, cooked, cut into bite size pieces
1/2	cup green onions (white part) sliced thin
1/2	cup radishes, sliced thin or jicama, shredded
1	cup snow peas, cooked crisp tender
1	cucumber, diced (or celery)
2	hard cooked eggs, chopped (yolks removed, if desired)
1/2	cup feta cheese, crumbled
1	cup olives, sliced (or cherry tomatoes)
2	cups spinach or radicchio, chopped
1	cup broccoli or sunflower sprouts
6	artichoke hearts sliced
2	tablespoons capers
1	cup cherry tomatoes

Health benefit

Artichokes are rich in cynarine, which stimulates the production of bile and helps break down fat faster.

Tomato and Mozzarella Salad

Serves 6 to 8

4	tomatoes, sliced
4	hard cooked eggs
8	slices mozzarella sliced thin
1	onion, sliced into thin rings
1	cup olives, sliced
2	avocados, sliced into rings
1/2	cup fresh basil, chopped
	salt, pepper and paprika to taste
1/4	cup lime or lemon juice
1/3	cup Marsala Olive Fruit Oil
6 to 8	Belgian endive, Boston or radicchio leaves

Line large platter with lettuce leaves.

Arrange tomatoes, eggs, onions, avocados and mozzarella slices overlapping on lettuce in serving platter.

In small bowl whisk together lime juice, oil, salt, pepper and paprika.

Spoon lime and oil mixture over salad evenly, sprinkle with basil.

Garnish with olives.

Variation:

1	cup cherry vinegar peppers
1	cucumber, sliced thin
1	cup shrimp or sea scallops, cooked
1	small eggplant sliced 1/4 inch thick, grilled
2	ounces sardines, water packed, crumbled
1	cup pimiento stuffed olives
1	cup musrhooms, sauteed
1-1/2	cups strawberries
1	cup mussels or clams, cooked
6	bocconcini (small fresh mozzarella balls)
1	cup goat cheese, crumbled
2	tablespoons poppy seeds

Health benefit

Basil, which is a key ingredient in pesto, soothes the stomach and kills many disease-carrying parasites in the intestines. Additionally, this herb stimulates the immune system by increasing the production of antibodies. Also contains: magnesium, a nutrient that relaxes blood vessels and helps ward off heart disease.

Turkey Salad With Polenta Cubes

Serves 4 to 6

2	cups turkey cooked, diced (or chicken)
4	green onions (white part) chopped
1	cup chayote cooked, diced
1	cup canned whole cranberry sauce, cubed
1	yam cooked, diced
4	cups mixed baby lettuce, radicchio shredded or spinach
4	radishes, sliced thin
2	cups polenta cubes
1	cup water chestnuts, sliced
6	cherry tomatoes, red or yellow
1	truffle, fresh, medium, grated (if available)

Dressing

	grated peel of 1 orange
	salt, pepper and paprika to taste
4	garlic cloves
1	teaspoon Dijon mustard
1/2	cup Marsala Olive Fruit Oil
1/3	cup lemon or lime juice
1/4	cup pure maple syrup, honey or corn syrup
1/2	cup fresh basil or mint
1	tomato

> **Health benefit**
>
> Ward off migraines with lettuce. This leafy green is chock-full of magnesium, a mineral that speeds, normal blood-vessel function and prevents serious headaches.

In jar of blender add dressing ingredients, whirl until well blended.

In large shallow serving salad bowl, add remaining ingredients, pour dressing mixture over, toss gently, sprinkle with truffle.

Variation:

1/4	pound fresh bean sprouts
1/4	pound pea pods, cooked crisp tender
1/2	head Boston, bibb, curly endive or frisee lettuce
1	cub butternut squash, cooked, diced
Substitute	
1-1/2	cups deli roast beef, cut into 3x1 inch strips for turkey

Waldorf Wheat Salad

Serves 4 to 6

1/3	cup mozzarella, cubed small
1	cup artichoke hearts, sliced
2	apples peeled or unpeeled, diced
1	persimmon, sliced
1	cup celery, sliced thin
1/4	cup pine nuts or walnuts
1-1/2	cups orange segments (or tangerine)
3/4	cup currants, golden raisins or dried cherries
2	cup whole wheat, cooked
1/2	cup Marsala mayonnaise (or to taste)
	pinch of cinnamon or cardamom
1	mango or papaya, diced
1	head butter or red lettuce leaves
	mint, basil or parsley sprigs
	salt and pepper to taste

In large bowl combine all ingredients, except lettuce and mint, toss gently.

In serving platter or shallow bowl arrange lettuce leaves on bottom.

Spoon wheat mixture over evenly, garnish with mint sprigs.

Variation:

2	tomatoes, chopped
1/2	pound grapes, seedless
2	cups turkey or chicken, cooked, diced
2	teaspoons tarragon
1/2	cup scallions, sliced
1	cup olives
1	cup shrimp, cooked
4	kumquats, sliced thin, remove seeds
1/2	cup dried cherries, cranberries or prunes, chopped

Whole wheat may be purchased at Italian specialty stores. The light colored pearl wheat cooks quickly.

Yuri's Oriental Cabbage Salad

Serves 6 to 8

1	small head cabbage, shredded fine
6	green onions, sliced thin diagonally
1	package (3 oz.) Oriental noodle soup mix (any flavor)
2	tablespoons sugar
1/2	cup Marsala Olive Fruit Oil
1/3	cup white vinegar
1	tablespoon soy sauce
1/2	teaspoon white pepper
1/4	cup sesame seeds toasted

In large shallow bowl, combine cabbage and green onions. Break the uncooked noodles into small pieces, mix into cabbage.

(Save the seasoning packet for other uses.)

Dressing

Stir together sugar, olive oil, vinegar, soy sauce and pepper in mixing bowl.

Pour over cabbage mixture, toss well. Cover, chill 2 to 4 hours.

Stir before serving; sprinkle with sesame seeds.

Tomato and Basil Salad

Serves 4

4	tomatoes, sliced
6 to 8	fresh basil leaves
1/4	cup pine nuts
	oil and vinegar dressing

Place tomatoes overlapping in serving plate. Arrange basil leaves in center.

Sprinkle with pine nuts, drizzle with dressing.

Garnish with tomato rose.

Variation:

1	cup dried ricotta, shaved

Health benefit
Cider vinegar eases sore throats. Apple cider vinegar is an antiseptic that fights infection and soothes laryngitis symptoms.

Persimmon and Grapefruit Salad

Serves 6

3	grapefruits (red or yellow) sectioned
1	orange (red or orange) sectioned
6	large persimmons, Fuyu
1	cup pomegranate seeds
6	ounces frisee, cut into bite size pieces
2	cups Belgian endive cut crosswise into 1/4 inch slices
1	cup French dressing (made with Marsala Olive Oil)
4	tablespoons honey or pure maple syrup
12	sugared pecans

Place persimmons stem side down, cut each into 6 sections, without cutting all the way through.

Place persimmons on a serving platter lined with a bed of frisée and endive.

Spread persimmons open, petal fashion. Arrange grapefruit and orange in center and around each persimmon.

Stir honey into French dressing, serve with salad.

Garnish with pomegranate seeds and sugared pecans.

Variation:

avocado, sliced
chicken, grilled, cubed
1 mango cubed

French Dressing

Makes about 1 cup

1/4	cup vinegar
1/3	cup catchup
2	tablespoons sugar
2	teaspoon onions, minced
3/4	teaspoon salt
1/2	cup Marsala Olive Oil
1/4	teaspoon pepper, black

> ## Health benefit
> Oranges are full of folic acid (17% of the RDA), a B vitamin that may help prevent heart disease.

Mustard and Olive Oil Dressing

!/3	cup Dijon mustard
1/2	cup Marsala or Sciabica olive oil

In mixing bowl whisk together mustard and olive oil until emulsified. Keep refrigerated until ready to serve. Serve over poached fish, meats, and in sandwiches in amount desired.

Endive Boat Salad

Serves 4 to 6

12	large Belgian endive leaves
1	grapefruit in segments
2	mandarin oranges, fresh or canned, segments
1	cup goat, feta, ricotta (or cheese of your choice)
12	glazed pecans

Dressing

1/4	cup lime or lemon juice
1/4	cup honey or pure maple syrup
	pinch of ginger
	salt and white pepper to taste
1	teaspoon Dijon mustard
1/4	cup Marsala or Sciabica's orange olive oil

Place endive leaves decoratively on serving plate. Place 1 grapefruit and orange segment on each leaf.

Distribute cheese in leaves evenly, top with pecans. Combine dressing ingredients, blend, pour over salad evenly.

Refrigerate until ready to serve.

Waldorf Salad

Serves 4 to 6

3	apples, yellow delicious, cut into 1/2 inch chunks
5	celery stalks, cut into 1/2 inch slices
1	cup walnuts, chopped
1/2	cup Sciabica's orange olive oil
1	cup pineapple, tidbits
	salt, white pepper and sugar to taste
	juice of 1/2 lime (or to taste)
1	head Bibb lettuce

In bowl, combine all ingredients, except lettuce, toss gently. Keep refrigerated until ready to serve. Line shallow salad bowl with Bibb lettuce. Arrange salad ingredients on top evenly when ready to serve.

Variations:

blue or goat cheese, crumbled
grapes, seedless
avocado, diced

Stuffed Eggs Pg 69   ~   Pasta with Pesto Sauce and Ricotta Pg 185

Pizza Pg 156   ~   Torta Rustica Pg 34   ~   Empanadas Pg 252

Egg Pockets

Makes 6

1   recipe for pie crust pastry
6   eggs (small)
1   cup mixed vegetables, (fresh or frozen, chopped)
1/2   cup Cheddar cheese, shredded
1/2   cup prosciutto, ham or lean turkey, bacon, cooked, crumbled
1/4   cup Marsala Olive Oil
1/4   cup parsley or basil, chopped

Saute vegetables in a non stick skillet with olive oil until tender, cool. Add cheese, ham and parsley.

Roll pastry out onto lightly floured surface. Cut into about 5 inch circles. Place circles in lightly greased muffin cups or place inside of a dumpling maker.

Place 1 egg into each pastry lined cup, top with a little vegetable mixture. Moisten edges with water. Pinch edges together forming a semi-circle.

If using a dumpling maker, fill, moisten edges, snap closed to seal.

Bake on a greased baking pan in a 350 degrees oven for 15 to 20 minutes or until golden brown.

Nick had these turnovers for breakfast when in Tunisia, but said they were deep fried.

The filling is as close as he could remember.

Coucous was served often and he found it very good. He also liked Harissa, which is a paste made from very hot peppers. He brought a tube of it home, believe me, it lasted a long time.

Coucous and Harissa are available at Middle Eastern grocery stores.

Coucous is a granulated pasta (semolina) made from the heart of durum wheat.

Shirred Eggs

Serves 2

4   eggs
        salt and pepper to taste
2   tablespoons Marsala Olive Fruit Oil

Preheat oven to 375 degrees. In 2 greased ramikins add 2 eggs in each one.

Sprinkle with salt and pepper.

Drizzle with olive oil, cover with foil tightly.

Bake for 12 to 15 minutes.

Variation:

4   tablespoons chopped ham
4   tablespoons fontina, shredded (or cheese of your choice)

Whole Eggs with Tomato Gravy

Serves 4

1/2	recipe for chunky tomato gravy, heated
1/4	cup Marsala Olive Fruit Oil
4	eggs
1/4	cup Romano cheese
1/4	cup mozzarella cheese, shredded
	basil or parsley, chopped fine

In non stick skillet over medium heat add oil. Break one egg at a time in saucer, slide into skillet, careful not to break yolk.

Cook until set, turn over easy for a few seconds. Lift egg into heated gravy. Repeat with remaining eggs.

Simmer about 5 to 10 minutes. Serve over cooked pasta, rice, couscous or whole wheat.

Garnish with basil.

Variation:

add 1 cup fresh mushrooms, sliced, to gravy.

Eggs cooked in this manner were a good substitute for meat; very popular in the 30's and 40's. Bread balls were also substituted for meat in the gravy.

My Mom would say eggs are the cement of cooking.

Scrambled Eggs

Serves 2

2	tablespoons Marsala Olive Fruit Oil
	salt, white pepper to taste
2	tablespoons orange juice or milk (non fat)
4	eggs (or 2 eggs and 4 egg whites)

Place oil into nonstick skillet over medium heat.

In mixing bowl combine eggs, orange juice, salt and pepper, beat until blended.

Pour egg mixture into skillet, stir gently until eggs are cooked through but still moist.

Variation:

2	tablespoons Romano cheese, grated or cheese of your choice
4	strips lean turkey bacon, cooked, well drained, crumbled
4	tablespoons ricotta, low fat
	mushrooms, chopped

Scrambled Eggs with Tomatoes

Serves 4

1/4	cup Marsala Olive Fruit Oil
6	eggs (or 3 eggs and 6 egg whites)
4	tablespoons milk, non fat
	Salt and white pepper to taste
2	tablespoons Romano cheese, grated
1/4	cup fresh basil, parsley, mint or cilantro, chopped
2	tomatoes, chopped
2	green onions (white part) chopped

In mixing bowl beat eggs, milk, salt, pepper, cheese and basil together.

In large nonstick skillet add oil and onions, cook until soft.

Add tomatoes, cook about 4 minutes. Pour in egg mixture, stir gently until eggs are cooked through but still moist and creamy in consistency.

Variation:

Substitute one of the following for tomatoes:

ham, chopped
cheddar, Monterey Jack or Swiss cheese, shredded
zucchini, sliced thin
peas or corn
asparagus tips
olives, sliced
artichoke hearts
potato cooked, sliced
spinach, cooked, well drained, chopped

> ### Health benefit
> Keep your eye on eggs. Egg yolks are high in lutein, the carotenoid that prevents macular degeneration.

Breakfast Eggs

Serves 2

2	tablespoons Marsala Olive Fruit Oil
4	eggs
	salt and white pepper to taste

In nonstick skillet over medium heat add oil.

Break eggs into pie plate, add salt and pepper, slide into skillet.

Cook until set to your liking. If desired, turn over easy for a few seconds.

Years ago I read somewhere that 1 fresh egg will do more for you than a whole bottle of pills.

Frittata With Potatoes

Serves 4

1/2	cup artichoke hearts, chopped
1/4	cup Marsala Olive Fruit Oil
1	onion, chopped
1/4	cup basil or parsley, chopped
2	potatoes peeled, sliced thin
4	garlic cloves, chopped
	salt, pepper and cayenne to taste
1/3	cup Cheddar, provolone or cheese of your choice, shredded
1	bell pepper, chopped small
8	eggs (or 4 eggs and 8 egg whites)

In a large non stick skillet with oven proof handle, over medium heat add oil.

In mixing bowl beat eggs to blend.

Add potatoes, onion, salt, pepper and cayenne to skillet, cook for about 4 minutes or until golden.

Add bell pepper, basil and artichokes. Turn mixture with a spatula, cook until all is tender.

Pour eggs over potato mixture. As the mixture sets run a spatula around edge of skillet.

Lift egg allowing the uncooked portion to flow underneath.

Bake in a 350 degrees oven for about 10 minutes or until golden and knife inserted in center comes out clean.

Sprinkle with cheese, cut into wedges. Serve with sliced tomatoes or avocado, if desired.

Variation:

	zucchini blossoms
1	cup spinach, cooked, well drained, chopped
1/2	cup olives, sliced
1	cup arugula or greens of your choice
2	leeks or green onions (white part) sliced thin
1	zucchini, medium, sliced thin
1/2	cup ricotta, low fat
2	tablespoons fresh chives
1/3	cup dried tomatoes, chopped

Health benefit

Zucchini contains the antioxidant glutathione, which boosts the body's immune system and helps detoxify chemicals which can build up in the liver.

Omelet

Serves 1

2   **eggs (or 1 egg and 2 egg whites)**
2   **tablespoons water**
       salt and pepper to taste
       Marsala Olive Fruit Oil

Whisk eggs, water, salt and pepper in mixing bowl.

Heat 1 tablespoon olive oil in a nonstick 10 inch skillet over medium heat.

Add eggs mixture, cook until edges are set.

Pull cooked egg toward center, tilting pan to let uncooked egg flow underneath.

Repeat until egg stops flowing, but top is still moist.

For filled omelet, place about 1/2 cup filling on one half. Fold unfilled side over filling.

Holding skillet in one hand, take a plate with the other. Invert skillet so omelet falls upside down onto plate.

> ### Boost brainpower with eggs
> The yolks contain high amounts of acetyl-choline, a compound that has been shown to improve memory.

Fillings

Add one of the following

      crushed pineapple with 2 tablespoons brown sugar
      cooked spinach, broccoli or greens of your choice
      sauteed onions, peppers and mushrooms
      Monterey Jack, mozzarella or Swiss cheese, shredded
      applesauce, pinch of cinnamon
      ricotta with fresh berries or fruit of your choice
      jams or jellies with ground nuts
      ham, smoked salmon with green onions, chopped
      asparagus tips, cooked crisp tender
      avocado, sliced
      Spanish omelet sauce

For larger omelet you may double or triple ingredients.
For each omelet use about 1/2 cup egg mixture.

Omelet Roll

Serves 4 to 6

6	eggs (or 4 eggs and 4 egg whites) beaten
	salt and pepper to taste
1/3	cup Marsala Olive Fruit Oil

Filling

1/4	cup raisins, currants or pine nuts
1	egg white
	pinch of cayenne
1-1/4	cups spinach, cooked, well drained and chopped
1/3	cup Romano cheese, grated or provolone, shredded
1/2	cup mozzarella, shredded (or goat cheese)
2	green onions, chopped
1/2	cup fresh mushrooms, chopped
1/2	cup rice, cooked
1/4	cup fresh basil, parsley or cilantro
2	garlic cloves, minced

In small skillet, over medium heat add 3 tablespoons olive oil, onions, mushrooms and garlic, cook until tender.

In mixing bowl combine onion mixture with remaining filling ingredients.

In large non stick skillet add remaining oil, place on medium heat. Pour in eggs, add salt and pepper, cook on one side until set.

Left edges around to let uncooked egg flow underneath to cook.

Slide omelet onto greased baking sheet. Spread with filling to 1 inch edge all around.

Roll omelet jelly roll fashion with seam side down.

Bake in a 350 degrees oven for about 10 to 15 minutes.

To serve, slice into about 1-1/2 inch pieces. Arrange on serving platter.

Garnish with avocado, mango or papaya slices and mint, parsley, rosemary or basil sprigs.

Place yellow or cherry tomatoes on each side.

Variation for filling:

> sausage, ham, turkey or meat of your choice, cooked and chopped
> zucchini, corn, green beans, asparagus tips, peas, carrots, broccoli or a variety of vegetables, cooked crisp tender
> olives, sliced
> shrimp, scallops, crab, tuna or fish of your choice
> mashed potatoes or roasted peppers

Peppers, Onions With Eggs

Serves 4 to 6

2	bell peppers, sliced thin
1	onion, sliced thin
1/4	cup Marsala Olive Fruit Oil
2	cups fresh or canned tomatoes
1/2	cup fresh basil or parsley, chopped
	salt, pepper and cayenne to taste
4	eggs (or 2 eggs and 4 egg whites)
4	garlic cloves, chopped

> **Look younger with bell peppers.**
> These sweet vegetables are loaded with vitamin C, an antioxidant that boosts your skin's production of collagen, which erases fine lines.

In large skillet add oil, onions, garlic and peppers. Cook covered on medium heat until crisp tender.

Add tomatoes, salt, pepper, basil and cayenne, cook 2 or 3 minutes.

In mixing bowl lightly beat eggs, pour into vegetable mixture.

Stir until eggs are cooked and still creamy.

Serve with toasted Italian bread.

This recipe was often served by Mom when we would come home from school on the lunch hour.

Mom canned many jars of peppers and tomatoes.

Pastina With Eggs

Serves 2

2	eggs (or 1 egg and 2 egg whites)
1	cup pastina (tiny pasta)
3	cups water
	white pepper to taste
2	tablespoons Marsala Olive Fruit Oil
1/4	cup Romano cheese, grated

Cook pastina in small sauce pan in boiling water until tender.

Drain most of the water out. In small bowl add eggs, cheese, oil and pepper.

Beat slightly and pour into pan with pastina. Cook over medium heat, stirring gently until egg is set.

Do not overcook.

This is one of my grandchildren's favorite recipe.

When they were very little they would say "Bana stina" — (Grandma pastina).

Even now that they have grown, they still like pastina.

Stuffed Eggs

Serves 6 to 8

6	hard cooked eggs
3 or 4	tablespoons Marsala Mayonnaise
4	tablespoons sweet pickle relish
1	teaspoon Dijon mustard
	pinch of white pepper
	paprika
12	slices sweet or dill pickles (midget)
4	olives, chopped (pimiento stuffed)
	cilantro sprigs
4	radish roses (for garnish)

Cut eggs in half lengthwise, remove yolks, place in mixing bowl.

Add mayonnaise, relish, mustard, pepper and olives, stir to blend.

Stuff egg white halves, sprinkle with paprika. Place in egg platter with indented cups. Garnish with midget pickles, olives, cilantro and/or radish roses.

Variation:

4	tablespoons ricotta
	pinch of nutmeg
1/4	cup tuna, canned, water packed or smoked salmon
1/4	cup ham, chopped small
1/4	cup dried tomatoes, chopped
1	tablespoon capers
1	anchovy, rinsed, minced or sardines
1	garlic cloves, minced
1	tablespoon parsley or tarragon, minced
2	tablespoons pure maple syrup or honey

Stuffed Tomatoes

6	large Roma tomatoes, peeled

Cut tomatoes in half lengthwise, scoop out pulp. (save for another use.)

Place the stuffed egg halves in tomato halves.

Arrange in egg serving plate with indented cups.

Garnish as desired.

> ### Ham reduces the risk of stroke
> A quarter-pound of lean ham contains more potassium than a banana.
> Potassium reduces the risk of stroke and high blood pressure.

Curry Rice and Chicken
Serves 4

1/3	cup chicken broth
2	tablespoons flour
1-1/2	pounds boneless, skinless chicken (or turkey)
1	onion, chopped
2	teaspoons curry (or to taste)
2	golden delicious apples, diced (or pears)
	salt and pepper to taste
1/3	cup Marsala Olive Fruit Oil

Cut chicken into bite size pieces, dust with flour. In large skillet, over medium heat, cook chicken in oil until golden.

Add onion, apples, salt, broth, pepper and curry. Cook covered on low heat until tender.

Rice

1	cup rice
	salt and pepper to taste
2	cups chicken broth
1	onion, chopped
2	tablespoons Marsala Olive Fruit Oil
1	cup fresh mushrooms, sliced
1/4	cup white wine

In saucepan add oil, onion and rice, cook over medium heat until rice is golden. Add wine, cook about 30 seconds.

Add broth, bring to a boil, Cook about 5 minutes on a low boil, add mushrooms, turn off heat.

Let stand covered 10 to 15 minutes. Spoon rice onto a large platter. Cover with sauce and chicken.

Variation Rice-a-Roni:

Substitute 1/2 cup of any short macaroni, for rice.

Oven Risotto
Serves 4

1	recipe for Quick Risotto

Add quick risotto ingredients into a 2-1/2 quart greased casserole, stir.

Bake covered in a 350 degrees oven for 55 to 60 minutes or until rice is tender.

Stir twice during baking.

Variation:

1	cup peas or carrots, diced (or vegetable of your choice)
1/4	cup pine nuts or nuts of your choice, chopped
1/3	cup Romano cheese, grated
1	cup raisins, banana, apricots, quince or prunes, chopped

Oven Baked Polenta

Serves 6

1 cup polenta
3-1/2 cups broth, milk, non fat (or water)
2 tablespoons Marsala Olive Fruit Oil
   salt and pepper to taste

Preheat oven to 350 degrees. Combine all ingredients in a lightly greased 9x13x3 inch baking dish, stir.

Bake about 40 minutes or until all liquid is absorbed. Stir several times during baking.

Serve with your favorite meat, fish or vegetable sauce.

Variation:

Stir in when cooked - 1/2 cup Cheddar, provolone or Monterey Jack cheese, shredded or goat cheese, crumbled
1-1/2 cups mushrooms, sauteed in a little olive oil
1/2 cup fresh basil or parsley, chopped

Grilled Polenta With Garbanzo

Serves 6

1 recipe for baked polenta
1 to 1-1/2 cups garbanzo or dried beans, cooked, drained
   Marsala Olive Fruit Oil

Add garbanzo to polenta when cooked. Pour into prepared lightly greased 9 by 12 inch pan, cool.

Cut into about 3 inch squares or triangles, brush with olive oil. Grill on both sides until golden brown.

Sprinkle with pepper and grated cheese if desired.

Note:

For thicker polenta, reduce liquid about 1 cup.

For thinner polenta add 3/4 to 1 cup more liquid.

Variation:

  substitute 1/3 cup semolina for 1/3 cup polenta

Paella

Serves 6 to 8

1-1/2	pounds chicken, skinless and boneless, cut bite size
1/2	pound Italian sausage, cooked, well drained
1/3	cup Marsala Olive Fruit Oil
1	large onion, chopped
6	garlic cloves (or to taste) chopped
1-1/4	cups long grain rice
2	red, green or yellow bell peppers, chopped
3 or 4	tomatoes or tomatillos, chopped
2	cups chicken or beef broth
1/4	pound clams or mussels in shell
1/4	pound squid cut into rings
1/4	pound shrimp, scallops or lobster, chopped
1/2	teaspoon tabasco (or to taste)
	pinch of saffron
1-1/2	cups fresh or frozen peas or green beans
1	cup asparagus tips
	salt, pepper and cayenne to taste
2	bay leaves
1/2	cup fresh basil, parsley or cilantro, chopped
1/2	cup white wine
1/2	pound fresh mushrooms, sliced
	Romano cheese, grated
2	lemons, quartered for garnish

In large paella pan or Dutch oven, brown chicken in oil on all sides.

In another pan, cook sausage in 1 cup water until browned. Lift out with slotted spoon, drain well, slice 3/4 inch thick.

Add onions, garlic, peppers and sausage to chicken, cook a few minutes. Add tomatoes, bay leaves, broth, wine and rice.

Cook covered on low heat for about 20 minutes. Add clams, squid, shrimp, basil, saffron, salt, pepper and cayenne.

Stir gently, cover, cook another 5 minutes. (remove any unopened clams.)

Add peas, asparagus and mushrooms. Cook 1 minutes covered. Turn heat off.

Let stand 10 minutes. Remove bay leaves before serving. Sprinkle with cheese if desired, garnish with lemon wedges.

Continued

Paella
Continued

Variation: Portions may vary

2	cups spinach, swiss chard or escarole, chopped
1	cup artichoke hearts or green beans
2	small chili or jalapeno peppers, minced
1	cup carrots or beets, cubed
1/2	pound halibut, bass or crayfish
1/2	pound pork loin or ham, cut into strips
4	lobster tails or 1-1/2 cups crab meat, cleaned
1	pound rabbit or duck meat, cubed
2	cups dried white beans, cooked
4	ounces spaghetti cut into 2 inch pieces, cooked
	paprika
	oyster crackers
1-1/2	cups pumpkin, fresh cubed

Polenta Lasagna
Serves 4 to 6

1	polenta recipe (using 1-1/4 cups polenta)
1	recipe for mini meatball gravy
1-1/2	cups ricotta (low fat)
1	cup mozzarella, shredded
1/2	cup Romano cheese, grated
1-1/2	cups swiss chard, cooked crisp tender, chopped
1	cup fresh or frozen peas

Pour cooked polenta into lightly greased 10x15 baking pan, spread evenly, let cool.

Lightly grease lasagna pan or casserole. Cut polenta into slices to fit pan. Pour in about 1/2 cup gravy covering bottom evenly.

Layer polenta slices over gravy, place on 1/2 of the ricotta, mozzarella, swiss chard and peas evenly. Cover with about 1 cup gravy. Repeat with polenta slices, peas, ricotta, mozzarella, swiss chard and gravy.

Sprinkle with grated cheese, cover loosely with foil. Bake in a 350 degrees oven for 25 to 35 minutes or until bubbly.

Variation:

Substitute eggplant, broccoli, artichoke hearts or vegetables of your choice for swiss chard.

Polenta Cubes for Salads

2   cups broth or water
2/3   cup polenta
2   tablespoons Marsala Olive Fruit Oil
       salt and pepper to taste
1/4   cup Romano cheese

In saucepan add broth, polenta, salt and pepper. Bring to a boil, lower to simmer.

Cook stirring frequently until very thick, about 10 to 12 minutes. Blend in olive oil and cheese.

Grease an 8x8 baking pan. Pour polenta mixture into pan, spread in a smooth even layer.

Cool completely, cut into 1 inch cubes. Toss as many cubes in salad as desired.

Any left over cubes may be refrigerated covered, for later use.

Variation:

1/4   cup provolone, shredded
1   tablespoon rosemary, thyme or tarragon, chopped
1   tablespoon pesto sauce
1   egg white lightly beaten

Note: Cut polenta in desired shapes (hearts, diamonds, rounds, leaves, triangles, etc.)

Breathe easier with thyme
This flavorful herb contains thymol, a volatile oil that helps clear congested airways.

Easy Spanish Rice
Serves 4

In large non stick skillet add 1/4 cup Marsala Olive Oil, 1 onion chopped and 1 bell pepper sliced, cook until tender.

Add 1/2 pound lean ground turkey, beef or lamb, saute about 10 minutes. Add 1 cup long grain rice, 2 cups tomato juice, salt, pepper and paprika to taste.

Pour into a greased casserole, bake covered in a 350 degrees oven until rice is tender, about 25 minutes. Add 1 cup sliced fresh mushrooms, bake another 5 minutes. Add a little more liquid if needed.

Quick Risotto

Serves 4

1-1/4	cups rice, long grain (or Italian Arborio)
1	onion, chopped
1/4	cup Marsala Olive Fruit Oil
	salt and white pepper to taste
2	garlic cloves, chopped
1/2	cup white wine
2-1/2	cups broth
	pinch of saffron, curry or nutmeg
1/4	cup Romano cheese (or to taste)

In saucepan, over medium heat add oil, onions and garlic. Cook until soft.

Add rice, cook until golden, stirring often. Stir in wine, cook 1 minute.

Add broth, salt, pepper and saffron, bring to a boil.

On medium heat, cook rice 5 minutes, stirring occasionally.

Turn heat off, cover, let stand 10 to 15 minutes. Fluff with a fork when ready to serve.

Variation:

1	cup fresh mushrooms, sliced
1	cup prosciutto or lean ham, chopped
1	cup fennel bulb, sliced thin (cooked crisp tender)
1/3	cup raisins or dried apricots, chopped (or berries)
2	potatoes, diced, cooked
1/3	cup dried tomatoes, chopped
1/2	cup olives of your choice, chopped
2	cups curly endive or arugula, chopped
1	cup zucchini diced or asparagus tips
1	cup fresh or frozen peas (or corn)
4	tomatoes, plum, diced
1	cup bell pepper, diced
	grated peel of 1 orange or lemon
1/4	pound Italian sausage, cooked, drained, crumbled
1	cup pumpkin or butternut squash, shredded
1	cup shrimp, crab or scallops, sliced (cooked)
1/2	cup fontina, mozzarella or provolone, shredded
2	cups escarole, radicchio, beet greens or greens of your choice, par boiled, chopped

Notes: When adding vegetables, stir in just before heat is turned off, cover.

For creamier risotto use Arborio Italian rice. I prefer Uncle Ben's long grain rice.

Rice and Beans

Serves 4 to 6

1/2	cup fresh basil or parsley, chopped
3 or 4	slices lean turkey bacon, chopped
2	cups white or brown cooked rice
1/2	pound dried beans (or lentils)
1/4	cup Marsala Olive Fruit Oil
1	large onion, chopped
1	cup celery, sliced
4	garlic cloves, chopped
	salt, pepper and cayenne to taste
1	bell pepper, chopped
2	bay leaves
1/3	cup rum liqueur
1	cup lean ham, chopped
1	teaspoon Worcestershire sauce
1	cup Cheddar cheese

Pick beans over, rinse, place in a large pot. Cover with water, let stand covered overnight.

Next day, cook beans on low heat until tender. Add more water if needed to just covering beans.

In saucepan, over medium heat add onions, celery, pepper and garlic.

Cook until tender. Add salt, pepper, basil, cayenne, bay leaves, Worcestershire sauce, rum, ham and bacon. Cook simmering about 10 minutes.

Add vegetable sauce to cooked beans, remove bay leaves.

Serve beans over cooked rice, sprinkle with cheese, (or serve rice and beans side by side).

Variation:

2 or 3	tomatoes
1	carrot, diced

Serve beans over cooked whole wheat.

Garnish with 2 hard cooked eggs, sliced and 2 small onions sliced into thin rings.

Rice Pizza Casserole

Serves 4 to 6

2	onions, sliced
1/4	cup Marsala Olive Fruit Oil
3	cups spinach, cooked, chopped
1-1/2	cups Cheddar, Swiss or mozzarella cheese (low fat)
1-1/2	cups ham, chopped
1	cup beef or chicken broth
1/2	cup white wine
2-1/2	cups milk (non fat)
1-1/2	cups rice (Italian arborio)
1/2	cup fresh basil or parsley, chopped
1	cup fresh mushrooms, chopped
	pepper and cayenne to taste
1/2	cup Romano cheese, grated
4	garlic cloves, minced

Preheat oven to 350 degrees. Lightly grease large casserole or baking pan.

In skillet cook onions and garlic in olive oil until crisp tender. Spread mixture in pan evenly, top with spinach, then ham and cheese.

Sprinkle over with rice, add remaining ingredients. Pour in broth, wine and milk. Cover with foil.

Bake 45 to 50 minutes or until rice is tender.

If needed pour 1/2 cup milk over top, to prevent drying.

Orzo Pilaf

Serves 3 to 4

Cook 1 cup orzo (rice shaped pasta) in 1/4 cup Marsala Olive Oil until lightly browned. Add 1 chopped onion, cook until soft. Add 2 cups broth or consomme, bring to a boil, lower to simmer. Cook covered until liquid is absorbed and orzo is tender. Add 1 cup mushrooms, 1/2 cup fresh basil or parsley chopped, salt, pepper and cayenne to taste. Cook 1 more minute. Serves as a side dish.

Variation:

2	tomatoes, chopped

Socca
(Chickpea Fritters)

Serves 6

2-1/4	cups chick pea flour (garbanzo)
2	cups water
1/4	cup Marsala Olive Oil
	salt, pepper and cayenne to taste
2	tablespoons fresh basil, parsley, rosemary or lavender
4	garlic cloves, minced

Wisk all ingredients together until smooth or use a blender. Let stand about 1 hour.

Lightly grease a 12 or 14 inch pizza pan. Drizzle with 2 or 3 tablespoons olive oil.

Pour batter into pan evenly, bake in a 400 degrees oven for about 15 minutes or until golden, cool.

Cut into irregular pieces about 2 by 3 inches.

In a non stick skillet with 2 or 3 tablespoons olive oil, cook until golden on both sides; avoid crowding.

Variation:

1	onion, sliced, caramelized
1/4	cup raisins or currants
1/4	cup green onions (white part) chopped
1/4	cup pine nuts
1	tablespoon fresh sage or mint, chopped
1/4	cup Romano cheese or provolone cheese, shredded

To make 1/2 socca recipe bake in a 10 inch greased pizza pan.

Note: Chick pea flour may be found in Italian specialty stores.

Quick Rice Balls

Serves 4 to 6

In mixing bowl add 2-1/2 cups of cooked rice, 2 eggs, 1/3 cup provolone or Romano cheese grated, salt, pepper and cayenne to taste, 1/2 cup fresh basil or parsley and 1 green onion, finely chopped.

Place 1 cup bread crumbs in pie plate, make rice mixture into 1-1/2 inch balls.

Roll into crumbs all around. Cook in a large non stick skillet with 1/4 cup Marsala Olive Oil until golden brown.

Fish Soup

Serves 6

1/3   cup Marsala Olive Fruit Oil
2   tomatoes, chopped
1-1/2   cups celery, sliced thin
1/4   cup flour
2   onions, sliced thin
2   carrots, shredded
2   quarts fish stock
1   cup white wine
    pinch of saffron
2   bay leaves
    salt, pepper and red pepper flakes (to taste)
1/2   pound swordfish, cut into 1 inch pieces
1/2   pound salmon, cut into 1 inch pieces
1/2   pound shrimp or scallops, halved
1/3   cup cognac or vermouth
1/4   cup fresh rosemary or tarragon
1/2   cup fresh basil or parsley, chopped
1-1/2   cups fresh or frozen peas or asparagus tips
1/2   cup almonds, ground
6   garlic cloves

In soup pot add olive oil, onions, carrots, celery and garlic, cook until crisp tender.

Add tomatoes, fish stock and wine, cook several minutes.

Add bay leaves, salt and peppers, simmer covered about 10 minutes.

Coat fish with flour, remove any excess. Heat 2 tablespoons olive oil in large non stick skillet.

Brown fish in batches if necessary, tossing gently until just cooked, about 2 minutes. Do not overcook.

Add cognac and fish to soup with remaining ingredients. Stir gently; simmer covered for about 2 minutes.

Remove bay leaves before serving. Serve with toasted Italian bread.

Variation:

2   potatoes, diced
1   cup radiator or wagon wheel pasta, cooked
    pinch of saffron
4   bay leaves, remove before serving

Fresh Tomato Soup

Serves 4 to 6

4	cups chicken broth
1/4	cup fresh basil or parsley, chopped
4	garlic cloves, chopped
1	onion, chopped
1/4	cup Marsala Olive Fruit Oil
1	cup sherry or white wine
3	tablespoons flour
2	pounds tomatoes, fresh, peeled, diced
	salt, pepper and cayenne to taste
2	bay leaves
1	teaspoon celery seeds, ground
2	cups croutons
	Romano cheese, grated or mozzarella, shredded

In Dutch oven, over medium heat add oil, onions and garlic, cook until soft.

Stir in flour, cook until smooth. Add sherry, simmer a few minutes.

Add tomatoes and remaining ingredients, (except croutons and cheese) cover and simmer 20 to 30 minutes.

Remove bay leaves before serving. Serve with cheese and croutons.

Garnish with celery leaves (center part)

Variations:

	substitute green tomatoes with pink blush
1	cup carrots or asparagus, chopped
1	cup celery, chopped (or fennel bulb)
2	bell peppers, chopped
2 to 3	cups arugula or spinach, chopped
	pinch of nutmeg or cinnamon
1	teaspoon paprika or cumin
	grated peel of 1 orange or lemon
1	yam shredded
1	cup mushrooms, chopped
6	ounces cheese tortellini
	fresh rosemary to taste
1	pound small fresh clams, well scrubbed

Cover, cook just until clams open, about 5 to 7 minutes. Discard any unopened clams.

Note: For smooth tomato soup, whirl in jar of blender. May have to be made in 2 batches.

Every summer we all looked forward to fresh tomato soup.

Gazpacho

Serves 6

1	cup celery, chopped
1	avocado, diced
6	tomatoes, red or yellow, peeled, chopped
1/2	cup Marsala Olive Fruit Oil
1/2	cup white wine vinegar
	salt, pepper and cayenne to taste
2	radishes, chopped
2	tablespoons lime or lemon juice
1/2	cup green onions (white and light green parts, chopped)
1/2	cup fresh basil, parsley or cilantro, chopped
2	cucumbers, diced
4	garlic cloves, minced
1	cup chicken broth
2	cups tomato juice
1/2	teaspoon Worcestershire sauce
	garnishes

Garnishes

red or yellow cherry tomatoes
celery sliced thin
fennel bulb sliced thin
mint sprigs
yellow squash sliced thin
shrimp, crab, chicken or lobster, cooked, chopped
avocado diced

Puree gazpacho ingredients in jar of blender or food processor. May have to be made in 2 batches.

Chill until ready to serve. Pour gazpacho into individual soup bowls. Serve with desired garnish.

Variation:

1	cup garbanzo, cooked
1-1/2	cups croutons, toasted
1/4	cup almonds toasted, slivered
1	apple, chopped or grapes, seedless
1/2	teaspoon chives or tarragon
2	green tomatoes with pink blush

Chunky Gazpacho With Pasta

Finely chop vegetables, add remaining ingredients, then add 2 cups small shell pasta, cooked.

Dan said he got to like this soup when he was in Spain.

Lentil Soup

Serves 6 to 8

1	pound lentils
2-1/2	quarts water (10 cups)
1	cup carrots, diced
1	cup celery, diced
	salt and pepper to taste
3	cups tomatoes, fresh or canned, chopped
1	onion, chopped
6	garlic cloves, chopped
1/2	cup fresh basil or parsley, chopped
2	bay leaves
1-1/2	cups elbow, any small pasta or rice
	mini meatballs
1/2	cup Marsala Olive Fruit Oil

Note: A friend adds 1 cup pomegranate juice to lentil soup.

Mini Meatballs

1/2	pound lamb, lean, ground
	salt, pepper and cayenne to taste
1	egg (or 2 egg whites)
1/2	teaspoon fennel or anise seeds
1/2	cup bread crumbs
1/4	cup Romano cheese, grated
1/4	cup fresh basil or mint, chopped
2	tablespoons Marsala Olive Fruit Oil
	flour (to coat meatballs)

Pick over lentils, rinse, place in large pot.

Add water, salt, pepper, carrots, celery, tomatoes, onion, garlic and bay leaves.

Cook over low heat, covered for about 40 minutes or until lentils are tender.

Combine meatball ingredients, working lightly; form into mini meatballs.

Roll balls in flour, then brown in olive oil in a non-stick skillet over medium heat. Add to soup.

Cook pasta (al dente) not too soft, drain, add to soup. Stir in olive oil, remove bay leaves before serving.

Sprinkle with Romano cheese, grated, if desired

Variation:

1	turnip, diced
1	potato, diced (or yam)
1	head escarole, chopped

Minestrone with Potato Dumplings

Serves 4 to 6

1/2	cup barley
6 to 8	cups chicken broth or water
2	cups celery, diced
1	onion, chopped
4	garlic cloves, chopped
4	carrots, diced
4	tomatoes, chopped
1	cup dried beans, cooked (or garbanzo)
1	zucchini, diced (or chayote)
1-1/2	cups pumpkin, diced (or potatoes)
1	cup fresh or frozen peas
1/2	cup fresh basil, mint or parsley, chopped
1	small eggplant, diced
1	turnip or parsnip, diced
1	jalapeño, minced
2	cups cabbage, escarole, kale or greens of your choice
1/4	pound lean meat ground, made into mini meatballs
1/4	cup pesto sauce
1/4	cup Marsala Olive Fruit Oil
	salt, pepper and cayenne to taste

> **Mint makes meals easy to digest**
> Menthol, the volatile oil found in mint, is a stomach-soothing compound that aids in digestion.

In large pot add oil and mini meatballs; cook until brown on all sides.

Add onion, cook until tender. Add broth and remaining ingredients, bring to a boil, lower to simmer.

Cook until vegetables are tender. Add dumplings, dropping dough by tablespoons. Simmer 10 to 12 minutes, covered.

Potato Dumplings

Makes 8

2	cups potatoes, mashed
1/2	cup flour
1	teaspoon baking powder
1/2	teaspoon each salt and pepper
2	egg whites and 1 egg yolk
1/4	cup fresh basil, parsley or cilantro, chopped
1	tablespoon Marsala Olive Fruit Oil
2	tablespoons Romano cheese, grated
1/4	teaspoon nutmeg
2	garlic cloves, minced

Combine all ingredients in mixing bowl until well mixed.

Potato Soup

Serves 4 to 6

1	bell pepper, diced
3	large potatoes, diced
1	onion, chopped (or leeks)
1	small cabbage, shredded
1/4	cup Marsala Olive Fruit Oil
1/4	cup fresh basil or parsley, chopped
	salt, pepper and cayenne to taste
2	bay leaves
6	cups chicken or beef broth
6	garlic cloves, chopped or 1 head of garlic, roasted
1	cup cheddar, Monterey Jack or Swiss cheese, shredded
1-1/2	cups croutons or oyster crackers

> **Quell coughs with carrots**
>
> Bugs Bunny's favorites contain beta-carotene, which has been shown to open up airways and relieve asthmatic symptoms.

In a large skillet over medium heat add oil, potatoes, onion, garlic, pepper and cabbage.

Cook covered until vegetables are almost tender, add bay leaves.

In large pot combine broth with vegetables, bring to a boil, lower to simmer. Cover and cook 20 to 30 minutes.

Stir in salt, pepper, cayenne and basil. Remove bay leaves, sprinkle with cheese. Serve with croutons.

Variation:

1	cup mini meatballs, cooked
1	cup carrots, diced
1-1/2	cups spinach, chopped
1	cup celery, zucchini, diced or fennel, chopped
1/2	pound broccoli, chopped
1	cup mushrooms, chopped
1	cup peas, corn or lentils
2	jalapeño peppers, minced
1/4	pound Italian sausage, cooked, well drained and crumbled
1-1/2	cups sweet potatoes, diced
1-1/2	cups fresh or canned tomatoes, chopped

One of Grandson Joseph's favorite soup.

Croutons

2	cups Italian or French bread, cubed
3	tablespoons Marsala Olive OIl
2	tablespoons Romano cheese, grated

Place bread on baking sheet, drizzle with oil, toss.

Bake in a 400 degrees oven 5 to 10 minutes or until golden. Sprinkle with cheese.

Pea Soup

Serves 4 to 6

4	garlic cloves, chopped
2	cups split peas, green or yellow
1/2	cup Marsala Olive Oil
3	carrots, diced
2	celery stalks, chopped
1	onion, chopped small
1/2	cup fresh basil or parsley, chopped
	salt, pepper and hot pepper flakes to taste
3	bay leaves
6 to 8	cups broth or water
1-1/2	cups pasta (shells, dubettini, elbows, etc.)

In large pot add broth and peas. Cook on medium heat until almost tender.

Add carrots, onion, celery and bay leaves. Cook until all vegetables and peas are tender.

Add remaining ingredients except pasta; cook several minutes.

Cook pasta according to label directions, drain, stir into pea soup. Remove bay leaves before serving. Serve with grated cheese if desired.

Variation:

For thicker soup stir in 2 or 3 tablespoons semolina, in a slow stream, stirring constantly.

2 or 3	cups spinach leaves, chopped
1	cup ham, lean, diced
2	tomatoes, chopped
1	cup fresh mushrooms, chopped
1	teaspoon thyme or sage
1	zucchini, green or yellow, diced
1-1/2	cusp broccoli, chopped
1	avocado, diced
1	cup corn niblets

Substitute:

1 or 2	potatoes, diced for pasta
1	cup rice, cooked, for pasta
1-1/2	cups croutons for pasta

Pumpkin Soup

Serves 4 to 6

1	jalapeno pepper, minced
1	cup mushrooms, chopped
3 or 4	slices Canadian bacon (lean) chopped
1	tablespoon tarragon, fresh, minced
5	cups chicken or beef broth
2	bay leaves (remove before serving)
1	onion or leek, chopped
1	bell pepper, red, roasted, chopped
1-1/2	pounds small sweet pumpkins, cubed
1/3	cup Marsala Olive Oil
1	cup milk
4	garlic cloves, minced
1/2	cup wine, white
1	cup celery or parsnip, diced
	salt and white pepper to taste
2	apples, chopped
1/2	cup basil and / or parsley, chopped
1/2	cup pumpkin seeds, toasted (to sprinkle on top of each serving)

In large stock pot add olive oil, onions, garlic, jalapeno, bell peppers, celery and pumpkin.

Cook until tender about 20 minutes.

Add wine, cook 5 minutes. Stir in remaining ingredients, bring to a boil, lower to simmer. Cook until all is tender.

(If smooth soup is desired, blend in jar of blender). May have to be done in batches.

> ## Health benefit
> See clearly with squash. Zucchini contains lutein, an antioxidant that protects eyes from macular degeneration.

Note:

For best results make this soup with small, sweet sugar pumpkins.

To serve - sprinkle each serving with pumpkin seeds or 4 corn tortillas, cut into 3/4 inch strips.

Variation:

	butternut squash, cubed
	Curry, thyme, mint or rosemary to taste
1/4	pound ham, chicken or veal, cooked, diced
1	cup pasta, dubetti or shape of your choice
1/2	pound chestnuts, cooked, peeled, mashed
1/2	pound shrimp, crab, scallops or lobster cooked, diced
1/2	pound spinach, escarole or greens of your choice

Continued

2	cups tomatoes or 2 avocados, diced
8	baby artichoke hearts or carrots, diced
2	small beets or potatoes, diced
1	cup asparagus tips, corn or peas

Spice Pumpkin Soup

1	teaspoon cinnamon
1	teaspoon chili powder
1	tablespoon ginger, fresh

For smooth soup, blend in batches. For sweet potato soup - substitute sweet potatoes for pumpkin.

Bean Soup

Serves 6

1/2	cup Marsala Olive Oil
1	pound dry navy beans
4	ounces ham diced, cooked
	salt, pepper and cayenne to taste
1	onion, chopped
2	cups celery, chopped fine
1/2	cup basil and/or parsley chopped
4	garlic cloves, minced
1/2	teaspoon oregano
1	carrot, diced

In large sauce pot or Dutch oven, soak (picked over and rinsed) beans in 6 cups of water overnight, covered.

Next day bring to a boil, lower to simmer, cook until almost tender. Add onion, celery, garlic and carrot. Cook until beans and vegetables are tender.

Add basil and ham, cook about 6 more minutes. Drizzle with olive oil.

Serve with crusty Italian of French bread.

Variation:

2	bay leaves, remove before serving
1	cup pearl barley, cooked
1/2	teaspoon nutmeg or rosemary to taste
1	potato, diced (or yam)
1	small hot chili pepper, minced
	substitute garbanzo beans for navy beans.
	Italian sausage, cooked, well drained and crumbled
1	cup corn, fresh or frozen

Rose's Chicken Soup

Serves 6 to 8

1	chicken (2 or 3 pounds)
4	carrots, diced
1-1/2	cups celery, diced
1/2	pound lean meat ground
1	onion, chopped
1/2	cup parsley, chopped
1	cup pastina (any small pasta)
1/4	cup Marsala Olive Fruit Oil
	salt, pepper and Romano cheese, grated

In large pot place whole chicken, cover with water. Bring to a boil, lower to simmer.

Cook until chicken is tender, remove from broth, place in large bowl to cool.

Remove meat from bones and skin; cut into small pieces.

Strain broth, let fat come to surface, remove.

Bring broth to a boil, add carrots, onions and celery. Cook until tender, simmering.

Make ground meat into mini meatballs. Cook in olive oil, over medium heat until brown all around in a non stick skillet.

Add 2 cups chicken pieces, cooked mini meatballs and pastina to broth.

Cook until pasta is cooked al dente. Add parsley, salt, pepper and cheese to taste.

Variation:

1	small head escarole (about 8 ounces) chopped
9	ounce package cheese tortellini

> ### Cheer up with chicken soup.
> Chicken meat and chicken broth both contain tryptophan, an essential amino acid the body uses to produce the feel-good neurotransmitter serotonin.

Olive You!

Cioppino Pg 93   ~   Free Form Apple Pie Pg 265   ~   Panzanella Pg51

Blueberry Pie Pg 293

Broiled Sea Scallops

Serves 4

1	pound sea scallops
1/4	cup Marsala Olive Fruit Oil
	salt, pepper and paprika
1/3	cup fresh lime or lemon juice
1/3	cup fresh basil, parsley, chives, mint or tarragon, minced

Preheat broiler, spread scallops on broiling pan with space between each one.

Brush with olive oil, sprinkle with salt, pepper and paprika.

Broil 3 inches from heat about 2 minutes, turn.

Sprinkle with lime or lemon juice, broil 2 minutes more or until tender.

Combine remaining oil and herbs, serve over scallops.

Scallops Piccata

Serves 4

1	pound scallops
1/4	cup Marsala Olive Fruit Oil
1/4	cup broth
1/4	cup white wine
	salt, pepper and paprika to taste
1/4	cup lime or lemon juice
1/2	cup fresh basil, mint or parsley, chopped
1/2	teaspoon Dijon mustard
1	whole lime or lemon quartered
2	basil or mint sprigs

In large non-stick skillet, over medium heat add oil. Cook scallops until opaque, about 2 to 3 minutes.

Remove scallops onto serving platter, cover, keep warm.

To skillet add broth, mustard, wine, salt, pepper, paprika, juice and basil.

Cook several minutes, pour over scallops. Garnish with lime wedges and sprigs of basil.

Variation:

Serve with 4 ounces of cooked linguine or fettuccine. Arrange scallops over hot pasta, spoon sauce over top.

Calamari Ripieni
(Stuffed Squid)
Serves 4

1/2	cup mushrooms, chopped small
1-1/2	pounds squid (calamari) whole, cleaned
2	garlic cloves, minced
1	cup ricotta, low fat
2	slices bread, crumbled
1/3	cup Romano cheese, grated
1/2	cup fresh basil, parsley or mint, chopped
1	egg (or 2 egg whites)
1/4	cup Marsala Olive Fruit Oil
	salt, pepper and cayenne to taste
1/2	cup mussels or shrimp, chopped
1/3	cup onion, chopped
2	tablespoons pine nuts or pistachio, chopped
2 or 3	cups chunky tomato gravy

Preheat oven to 350 degrees. Grease a deep baking dish.

In mixing bowl combine ricotta, bread, cheese, basil, egg, pine nuts, mussels, salt, pepper and cayenne.

In small non stick skillet, over medium heat add oil, onions, garlic and mushrooms. Cook until crisp tender.

Add to ricotta mixture. Stuff squid with filling, fasten with small poultry pins.

In non stick skillet add 2 tablespoons olive oil. Over medium heat brown squid all around until slightly pink.

Place half of gravy over bottom of baking dish, add stuffed squid, pour remaining gravy over.

Cover with foil, bake until tender, about 30 to 40 minutes.

Note: This stuffing is also good for a red snapper about 3-1/2 pounds.

Stuff fish, place in greased baking dish, drizzle with a little olive oil.

Bake in a 350 degrees oven for about 30 to 35 minutes or until fish flakes easily when touched with a fork.

Garnish with lime or lemon slices and sprigs of mint, parsley or basil.

Variation:
Add 1/2 cup vermouth

Christmas Eve Mixed Fish Fry

Serves 6

1/2	pound shrimp, large or medium
1/2	pound fresh small whole fish
	(such as anchovies, sardines, smelts)
1/2	pound baby squid
1	dozen clams
1/2	pound small sole
1/2	pound salmon, cut into 3x1 inch strips
1	cup parsley, chopped fine
	flour for dredging
1/2	cup Marsala Olive Fruit Oil
	salt, pepper and paprika to taste
4	lime or lemons cut into wedges

Clean fish, pat dry, dredge lightly in flour. In large skillet, (non stick) add oil and heat.

Cook fish on both sides until crisp and golden brown. Sprinkle with salt, pepper and paprika.

May have to be cooked in 2 or 3 batches.

Place fish on large serving platter, garnish with lime wedges and parsley.

Another tradition we had (and still have) for Christmas Eve is a fish dish along with pasta and walnuts.

Squid Rings

Serves 6

1/2	cup parsley, chopped
1/2	cup Marsala Olive Fruit Oil
1-1/2	pounds squid, cleaned, cut into rings
3/4	cup beer, room temperature
3/4	cup flour
	salt, pepper and paprika to taste
	pinch of rosemary or sage
2	lemons cut into wedges

> **Health benefit**
> Studies have found that sage boosts memory.

Heat oil in deep skillet. Pat squid dry in clean towel.

Combine in mixing bowl, beer, flour, rosemary, salt, pepper and paprika, stir until smooth.

Dip squid rings into batter, lift out with tongs or slotted spoon. Let excess batter drip back in bowl.

Cook squid on both sides until golden brown. Serve with lemon wedges, sprinkle with parsley.

Cioppino

Serves 6

1	onion, diced
1	bell pepper, diced
6	garlic cloves, chopped
1/4	cup Marsala Olive Fruit Oil
4	cups fresh or canned tomatoes, chopped
3/4	cup wine
1/2	cup fresh basil and/or parsley, chopped
	salt, pepper and red hot pepper flakes to taste
2	bay leaves, remove before serving
2	dozen clams or mussels
1	pound crab (Alaskan King, thawed)
1/2	pound shrimp
1/2	pound scallops
1/2	pound cod cut into 2 inch cubes
4	tablespoons tomato paste

In Dutch oven add oil, onions, garlic and pepper. Cook over medium heat until soft. Add wine, cook 1 minute.

Add tomatoes, tomato paste, salt, pepper and bay leaves. Simmer for 15 minutes covered, add basil.

Add cod and cook about 5 minutes. Add remaining fish, cook covered 5 minutes or until clams open. Any unopened clams, discard.

Serve in soup bowls with toasted crusty Italian bread slices.

Variation:

	flounder fillets cut in cubes or lobster
2	cups small potatoes, cooked
1	small head escarole, chopped
	snapper or seabass, cubed
1/4	cup pesto sauce

> ### Health benefit
> Clams provide five times the daily requirement of vitamin B12, which assists in converting food into energy and helps boost metabolism.

Note: *Cioppino is a favorite San Francisco seafood stew, served with sourdough bread and a bib.*

Halibut Grilled in Fig Leaves

Serves 4

4   slices halibut or swordfish about 1 inch thick
4   garlic cloves, minced
        salt, pepper and paprika to taste
4   tablespoons Marsala Olive Fruit Oil
1/2   cup lemon or lime juice
1/4   macadamia or cashew, ground
4   large fig leaves, washed (or large grape leaves)
2   mushrooms, chopped
1/3   cup fresh basil or parsley, chopped
4   tablespoons bread crumbs

Blanch fig leaves about 30 seconds in hot water.

On each leaf divide evenly garlic, bread crumbs, nuts, basil and mushrooms.

Place fish on crumb mixture, sprinkle with salt, pepper and paprika. Drizzle each slice with olive oil and lemon juice.

Fold fig leaves up and over top of fish. Place bundles folded side down in a grill basket.

Cook on grill about 5 minutes on each side or until desired doneness.

Serve with pineapple salsa.

Variation:

Substitute blanched large lettuce leaves for fig leaves.

Baked Scallops or Oysters

Serves 4

1   cup bread crumbs
1   egg (or 2 egg whites)
        salt, pepper and cayenne to taste
1-1/2   pounds scallops
1/4   cup Marsala Olive Fruit Oil
4   garlic cloves, minced
1/2   cup fresh basil or parsley, chopped
2   limes or lemons cut into wedges
1/4   cup pine nuts, lightly toasted

In pie plate add crumbs, salt, pepper, cayenne, garlic and basil.

In another pie plate add egg, beat lightly.

Dip scallops in egg coating on all sides, then roll in bread crumb mixture.

Place in greased baking dish, drizzle with olive oil.

Bake in a 400 degrees oven for 20 to 25 minutes or until golden brown.

Serve with lime wedges, sprinkle with pine nuts.

Mom's Baked Cod with Potatoes

Serves 4

1-1/2	pounds cod fillet (red snapper or any firm fish)
	salt, pepper and cayenne to taste
1	cup bread crumbs
1/4	cup Romano cheese, grated
1/2	cup fresh basil or parsley, chopped
4	fresh or canned tomatoes
4	potatoes, peeled, sliced thin or shredded
1/4	cup raisins
1/4	cup pine nuts or walnuts, chopped fine
1/2	cup Marsala Olive Fruit Oil
4	garlic cloves, minced
2	lime or lemons, quartered

Preheat oven to 350 degrees. Grease roasting pan, drizzle bottom with a little oil evenly.

Spread potatoes evenly in pan, sprinkle with raisins and nuts.

In pie plate, combine bread crumbs, garlic, cheese, basil, salt, pepper and cayenne.

Press fillets on both sides with crumb mixture, lay over potatoes evenly.

Slice tomatoes about 1/2 inch thick, place over fish. Drizzle a little olive oil over all, cover with foil. Remove last 10 minutes of baking.

Bake 30 to 40 minutes or until potatoes are tender and fish flakes easily. Serve with lime wedges. Garnish with chopped parsley.

Variation:

1	onion, sliced
1/2	cup olives or 1 cup fresh or frozen peas
2	tablespoons fresh rosemary or sage, chopped
2	tablespoons fresh tarragon, chopped
1/2	pound fresh mushrooms, sliced

Substitute yams or sweet potatoes for white potatoes.

Variation for fish:

Substitute dried cod (baccala) for fresh cod.

Soak in water several days. Change water daily, keep refrigerated.

Drain, proceed with recipe.

Olive You!

Mussels Marinara

Serves 4

4	**dozen mussels, cleaned well (or clams)**
4	**garlic cloves, chopped**
1	**onion, chopped**
4	**tomatoes, chopped**
1	**bell pepper, diced**
2	**jalapeno peppers, minced**
	salt, pepper and cayenne to taste
1/2	**pound Italian sausage, cooked, sliced thin**
1/2	**cup fresh basil, parsley or mint, chopped**
2	**bay leaves**
1	**cup white wine**
1/3	**cup Marsala Olive Fruit Oil**
1	**leek (white part only) chopped**
4	**slices crusty Italian bread, toasted**

Rinse mussels thoroughly in cold running water, scrub, pull off beard. Cover with water for 1 hour, discard mussels that float to the top or are opened.

Cook sausage with 1 cup water until browned. Lift out with slotted spoon, drain on clean paper towel.

In Dutch oven add oil, onion, garlic, leek and pepper, cook until crisp tender. Add tomatoes, basil, wine, bay leaves, salt, pepper and cayenne, bring to a boil.

Add mussels, cook covered 5 to 8 minutes. Stir in cooked sausage.

Discard any unopened mussels, remove bay leaves.

Place bread in soup bowls, place mussels and cooking liquid atop.

Mussels may be served over cooked pasta, polenta or rice. Add 3 or 4 tablespoons of tomato paste in liquid, cook about 10 minutes.

Add a little more wine if needed.

Variation:

1	**cup fresh or frozen peas, thawed**
1	**zucchini, sliced**

Omit sausage and bread, serve over cooked pasta shells, cavatelli or tagliolini.

Reserve a few mussels in shell for garnish.

Jalapeños relieve arthritis pain

Jalapeño peppers contain capsaicin, a natural anti-inflammatory that inhibits production of substance, P, a chemical involved with sending pain messages to the brain.

Mussels With Pasta

Serves 4 to 6

6	pints mussels, cleaned (or clams)
1	cup white wine
2	onions, chopped
1/2	cup Marsala Olive Fruit Oil
4	garlic cloves (or to taste) minced
1/2	cup fresh basil or parsley
	salt, pepper and paprika to taste
12	ounces shell or cavatelli pasta
4	tomatoes, chopped
	pinch of saffron or thyme

In large Dutch oven add olive oil, onions and garlic, cook until tender. Add wine, basil, salt, pepper, paprika, tomatoes and saffron.

Bring to boil, lower heat to simmer, cover, cook about 10 minutes. Add mussels, cover, cook over medium heat 3 to 4 minutes or until mussels open.

Discard any unopened mussels. Cook pasta according to package directions and almost tender.

Remove mussels from shells, place in sauce. Place pasta in large shallow serving bowl. Pour the mussels and sauce over pasta, toss gently. Cover, let stay in warm place about 10 minutes.

Reserve a few mussels in shell for garnish.

Variation:

1	small fennel bulb, chopped
	sea scallops or shrimp
1-1/2	cups spinach, cooked
1/2	cup Monterey Jack cheese (or feta)
1/2	cup olives, chopped

Health benefit

Fennel contains a substance called phytoestrogens, which herbalists say may help relieve menstrual cramping. And research has also suggested that phytoestrogens may help prevent breast cancer.

Oven Fried Fish

Serves 4

1/4	cup white wine
1	tablespoon Dijon mustard
1-1/2	pounds fish fillets (salmon, cod, red snapper, etc.)
1/4	cup milk
1	egg lightly beaten
	salt, pepper and paprika to taste
4	garlic cloves, minced
1/2	cup fresh basil, parsley or mint, chopped
1/3	cup Marsala Olive Fruit Oil
1/2	cup bread crumbs and 1/2 cup cornmeal
1/4	cup Romano cheese, grated
2	limes or lemon wedges
1/4	teaspoon ginger
1/3	cup pecans or hazelnuts, ground

In a pie plate combine milk, egg, salt, pepper, paprika and mustard.

Dip fish fillets in milk mixture on both sides.

In another pie plate add crumbs, cheese, garlic, cornmeal, ginger, basil and pecans.

Press fillets in crumb mixture on both sides. Place in greased baking pan with a little drizzle of olive oil over bottom.

Drizzle a little more olive oil over top of fish, sprinkle with wine evenly. Cover with foil.

Bake in a 400 degrees oven for 20 to 25 minutes or until golden and easily flaked with fork, but still moist inside.

Serve with lime wedges and roasted or mashed potatoes.

Fillet of Sole

Serves 4

Place 1-1/2 pounds sole fillet into a shallow lightly greased 2 quart casserole.

Add 1/2 cup white wine, 1 chopped onion, 2 garlic cloves minced, 1/4 cup Marsala Olive Oil, 2 bay leaves, 1/2 cup fresh basil chopped, salt, pepper and paprika to taste.

Cover, bake in a 375 degrees oven for 25 minutes or until fish flakes easily when tested with a fork.

Remove bay leaves before serving.

Serve with 2 lemons, cut into wedges.

Salmon Grilled in Spinach Leaves

Serves 4

1	teaspoon celery seeds
4	3/4 inch slices (about 2 pounds) salmon, swordfish, cod or halibut
	salt, pepper and cayenne to taste
1/4	cup Marsala Olive Fruit Oil
1/2	cup fresh basil or parsley, chopped
4	garlic cloves, chopped
4	tablespoons bread crumbs
4	large Swiss chard leaves, stems removed
1	egg white lightly beaten
1/2	teaspoon sage or tarragon
1/2	cup lemon juice
4	tablespoon pine nuts

In pie plate add egg white, coat salmon on both sides. In another pie plate, add crumbs, basil, olive oil, garlic, celery seeds, sage, salt, pepper and cayenne.

Press salmon in crumb mixture on both sides. Place each slice on a spinach leaf, fold over to cover fish.

Place packages, folded side down, in a wire basket with handle. Grill about 4 inches above hot coals for about 4 minutes on each side, or until fish flakes easily when tested with fork.

Place on serving platter, unwrap, drizzle with lemon juice, sprinkle with pine nuts. Serve with sauteed grapes.

Sauteed Grapes

2	tablespoons Marsala Olive Fruit Oil
2	cups grapes, seedless or cherries, pitted
2	tablespoons orange peel, grated
2	tablespoons brown sugar
1/4	teaspoon nutmeg or cinnamon
1/4	cup orange juice

In skillet add all ingredients, cook over medium heat 1 or 2 minutes.

Variation:

Add 2 or 3 shrimp on top of salmon slices before folding swiss chard over fish.

Add 2 slices of lemon, cut 1/4 inch thick before folding swiss chard over fish.

Drizzle 1 tablespoon honey on each slice.

Sauteed Salmon

Serves 4

1	egg white, lightly beaten
1	cup bread crumbs
4	garlic cloves, minced
	salt, pepper and paprika to taste
1/2	cup fresh basil, parsley or cilantro
4	salmon fillets (6 ounces each)
1/4	cup Marsala Olive Fruit Oil
1/4	cup macadamia or pistachio nuts, ground
4	lime or lemons, quartered
	pinch of sage

> **Salmon helps you sleep deep**
> This rich, flaky fish is full of calcium and magnesium, two minerals that balance brain chemistry and help the body relax.

In pie plate combine bread crumbs, garlic, salt, pepper, paprika, basil, sage and nuts.

In another pie plate add egg white lightly beaten.

Dip fillets into egg white on both sides then into crumb mixture.

In large nonstick skillet, over medium heat, cook fillets in hot olive oil.

Cook 4 to 5 minutes on each side, turning fillets once (carefully with large spatula) or until fish flakes easily when tested with a fork.

Serve with lime wedges and Italian mashed potatoes if desired.

Salmon With White Wine

Serves 4

4	garlic cloves (or to taste)
2	tablespoons flour
1/2	cup white wine
1	cup fresh mushrooms, sliced
4	salmon steaks, 1-1/2 inches thick
1/3	cup Marsala Olive Fruit Oil
1/2	cup fresh basil or parsley, chopped
	salt and white pepper to taste
1/2	teaspoon dry mustard
2	tablespoons fresh rosemary, chopped
1/4	cup lime or lemon juice

In large skillet add oil, heat. Dust salmon with flour on both sides, place in skillet. Cook until golden brown on both sides.

Add wine, juice, garlic, mustard, salt and pepper. Simmer about 3 to 4 minutes, covered. Add mushrooms, cook covered 1 more minute or until fish flakes easily.

Serve with fruit salsa if desired.

Squid Chowder

Serves 4

4	garlic cloves, minced
2	bay leaves
1/2	cup red or white wine
1	pound squid, cleaned, chopped small or ground coarsely
1/2	teaspoon rosemary
	salt, pepper and cayenne to taste
1	cup peas, fresh or frozen
1-1/2	cups fennel bulb or celery, chopped
4	green onions
1/3	cup Marsala Olive Oil
4	potatoes, cubed
1	teaspoon paprika
1/2	cup fresh basil, mint or parsley, chopped
2	cups fresh or canned tomatoes, chopped
1	bell pepper, chopped
2	tablespoons tomato paste

In Dutch oven add oil, onions, fennel, garlic, pepper and potatoes.

Cook covered on medium heat until tender, add wine, cook one or 2 minutes.

Add tomatoes, tomato paste, bay leaves, paprika, salt, pepper, cayenne and rosemary. Cook 10 to 15 minutes covered.

Add squid and basil, cook 3 to 5 minutes or until squid is tender.

Remove bay leaves before serving.

Variation:

2 to 3 cups spinach, swiss chard, curly endive or
greens of your choice, chopped
substitute 1-1/2 cups lobster meat, chopped, salmon cubed,
clams or fish of your choice for squid

Outsmart secondhand smoke with Swiss chard

Quercetin, an antioxidant in this leafy green vegetable, has been shown to protect lungs from the harmful effects of cigarette smoke.

Stuffed Jumbo Shrimp

Serves 4

1   egg white
1-1/2 pounds jumbo shrimp
1/2   cup bread crumbs
1/4   cup Romano cheese, grated
1/4   cup Marsala Olive Fruit Oil
4   garlic cloves, minced
1/3   cup fresh basil, parsley or cilantro, minced
1/4   cup pine nuts or currants
1/3   cup lime or lemon juice
1   tablespoon fresh sage, minced
           salt, white pepper and paprika to taste

> **It's _so_ good for you**
> Shrimp are a great source of iron, a nutrient necessary for the production of red blood cells, which carry oxygen to the brain.

In pie plate or bowl combine bread crumbs, salt, peppers, cheese, garlic, egg white, basil, sage and pine nuts.

Cut cleaned shrimp (leaving tail) along back curve. Open, clean, press flat, stuff, close with small poultry pins.

Arrange on greased baking dish, drizzle with olive oil and juice.

Bake in a 350 degrees for about 12 to 15 minutes or until shrimp turn pink. Do not over cook.

Variation:

1   shallot, finely chopped
1   tablespoon prepared horseradish (or to taste)

Poached Salmon

Serves 4

4   garlic cloves, minced
4   salmon steaks (about 1-1/2 pounds)
1/2   cup lemon juice or white vinegar
           salt to taste
2   bay leaves
2   tablespoons fresh ginger, chopped

In large skillet or sauce pot add enough water to cover fish.
Bring water, lemon juice, salt, ginger, garlic and bay leaves to a boil.
Add salmon, cook simmering for 8 to 10 minutes.
Remove salmon with slotted spoon, place on serving platter.
Spoon mango salsa over top evenly.

Variation:

1/4 cup parsley, 1 cup carrots, 1 cup celery and 1 cup onion, chopped.

Mike's Low Country Boil

Serves 6 to 8

Stock

1-1/2 to 2 gallons water
2   packages crab boil, dry (or 1 cup liquid crab boil)
1   small bottle tabasco or hot sauce
2   tablespoons salt (or to taste)
2   lemons, quartered
1   tablespoon creole seasonings
2   bay leaves (remove before serving)

Shrimp, Vegetable and Sausage

6   small new potatoes, red or white
2   medium onions, peeled, quartered
3   ears of corn, cut into thirds
6   carrots small and/or artichoke hearts, small
3   bell peppers, quartered
1   pound green beans and/or asparagus, chopped
3   pounds chicken sausage, cooked
2   pounds shrimp (about 30 count) and/or crawfish
10   garlic cloves, chopped
1/2   cup Marsala Olive Oil

In a large stock pot fitted with a basket insert combine stock ingredients, bring to a boil.

Add longer cooking vegetables first. Add potatoes, carrots and onions, cover, bring back to a boil, cook 5 minutes.

Add sausage, garlic and green beans, cover, return to a boil, cook another 5 minutes.

Add corn and bell peppers, cover, cook 5 minutes more.

When vegetables are tender, add shrimp, cover, turn off flame and let steep until all is tender.

Once the shrimp turns red and floating, lift the basket from stock, pour directly into large serving trays. Drizzle olive oil over mixture evenly.

Serve immediately with Italian or French bread and paper towels.

Note: Recipe may be doubled

> ### Keep arteries clear with artichokes
> Cynarin, an antioxidant in this vegetable, may lower levels of blood cholesterol.

Continued

Continued

Creole Seasonings

Yields about 2/3 cup

1	**tablespoon salt**
2	**tablespoons garlic powder**
1	**tablespoon onion powder**
1	**tablespoon cayenne**
1	**tablespoon black pepper**
1	**tablespoon oregano**
1	**tablespoon rosemary**
1	**tablespoon paprika**
1	**tablespoon thyme**
2	**tablespoons grated lemon peel, dried**

Combine all ingredients thoroughly, store in airtight containers.

May be used for meats, fish or vegetables.

> ### Health benefit
> The high zinc content in shrimp boosts immunity. Zinc is an essential mineral that helps the body fight bacterial infections.

Vanilla Shrimp

Serves 4

1	**pound shrimp, medium**
1/4	**cup Marsala Olive Oil**
1	**tablespoon corn starch**
1	**egg white lightly beaten**
1	**teaspoon vanilla**
1/2	**cup coconut milk, canned**
	salt and white pepper to taste

In mixing bowl add shrimp, egg white, corn starch, salt and pepper.

Stir to coat well, heat olive oil in large non-stick skillet.

Add shrimp, cook on both sides until pink.

Stir in coconut milk, heat through. Blend in vanilla.

Serve with cooked couscous or rice and sliced mango, pineapple or pears.

Grilled Trout

Serves 4

2	limes
4	3/4 pound each, trout
1/2	cup Sciabica's orange olive oil
	salt and white pepper to taste
1/4	cup parsley, minced (or herb of your choice)
2	tablespoon lemon juice
2	tablespoon ginger root, shredded (or to taste)
2	tablespoons honey
	fresh parsley sprigs

Place fish in glass baking dish. Combine remaining ingredients blending well. Pour mixture over fish, marinate about 1 hour.

Drain, reserve marinade, place trout on prepared grill for about 5 minutes on each side. Brush lightly with marinade from time to time.

Bring any remaining marinade to a boil. Arrange trout on serving platter, spoon marinade over evenly.

Garnish with parsley sprigs and lime wedges.

Lois' Christmas Eve Shrimp

Serves 4

12	jumbo shrimp, cleaned, butterflied, tail left on

Filling:

20	Ritz crackers, made into crumbs
1/4	cup Marsala or Sciabica lemon olive oil
1/4	cup white horseradish (bottled) or to taste

Mix all above ingredients together, adding more cracker crumb to hold mixture together if needed.

Spoon filling on shrimp, fold tail over to top of shrimp, press gently.

Place under broiler or bake in a lightly greased baking pan in a 350 degrees oven for about 18 minutes or until shrimp turn pink. May be served as an appetizer.

Lois told me that only the Ritz crackers bring a special taste to the shrimp. Lois got this recipe from her Mom many years ago.

Health benefit
Consume horseradish to prevent urinary tract infections. It's rich in mustard oil, an antibacterial agent that fights UTI germs.

Shrimp Tempura

Serves 4

1	pound shrimp, large, cleaned (or fish fillets cut into 1 inch pieces)
8	green beans
4	mushroom caps
8 to 10	asparagus spears
4	green onions, 4 inches in length
2	zucchini, sliced 1/4 inch thick
1	yam, sliced thin or carrots cut into 1/4 inch thick pieces
1	avocado, cut into wedges
1	cup ice water
1	cup flour
1	egg yolk
2	tablespoons Marsala Olive Oil
1	teaspoon sugar
1/2	teaspoon salt (or to taste)
1/2	teaspoon baking powder
	Marsala Olive Oil for cooking

> ### Health benefit
> Leeks beat bloating. These onion cousins contain potassium, which stimulates kidneys and reduces water retention.

Wash shrimp, prepare vegetables; wash and pat dry, refrigerate.

In blender or bowl, combine water, flour, yolk, olive oil, sugar, salt and baking powder, whip until smooth, refrigerate.

Heat 2 inches olive oil in small sauce pot or fry pan to 375 degrees.

Dip shrimp and vegetables a few at a time in batter, letting excess drain.

Cook in olive oil for 2 or 3 minutes until golden.

Keep warm on serving platter in oven at low temperature until cooking is completed.

Serve with or on cooked rice and oriental dip if desired.

Oriental Dip

Makes about 1-1/4 cups

1/2	cup parsley minced
3/4	cup water
1/4	cup soy sauce
3	tablespoons honey or pure maple syrup
1	tablespoon Marsala Olive Oil
1	tablespoon ginger, grated
1/2	cup chicken broth
	pinch of cayenne or paprika
1	garlic clove, minced

In small sauce pan, heat the above ingredients for 1 minute.

Lamb Shish Kabob with Risotto Pg 116   ~   Fresh Tomato Soup Pg 80

Ricotta Chocolate Cake Pg 285

Baked Lamb Chops

Serves 4 to 6

1/4	cup fresh mint, chopped
8	lamb chops (fat removed) about 1-1/2 pounds
4	potatoes cut into wedges
4	tomatoes, chopped
1/4	cup Marsala Olive Fruit Oil
4	bay leaves
4	garlic cloves (or to taste), chopped
1/3	cup Romano cheese, grated
	Salt, pepper and red hot pepper flakes to taste
1	onion, sliced
1/2	cup fresh basil or parsley, chopped
8	shallots or green onions, chopped
1/2	cup white wine

> ### It's **_so_** good for you
> Hot peppers contain capsaicin, a compound that fights pain by preventing the brain from receiving "pain messages."

Preheat oven to 350 degrees.

Grease a large casserole or baking pan. Add potatoes, onions, shallots, garlic, mint, basil, bay leaves, chops, wine, tomatoes and cheese.

Sprinkle with salt, pepper, red pepper flakes and drizzle with olive oil.

Bake covered with foil for about 1 hour or until vegetables and meat are tender.

Remove bay leaves before serving.

Garnish with celery leaves (center part). Serve with mint jelly.

Rabbit with Tomato

Serves 4

Lightly flour 1-1/2 pounds rabbit pieces. In large pot, cook rabbit in 1/4 cup Marsala Olive Oil over medium heat, until brown on all sides. Cool slightly, add 1/2 cup wine.

Add 1 onion chopped, 2 carrots chopped, 2 potatoes diced, salt, pepper and cayenne to taste and 1/2 cup fresh basil, chopped. Cook covered about 10 minutes. Add 2 tablespoons fresh rosemary, chopped and 2 cups fresh or canned tomatoes. Cover, simmer until meat is tender.

Add 1-1/2 cups fresh mushrooms sliced, and 1 cup artichoke hearts, cook covered 1 more minute.

Serve over cooked polenta or whole wheat.

Barbecued Leg of Lamb

Serves 8

1	4 to 5 pound leg of lamb, butterflied
1/2	cup fresh basil or parsley, chopped
4	garlic cloves (or to taste) minced
1	onion, chopped
1	tablespoon Dijon mustard
	Pinch of allspice and oregano
1	cup pomegranate juice, cranberry juice or wine
2	tablespoons fresh rosemary, chopped
1/2	cup Marsala Olive Fruit Oil
	Salt, pepper and powdered ginger to taste
1/2	cup fresh mint, chopped
1/2	cup lime or lemon juice

In large stainless, enamel or glass pan, place lamb cut side down, add remaining ingredients.

Cover with foil, refrigerate over night. Turn several times. Bring to room temperature before grilling.

Prepare grill for barbecuing. Over medium hot coals, on grill arrange lamb boned side down.

Cook about 20 minutes, brush with marinade. Turn several times, cook until thermometer inserted in thickest part registers 170 degrees.

Serve with Mango Salsa.

For Oven Broil

Preheat broiler, place lamb on rack in broiling pan. Broil 20 to 25 minutes or until desired doneness.

Brushing with marinade, turning lamb once. Serve with rice or potatoes, mint jelly and vegetables of your choice.

If preferred, roast in oven at 325 degrees for about 1 to 1-1/2 hours or until desired degree of doneness.

Variation:

1/4	cup soy sauce
1/4	cup pure maple syrup

Substitute red cactus pear puree for pomegranate juice.

Substitute 2 tablespoons fresh ginger, chopped for powdered ginger.

Note: Insert 2 or 3 skewers lengthwise through center of lamb pressing meat together to cook evenly.

Braciola (Meat Roll) With Pasta

Serves 4 to 6

1-1/2 to 2 pounds beef top round 1/4 inch thick (or veal)
Salt, pepper and cayenne to taste
6 to 8   garlic cloves, chopped
1/2   cup fresh basil or parsley, chopped
1/3   cup Romano cheese
1/2   cup provolone, shredded
1/4   cup pine nuts or pistachio
1/3   cup raisins, golden
2   teaspoons fennel seeds (or to taste)
3/4   cup spinach cooked, well drained, chopped
1/4   cup Marsala Olive Fruit Oil

Pound beef slice thinner with a meat mallet, working from center to edges.

Spread remaining ingredients evenly over meat.

Roll up jelly roll style beginning with shorter side.

Tie meat 4 or 5 places with clean heavy string. Tie string around length of roll.

In Dutch oven with olive oil, brown roll on all sides over medium heat.

Add onion and carrot, cover, lower heat and cook until crisp tender.

Add wine, cook about 1 minute, Stir in tomato, tomato paste, fennel seeds, cook until meat is tender, about 45 minutes.

Add basil, salt, pepper and red pepper flakes.

Stir in mushrooms, cook several minutes.

Sauce

1/4   cup Marsala Olive Fruit Oil
1   onion, chopped
1/2   cup wine, red
4   cups fresh or canned tomatoes, chopped
3   ounces tomato paste
2   teaspoons fennel seeds
1/2   cup fresh basil or parsley, chopped
Salt, pepper and red pepper flakes to taste
1   carrot, diced
1-1/2   cups fresh mushrooms, sliced
12   ounces pasta of your choice
Romano cheese, grated

Cook pasta according to package directions. Drain, place in shallow serving bowl.

Spoon sauce over pasta, toss gently. Slice braciola, arrange over top. Sprinkle with cheese.

Variation:

Serve over cooked rice or polenta.

Braised Pork Loin with Milk

Serves 6

3-1/2 to 4 pounds lean pork loin, boneless
      Salt, pepper and cayenne to taste
1   tablespoon fennel seeds or rosemary
1/4   cup Marsala Olive Fruit Oil
3   cups milk, low fat
1/3   cup white wine, sweet
1   pound fresh mushrooms, sliced
1/2   cup onion, chopped
1/4   cup fresh basil or parsley, chopped
4   garlic cloves (or to taste) chopped

Remove as much fat from pork as possible. In Dutch oven, over medium heat, brown pork in olive oil on all sides, add wine, cook 1 minute.

Add onions and garlic, cook until soft. Add milk and fennel seeds, cover, simmer 1-1/2 to 2 hours or until instant thermometer reaches 160 to 170 degrees.

Gravy will be golden brown. Add mushrooms, basil, salt, pepper and cayenne. Cook 1 more minute.

Place pork on serving platter, slice, spoon gravy and mushrooms over pork.

Serve with chunky applesauce.

Variation:

2   bay leaves, remove before serving
1/4   cup leek (white part) sliced thin
1   cup carrots, chopped small
1   cup celery, chopped small

Swedish Meatballs

Makes 12 to 16

1/4   cup broth
1/4   pound lean pork, ground
1   cup onions, minced
1   cup potatoes, shredded
2/3   cup bread crumbs
3/4   pound lean beef or turkey, ground
1/3   cup Marsala Olive Fruit Oil
      Salt and white pepper to taste
1   egg (or 2 egg whites)
1/4   cup parsley, chopped or fresh dill
1/2   teaspoon allspice, nutmeg, ginger or cardamom
      White sauce

In mixing bowl combine meats, onion, potatoes, crumbs, salt, pepper, parsley, and egg. Mix well, working lightly.

Shape into small meatballs. Cook in skillet with olive oil until browned all around. Add broth, cook 1 minute.

Serve with white sauce.

Chicken Nuggets

Serves 4

1-1/2	pounds skinless, boneless chicken breasts
3	tablespoons cornstarch
1	egg (or 2 egg whites) lightly beaten
2	tablespoons black or regular sesame seeds
	Salt, pepper and cayenne to taste
1/4	teaspoon paprika or nutmeg
1/2	teaspoon dry mustard
1/4	cup Marsala Olive Fruit Oil
4	garlic cloves (or to taste) minced
1/2	cup parsley or fresh basil, chopped

Cut chicken into about 3 by 1-1/2 inch pieces. In mixing bowl add chicken and cornstarch, stir until coated.

Add remaining ingredients (except olive oil) mix until well blended.

In a large skillet add oil, place over medium heat. Add chicken pieces, do not crowd, may have to be cooked in 2 batches. Brown on both sides.

Place chicken in a lightly greased baking pan, cover loosely with foil. Bake in a 350 degrees oven for about 15 to 20 minutes or until tender.

Serve with mushroom sauce.

Variation:

1	tablespoon fresh rosemary or sage, chopped
1/2	teaspoon ginger

Substitute turkey, veal, pork loin or fryer tenderloins for chicken.

Mushroom and Onion Sauce

1	tablespoon cornstarch
1/2	pound porcini mushrooms, sliced
1	onion, sliced
4	tablespoons Marsala Olive Fruit Oil
4	tablespoons sherry or port wine
1	tablespoon balsamic vinegar or lemon juice
	Salt and pepper to taste

> Sprinkle on sesame seeds for soft, shiny hair
> The seeds are a good source of methionine, an amino acid that builds hair follicles and promotes healthy hair growth.

In skillet add oil and onions, cook until crisp tender, add mushrooms.

Dissolve cornstarch in the sherry, stir into onion and mushrooms.

Cook until slightly thickened, add vinegar, salt and pepper, stir until blended.

Olive You!

Crumb Topped Rib Roast

Serves 6

1	3 rib beef roast (small end) about 3-1/2 pounds
	salt, pepper and cayenne to taste
1	lime, grated peel and juice
1-1/2	cups bread crumbs
1/2	cup fresh basil, parsley or cilantro, chopped
4	garlic cloves, chopped
1/4	cup macadamia or hazelnuts, finely chopped
1	tablespoon rosemary
1	tablespoon prepared mustard
1/2	cup onion, chopped
1/2	cup celery, chopped
2	tablespoons Marsala Olive Fruit Oil
1/4	cup sherry
1/2	teaspoon ginger

Preheat oven to 325 degrees. Lightly grease a roasting pan.

Rub salt, pepper, rosemary, cayenne and ginger over roast.

Roast beef 1-1/2 hours, prepare topping.

In small skillet add oil, onions and celery, cook until soft.

In mixing bowl add bread crumbs, basil, lime, sherry, olive oil, onion mixture, garlic and nuts.

After beef has roasted 1-1/2 hours, spread with mustard evenly, press on crumb mixture.

Roast 1 hour longer or until topping is golden and instant thermometer reaches 145 or until desired doneness.

(Careful that thermometer does not touch bone.)

Place roast on serving platter, let stand 10 to 15 minutes at room temperature.

Garnish with basil, mint or rosemary sprigs and orange slices.

Serve with Italian mashed potatoes or yams, roasted.

Beat the blues with these meatballs

Tryptophan, an essential amino acid found in turkey and beef, is converted into serotonin, the brain chemical that naturally fosters feelings of contentment and well-being.

Italian Meatballs

Makes 12 to 16

1/2	pound pork or lamb, lean, ground
1/2	pound veal or turkey (no skin) ground
1/2	pound beef, lean, ground
2 or 3	slices Italian bread
1/2	cup fresh basil and/or parsley, chopped
1/2	cup Romano cheese, grated
3/4	cup provolone, shredded
	Salt, pepper and cayenne to taste
1	egg and 1 egg white
1/3	cup Marsala Olive Fruit Oil
2	teaspoons fennel or anise seeds
1/2	cup red wine
1/2	cup raisins or currants
1/4	cup pine nuts
4	garlic cloves minced
	pinch of nutmeg, cinnamon or cloves
4	green onions (white part) chopped

Soak bread in water, squeeze water out and crumble into a mixing bowl. Add remaining ingredients, except oil.

Mix very lightly until well blended. Form into meatballs in size desired.

Pressing the mixture too tightly will make the meatballs too firm.

In large skillet heat olive oil, add meatballs. Cook until brown on all sides. May have to be cooked in 2 batches over medium heat.

Add to gravy, soups, stews, meat pies etc.

Note: Meatballs may also be added to gravies and soups without cooking first.

Variation:

1/2	cup carrots or zucchini shredded
	grated peel of 1 lemon
1/2	cup spinach well drained, chopped
1/2	cup cooked rice or potatoes mashed
1/2	cup tomatoes, chopped
1/2	cup eggplant cooked, mashed

Meatballs may be rolled in flour on a baking sheet, remove excess.

Meatballs may be baked on a greased baking sheet in a 375 degrees oven.

Drizzle with a little oil bake until golden brown for 15 to 20 minutes, depending on size.

Turn meatballs around half way through baking.

If serving meatballs only, dip in lightly beaten egg white, then roll in flavored bread crumbs all around, bake or cook in skillet.

Lamb and Beans

Serves 8

1	6 to 7 pounds leg of lamb
1	sprig fresh rosemary
	Pinch of tarragon
1/2	teaspoon oregano
1/2	teaspoon thyme
	Salt, pepper and cayenne to taste
1/2	cup fresh basil, parsley or mint, chopped
6	garlic cloves, chopped
1/4	cup fresh ginger, grated
1/4	cup Marsala Olive Fruit Oil
1	onion, chopped
1	cup red wine

Remove as much fat as possible from lamb. Brush with olive oil, sprinkle remaining ingredients on all sides of lamb.

Place in a greased roasting pan, pour in wine.

Insert meat thermometer into meaty part, not resting on bone.

Roast uncovered in a 325 degrees oven. Bake about 2-1/2 to 3 hours, or until thermometer reaches 175 degrees.

Let lamb stand about 15 minutes before slicing.

In large serving platter, add beans. Slice lamb, arrange over beans.

Decorate with rosemary or mint sprigs.

White Beans

1	pound dry white beans
6	garlic cloves
1/2	cup Marsala Olive Fruit Oil
2	onions, sliced thin
1/2	cup fresh basil, chopped
	Salt, pepper and cayenne to taste
3 or 4	cups fresh or canned tomatoes, chopped
1	cup celery, chopped
1/2	teaspoon sage
1	pound spinach or radicchio

Pick beans over, wash, place in large pot. Cover with water, 2 inches above beans, leave to soak overnight.

Next day over low heat, cook beans until tender but not mushy.

In saucepan add oil, onions, garlic, celery, salt, pepper, cayenne and sage.

Cook until tender, add tomatoes and basil, cook about 15 minutes, add to cooked beans.

Add spinach leaves, cover, cook until wilted, about 2 minutes.

Lamb Shish Kabobs

Serves 8

4 to 5	pounds leg of lamb
1/2	teaspoon ginger or to taste
1/2	cup Marsala Olive Fruit Oil
1/2	cup wine
1	tablespoon mustard, Dijon
4	garlic cloves, chopped
2	onions sliced about 1-1/2 inches wide
4	red or green bell peppers, sliced
	Salt and pepper to taste

10 to 12 mushrooms

1/3	cup soy sauce
2	tablespoons Worcestershire sauce
1/2	cup lemon juice
1	teaspoon oregano
1/2	cup fresh basil, mint or parsley, chopped
1	zucchini, sliced
1	cup pomegranate or cactus pear juice

Cut lamb into 1-1/2 to 2 inch cubes. Combines all ingredients in large pan, marinate several hours, turning several times.

Place meat and vegetables alternately on skewers and grill, turning on all sides.

Baste frequently with remaining marinade. Grill until cooked through. Serve with steamed or baked rice.

Garnish with lemon peel roses

Variation:

1	tablespoon fresh ginger, grated
1/2	eggplant, cubed

Substitute chicken, turkey, lean pork, beef or meat of your choice for lamb.

Swordfish, cut into 1-1/2 to 2 inch cubes

fresh fruit of your choice, cubed

jumbo shrimp, scallops or seafood of your choice

8	kumquats or loquats, halved, seeds removed
	green tomatoes with a pink blush, quartered

Lemon Roses:

Using vegetable peeler, peel lemon in about 3/4 inch wide strips. Starting from one end, roll peel forming a rose.

Meatballs and Peppers With Wine

Serves 4 to 6

Award Winning Recipe at Riverbank Cheese and Wine Exposition

1	recipe for Italian meatballs
1/4	cup red wine
1/4	cup Marsala Olive Fruit Oil
2	onions, sliced
4 to 6	bell peppers, red, yellow or green, sliced
	salt, pepper and red pepper flakes to taste
1-1/2	cups fresh mushrooms, sliced
2	cups fresh or canned tomatoes, chopped
3	tablespoons tomato paste
1	cup fresh basil or parsley, chopped or
1/3	cup pesto sauce
6	garlic cloves, chopped

In large skillet cook meatballs all around, in oil, over medium heat, set aside.

In greased roasting pan add a drizzle of olive oil. Add onions, garlic, wine and peppers.

Bake in a 400 degrees oven for about 30 minutes, covered loosely with foil.

Add tomatoes, tomato paste, salt, pepper, red pepper flakes and meatballs. Toss gently, bake covered about 15 minutes.

Add mushrooms and basil, continue baking until vegetables are tender and meat is well done.

Serve with crusty Italian bread and salad.

Barbecued Quail

Serves 4 to 6

1/2	cup lemon juice
8	dressed quail, butterflied (1/4 pound each)
	Marsala Olive Oil
	salt, pepper and paprika to taste
1	teaspoon dried rosemary or oregano
1	teaspoon garlic powder

Lightly brush quail with olive oil. Sprinkle each quail on both sides with salt, pepper, paprika, rosemary and garlic.

Grill quail 3 or 4 minutes on each side or until desired doneness.

Drizzle with lemon juice.

Mom's Lamb and Eggplant Roast

Serves 4 to 6

Filling for vegetables:

1/2   cup provolone, shredded
1/2   cup Romano cheese, grated
1/2   cup fresh basil or parsley, chopped
1/2   cup bread crumbs
2   eggs, small
        pepper and red hot pepper flakes to taste
1/2   teaspoon fennel seeds, ground

Combine filling ingredients in small bowl, set aside.

Roast Ingredients

1   large onion, sliced 1/4 inch thick
1/3   cup Marsala Olive Fruit Oil
4   potatoes, large, peeled or unpeeled
2   eggplants, small, sliced 1/4 inch thick
6   tomatoes, sliced
1   cup bread crumbs
1/2   cup fresh basil or parsley
6   lamb slices from leg or chops (1-1/2 to 2 pounds)
1/4   cup Romano cheese, grated
        salt, pepper and cayenne to taste
3/4   cup white wine

Lightly grease a large roasting pan. Drizzle with a little olive oil, add onion slices, spread evenly.

Slice potatoes in half lengthwise. Slice each half almost to end, making a sandwich.

Fill potatoes with about 1 tablespoon filling, lay over onions evenly.

Fill 2 slices of eggplant with 1 tablespoon filling. Repeat with remaining slices.

Place eggplant sandwiches over potatoes evenly.

Salt and pepper lightly (there is salt in the cheeses). Drizzle with olive oil, add wine, cover with foil loosely.

Bake in a 400 degrees oven for 30 to 40 minutes or until almost tender.

Combine bread crumbs, basil and cheese. Press lamb and tomatoes into crumb mixture on both sides.

Remove pan from oven, place breaded meat over eggplant evenly.

Place tomato slices over lamb, drizzle with remaining olive oil over all, cover loosely, return to oven.

Bake another 20 to 30 minutes or until vegetables and meat are tender. Check with a meat thermometer.

This roast is a family favorite. A sister-in-law would say "I don't know why, but when I make Mom's lamb roast, it never tastes like hers."

Mom's Meat Loaf

Serves 6 to 8

1	large onion, sliced across (for bottom of roaster)
1/2	cup dried tomatoes, crumbled
1/3	cup Marsala Olive Fruit Oil
2	pounds turkey, pork, chicken, beef or veal, ground
2	eggs (or 4 egg whites)
1/2	cup fresh basil or/and parsley, chopped
	Salt, pepper and cayenne to taste
1	cup bread crumbs
1/2	cup wine or milk
3/4	cup provolone, shredded
1/2	cup Romano cheese, grated
4	garlic cloves (or to taste), minced
2	green onions (white part), chopped
1	teaspoon fennel seeds
1	large tomato sliced across (for top)

Grease roasting pan, drizzle in 2 tablespoons olive oil, spread with onion slices.

Combine in mixing bowl, remaining ingredients (except sliced tomato) mix gently.

Roll mixture between 2 pieces of waxed paper to about 10 by 12 inches and 1/2 inch thick,

Combine all filling ingredients in mixing bowl (except hard cooked eggs and asparagus)

Spread filling on meat leaving 1 inch border all around.

Place eggs end to end in line down long side of roll.

Arrange asparagus along both sides of eggs.

Pick up waxed paper, starting at long side, near eggs, roll up meat, jelly roll fashion, enclosing filling.

Place meat on top of onions, drizzle with olive oil, arrange tomato slices on top over lapping.

Bake in a 350 degrees oven for 1 to 1-1/4 hours or use an instant meat thermometer registering at 160 degrees.

Filling

1/4	cup raisins or currants
1/2	cup olives, sliced
1/4	cup pine nuts
1	cup fresh mushrooms, chopped

Continued

1	egg (or 2 egg whites)
1	cup ricotta or mozzarella
	Pepper to taste
1	cup spinach or eggplant, cooked, chopped
1/2	teaspoon sage or tarragon
3 to 4	hard cooked eggs (for top of filling)
4	asparagus spears (for top of filling)

Variation: Potato Filling

1-1/4	cups yams or white potatoes, cooked, mashed
1/2	cup pineapple, crushed, drained
1/2	onion, chopped, cooked tender in 2 tablespoons olive oil
2	egg whites
1/3	cup macadamia nuts, chopped small
	Salt, pepper and cayenne to taste
1/3	cup dried cranberries or blueberries

In mixing bowl combine all ingredients, proceed with recipe.

Chicken With Lemon

Serves 4

1-1/2	pounds chicken, boneless, skinless, cut into serving pieces
	salt, pepper and cayenne to taste
1/4	cup flour
6	garlic cloves
1	teaspoon oregano
1/2	cup fresh basil or parsley, chopped
1/2	cup Marsala Olive Oil
3/4	cup fresh lemon or lime juice
	rosemary to taste

Coat chicken pieces with flour. Place olive oil in lightly greased roasting pan. Add chicken, bake in a 350 degrees oven for about 20 minutes, turning halfway through.

Add remaining ingredients, cover with foil, bake until tender, about 30 more minutes.

Serve with cooked rice, salad or mango salsa.

> ### Fight infections with garlic
> This flavor enhancer has antimicrobial properties, which combat Candida yeast infections.

Oven Baked Barbecued Spareribs

Serves 4

1-1/2	cups water
1	onion, chopped
1	teaspoon anise or fennel seeds
2	tablespoons Worcestershire sauce
4	pounds spareribs
4	garlic cloves (or to taste) minced
1/4	cup Marsala Olive Oil
1	cup tomatoes, diced
1	green bell pepper, minced
1/4	cup ketchup or chili sauce
1/4	cup brown sugar, pure maple syrup or honey
1	teaspoon mustard, curry powder or ginger
	salt, pepper and cayenne to taste
1-1/2	cups pineapple, crushed with juice
1/4	cup lemon or lime juice
4	tablespoons molasses

> **Stop bacteria with ginger**
> This spicy root contains gingerols, compounds that promote toxin-flushing sweating and fight E. Coli

Place ribs in large baking pan, add water, roast for 30 minutes in a 350 degrees oven, covered.

Pour off fat. In skillet saute onion, garlic and pepper in olive oil until tender.

Add remaining ingredients, stir, cover, simmer about 20 minutes.

Pour sauce over ribs, roast about 45 minutes longer or until tender, basting frequently.

To brown ribs, place under broiler 3 or 4 minutes

To cook spareribs on grill, prepare and preheat grill. Grill is ready when temperature reaches 200 to 225 degrees.

Place ribs on grill rack, baste with sauce, close lid. Cook until meat shrinks about 1 inch up the bone and they "give" when you wiggle the bones.

Pork Loin With Dried Fruit

Serves 6

1/2	cup bread crumbs
3 to 3-1/2 pounds pork tenderloin
2	onions, sliced across 1/4 inch thick
4	carrots, cut in half across
8 to 10 garlic cloves
1	tablespoon fresh sage, chopped
1	cup dried apricots or apples
1	cup dried prunes, pitted (or dried figs)
3/4	cup kumquats, quartered, seeded
1	teaspoon fennel or anise seeds
	Salt, pepper and cayenne to taste
1/2	cup fresh basil or parsley, chopped
3/4	cup wine
1/4	cup Marsala Olive Fruit Oil
1	cup celery, chopped
1	tablespoon fresh rosemary, chopped

Lightly grease roasting pan. Drizzle bottom with a little olive oil. Place onion slices, celery and carrots in pan, pour in wine.

Cut pork in half lengthwise, about 3/4 way. Stuff with prunes, apricots, rosemary, garlic, salt, pepper, cayenne and fennel seeds.

Close with poultry pins, lay on top of vegetables.

Sprinkle loin with bread crumbs, place remaining ingredients around evenly.

Drizzle loin with olive oil, cover with foil.

Bake in a 350 degrees oven for about 45 to 55 minutes or until instant meat thermometer reaches 170 degrees or desired doneness.

Slice, place on serving platter, arrange fruit around.

Variation:

10 to 12 fresh figs, whole - add last 10 minutes of baking

1	cup dried cherries, blueberries or cranberries
	garnish with 3 or 4 rosemary sprigs
2	quince, quartered
1	orange sectioned

Note:

If pork loin comes packaged in two pieces, place stuffing in between and tie with kitchen twine. When we have this for company, they always ask for the recipe.

Pork With Rhubarb

Serves 4

1-1/2   **pounds pork loin, cut into 1-1/2 inch thick slices**
        salt, pepper and cayenne to taste
1/4   **cup flour**
1/4   **cup Marsala Olive Oil**

Pound each piece of pork to about 1/4 inch thick, sprinkle with salt and peppers.

Cover both sides with flour, removing excess.

In large non stick skillet, lightly brown pork slices on each side in olive oil over medium heat.

Remove pork to platter, keep warm.

Rhubarb Sauce

1   **pound fresh or frozen rhubarb, chopped**
2   **tablespoons Marsala Olive Oil**
1/4   **cup brown sugar (or to taste)**
2   **tablespoons flour**
1/2   **teaspoon cinnamon**
1   **teaspoon fennel seeds**
2   **tablespoons lemon juice**
2   **cups soft bread crumbs**

In mixing bowl combine sugar, flour, cinnamon, fennel seeds, juice and rhubarb.

Toast bread crumbs in olive oil and place half on bottom of a lightly greased casserole.

Spoon half of rhubarb mixture over crumbs, arrange pork on rhubarb.

Place remaining rhubarb on pork, cover with foil.

Bake in a 350 degrees oven for 25 to 30 minutes.

Remove foil, cover with remaining crumbs, bake another 10 minutes.

Rack of Lamb

Serves 4 to 6

2   pounds rack of lamb (6-8 ribs) trimmed
1   tablespoon mustard, mild
1   egg white
2   tablespoons milk, non fat
1   onion, chopped
1/2   cup fresh mint, basil or parsley, chopped
4   garlic cloves, minced
1   cup fresh bread crumbs
1/4   cup Marsala Olive Fruit Oil
       Salt, pepper and cayenne to taste
1/4   cup Romano cheese, grated
3/4   cup wine, white
3   teaspoons fresh ginger, grated
1/2   cup pecans, almonds or walnuts, chopped fine

Sprinkle lamb with salt, pepper and cayenne.

In large skillet add olive oil, garlic, onion and ginger, cook until crisp tender. Remove from heat, add cheese, bread crumbs, mint, nuts, milk and egg white.

Remove as much fat from lamb as possible. In large skillet brown lamb in olive oil on both sides and ends.

Brush with mustard, pat crumb mixture over top of rack of lamb. Place in baking pan, add wine, roast in a 400 degrees oven for about 20 minutes for medium rare, 5 to 10 minutes longer for well done.

If browning too quickly, add 1/2 cup water in bottom of pan. Cover with foil. When done slice rack into chops, cutting between ribs.

Serve with apricot sauce or mint jelly.

Apricot Sauce

1   cup dried apricots
1/2   onion, chopped
2   garlic cloves, minced
1   cup broth
1/2   cup apricot nectar or orange juice
1   tablespoon honey or maple syrup
2   tablespoons Marsala Olive Fruit Oil
2   tablespoons fresh mint, chopped

In skillet add oil, garlic and onion, cook until crisp tender. Add remaining ingredients, cook simmering about 15 minutes.

Roasted Stuffed Turkey

Serves 6 to 8

1	12 pound turkey
1/4	Italian sausage cooked, well drained crumbled
3/4	cup each onion and celery
5	cups bread cubed
1	apple chopped
1/2	cup raisins, apricots or prunes, chopped
1/2	cup Romano cheese, grated
3/4	cup provolone, shredded
1/2	cup mozzarella, shredded
3	eggs or 6 egg whites
3/4	cup milk, non fat (or broth)
3/4	cup fresh basil and/or parsley
1	liver from turkey, chopped
1	cup chestnuts, cooked, peeled, chopped
1/3	cup Marsala Olive Fruit Oil
1/3	cup pistachios, pine nuts or walnuts, chopped
1	cup fresh mushrooms, chopped
	pepper to taste

In skillet over medium heat add olive oil, onion, celery and mushrooms, cook until tender. Add liver, cook a few seconds more.

Add mixture into a large mixing bowl together with remaining ingredients except turkey. Stuff turkey, truss. Stuff neck cavity, secure with poultry pins.

Roast in a 325 degrees oven about 3-1/2 to 4 hours or until internal temperature of 185 degrees and leg moves easily.

Baste with a drizzle of olive oil several times during baking.

Try not to open oven door too many times, as heat escapes. Cover with foil if browning too quickly.

Any stuffing left over, bake in greased muffin tins at 325 degrees for about 15 minutes or until golden.

Variation:

1	cup ham chopped
1/2	cup prosciutto chopped
1	cup rice, parboiled
1	pear, diced
1/2	cup dried cranberries, cherries or blueberries
1	cup spinach cooked, well drained, chopped

This stuffing may be used for chicken, capon, cornish hens or guinea hens only in smaller quantities.

Sarah's Pork Roast With Bread Dressing

Serves 6 to 8

1   4 to 5 pound pork roast

Dressing

4   slices Italian bread, several days old
2 or 3   onions, chopped
1/2   cup Romano cheese, grated
1/2   cup provolone, shredded
         Salt and pepper to taste
1   teaspoon fennel seeds
2   small eggs
1   cup milk (more if needed)
1/4   cup Marsala Olive Fruit Oil
2   tablespoons pine nuts
1/2   cup raisins

Cube bread, place in mixing bowl with milk to soak.

In skillet over medium heat add oil and onions, cook until crisp tender.

Squeeze milk from bread. Combine in bowl with eggs, cheeses, salt, pepper, fennel seeds, pine nuts, raisins and onion mixture.

Place pork roast in greased baking pan. Bake in a 350 degrees oven until thermometer reaches 170 degrees.

Spread dressing on top of pork roast evenly about 20 minutes before roast is ready.

Bake until dressing is golden. Cover with foil loosely if browning too quickly.

Variation:

1/2   cup apple butter
1/2   cup prunes, pitted, chopped
1/2   cup dried apricots, pears or apples, chopped
1/2   cup dried cherries, cranberries or blueberries
1   teaspoon Dijon mustard
2   tablespoons honey or pure maple syrup
1   cup carrots, shredded
1   cup celery leaves, chopped
1/4   teaspoon saffron

> ### Health benefit
> Boost brainpower with blueberries. New studies show that
> antioxidant-rich blueberries may keep your memory strong.

Terese's Spaghetti Squash With Chicken Cacciatore

Serves 4 to 6

Cut squash in half lengthwise, spoon out seeds. Place cut side down in large baking pan with 1 inch of water.

Bake in a 400 degrees oven for 50 to 60 minutes or until tender when pierced with fork.

With fork, remove spaghetti like strings from squash, place in a large shallow serving bowl.

Cover with chicken cacciatore sauce, place chicken around or on top of squash. Decorate with sprigs of basil.

If squash is too hard to cut, punch a hole in each end, wrap in foil. Bake 1-1/2 to 2 hours in a 400 degrees oven (depending on size) or until soft when pierced with fork. (or cook in microwave)

Chicken Cacciatore

Serves 4

3/4	cup flour
1/3	cup Marsala Olive Fruit Oil
2-1/2 to 3 pounds chicken pieces, boneless and skinless	
1	cup fresh or frozen peas
2	onions, diced
2	bell peppers, sliced
6	garlic cloves (or to taste) chopped
4	cups fresh or canned tomatoes, chopped
3	ounces tomato paste
1/2	cup wine
	Salt, pepper and red pepper flakes (to taste)
1/2	cup basil, parsley or cilantro, chopped
2	bay leaves (remove before serving)
1-1/2	cups mushrooms, sliced
1	cup celery or carrots, chopped

Coat chicken with flour, salt and peppers. In Dutch oven, heat oil, cook chicken on both sides until golden brown.

Add onion, garlic bell peppers and celery, cook until crisp tender over medium heat. Add tomatoes, tomato paste, wine, and bay leaves.

Simmer about 30 minutes or until chicken is tender. Add mushrooms, peas and basil, cook 1 or 2 minutes.

Variation:

Substitute rabbit, duck, veal or Italian meatballs for chicken

2	tablespoons fresh rosemary, chopped
1	cup olives, sliced

Variation:

Serve chicken cacciatore over 12 ounces of cooked "al dente" perciatelli or fusilli or cooked polenta.

Veal or Chicken Parmesan
(Veal Parmigiana)

Serves 4 to 6

1-1/2	pound veal steak, chicken or turkey, skinless, boneless
	Salt, pepper and cayenne to taste
1	egg (or 2 egg whites) slightly beaten
1/3	cup Romano cheese, grated
1/2	cup bread crumbs
1/3	cup Marsala Olive Fruit Oil
1	onion chopped fine
3	cups fresh or canned tomatoes chopped
1	teaspoon rosemary
1/2	cup fresh basil chopped
1-1/2	cups fresh mushrooms, sliced
1/2	pound Swiss, Monterey Jack or mozzarella cheese
1/2	cup red wine or vermouth
4	tablespoons tomato paste
6	garlic cloves, chopped

Slice veal into 8 or 10 very thin pieces. Place egg in pie plate.

In another pie plate combine bread crumbs, grated cheese, salt, pepper and cayenne.

Dip veal slices into egg, then in crumb mixture on both sides.

In skillet, over medium heat, cook veal in olive oil 3 or 4 pieces at a time.

When brown on each side, place on large plate, keep warm.

In same skillet, cook onions and garlic with a little olive oil, until tender. Add tomatoes, tomato paste, rosemary, basil and wine.

Cook about 15 minutes. In greased baking pan add a little tomato sauce on bottom evenly.

Place veal on top, add mushrooms, pour 3/4 of sauce over veal. Cover with thin slices of cheese, spread with remaining sauce evenly.

Bake in a 350 degrees oven for about 35 minutes covered with foil if desired.

Variation:

1	teaspoon Worcestershire
1	teaspoon thyme, sage or oregano
3/4	cup olives, sliced
1	bell pepper, chopped
1	cup celery, chopped
1/2	cup coconut, flaked

Veal Roast with Prunes

Serves 6

3-1/2 to 4 pounds veal, rolled, tied
      Salt, pepper and cayenne to taste
1/2   teaspoon ginger
2   onions, sliced
3/4   cup wine
4   garlic cloves, chopped
3/4   cup water
1-1/2 cups prunes, pitted, (dried peaches, apricots or cherries)
1/3   cup Marsala Olive Fruit Oil
2   celery stalks
2   carrots
1/4   cup brown sugar
1/2   teaspoon sage

Rub ginger, salt, pepper, sage and cayenne all around veal. Lightly grease roasting pan.

Add to pan onions, carrots, garlic and celery, place roast on top, drizzle with oil. Bake in a 325 degrees oven for 2-1/2 hours or until meat thermometer reaches 170 degrees.

In saucepan combine sugar, wine, water and prunes, bring to a boil. Lower to simmer, cook for 20 minutes.

Add to veal last 20 minutes of baking. Serve with cooked rice, wheat, couscous or polenta.

Variation:

1/2   cup fresh basil, chopped
      grated peel of 1 orange or 1 lemon

Porcupine Meatballs

Serves 4

1   recipe for Italian meatballs
1/3   cup rice
1/2   cup tomato soup or tomato juice
1/4   cup Marsala Olive Fruit Oil
1   recipe for chunky tomato gravy

Add rice and tomato soup to meatball mixture. Brown in olive oil on all sides.

Add to chunky tomato gravy. Simmer about 30 minutes or until rice is tender.

Note: for meat rolls, shape 1 heaping tablespoon of ground meat mixture into a small roll, 1 inch thick, 4 inches long. Press ends to flatten.

Veal Rolls

Serves 4 to 6

8	slices veal, 1/4 inch thick, 4x6 (about 1-1/2 pounds)
8	thin slices prosciutto, 4x4 inches
8	slices Monterey, fontina or Swiss cheese
8	large spinach leaves, radicchio or greens of your choice
1/4	cup Marsala Olive Fruit Oil
4	tablespoons lemon juice
1/4	cup flour
1	onion, sliced
1/2	cup white wine
	Salt, pepper and paprika to taste
1/2	teaspoon sage
1/4	cup pine nuts or currants
1/2	cup fresh basil or parsley
	Pinch of rosemary or nutmeg

Place 1 slice each of prosciutto, cheese and spinach leaf on each veal slice. Sprinkle with nuts.

Turn veal slices over about 3/4 inch on each side, roll up and secure with poultry pins or toothpicks. Dust with flour lightly.

In large skillet add oil and onions. Over medium heat cook rolls until golden on all sides.

Add lemon juice, rosemary, wine and remaining ingredients. Cook on low heat about 20 minutes. Serve with cherry salsa.

Cherry Salsa

1-1/2	cups bing cherries pitted, chopped
1/4	cup orange juice
2	tablespoons Marsala Olive Fruit Oil
1/4	cup pistachio or almonds, sliced, lightly toasted
2	tablespoons fresh mint, chopped
1/4	teaspoon almond flavoring
2	tablespoons amaretto liqueur

In mixing bowl combine all ingredients, refrigerate until ready to serve.

Health benefit

Dodge varicose veins with cherries. Bioflavonoids in these jewels strengthen blood vessels to prevent leg blemishes.

Veal Scallopini With Peppers

Serves 4

1	cup celery, sliced
1	cup fresh mushrooms, sliced
4	bell peppers, red, green or yellow, sliced
1	onion, sliced
1/3	cup Marsala Olive Fruit Oil
1-1/2	pounds veal, cut for scallopini
4	garlic cloves (or to taste) chopped
4	tablespoons flour
	Salt, white pepper and cayenne to taste
1/2	cup white wine or sherry
1	lime or lemon
1/4	cup fresh basil or parsley, chopped
1/2	teaspoon sage or rosemary

In large skillet add oil, onions, celery, peppers and garlic. Cook until crisp tender, add mushrooms and basil.

Coat veal with flour, salt, peppers, and sage. Remove vegetables from skillet with slotted spoon onto serving plate.

Add to skillet 2 to 3 tablespoons olive oil, cook veal on both sides until golden brown.

Place vegetables back in pan with veal, pour in wine, cook covered 5 to 8 more minutes on low heat. Serve with lemon.

Variation:

Substitute turkey or chicken scallopini, or meat of your choice for veal.

1 can whole baby corn (15 ounce) drained.

Meat Stew

Serves 4

In large saucepan cook 1-1/2 pounds of cubed meat of your choice until brown in 1/4 cup Marsala Olive Oil. Add 1/4 cup wine, 1 onion chopped, 4 garlic cloves and cook covered about 5 minutes. Add 2 carrots, 2 celery stalks, 2 potatoes, 1 turnip, chopped and cook covered until meat and vegetables are tender.

Add 2 cups tomatoes chopped, 1/2 cup fresh basil chopped, 1 teaspoon fennel seeds, salt, pepper and cayenne to taste. Cook covered 5 minutes. Add 1-1/2 cups mushrooms and 1 cup fresh or frozen peas, cook a few more minutes. Serve with green salad and crusty bread.

Veal Scallops

Serves 4 to 6

1/4	cup lemon juice

10 to 12 scallops 6x4 about 1/4 inch thick

1/3	cup flour
1/3	cup Marsala Olive Fruit Oil
1	onion, chopped
4	garlic cloves (or to taste) chopped
1-1/2	cups fresh mushrooms, sliced
1/2	cup parsley, chopped
1/3	cup cognac, brandy or rum
1/2	cup broth
1	cup cherries, pitted
	Salt and white pepper to taste

Dust veal on both sides with flour.

In large non-stick skillet, over medium heat add oil, cook veal 2 minutes on both sides.

Remove to serving platter. In same skillet add 2 tablespoons olive oil.

Cook onions and garlic until soft. Add mushrooms, parsley, salt, and pepper, cook about 2 minutes.

Return veal to skillet, add broth, lemon juice, cherries and cognac. Bring to a boil, lower to simmer for about 10 minutes.

Pizzaiola

Serves 4

Pound 1-1/2 pounds boneless round steak, cut into serving pieces. Dust with flour, brown in large non stick skillet with 1/4 cup Marsala Olive Oil. Add 1/2 cup red wine, 1 onion chopped and 4 garlic cloves, cook covered until soft. Add 2 cups tomatoes chopped, 3 ounces tomato paste, 1/2 cup fresh basil chopped, salt, pepper, cayenne and oregano to taste.

Cover, simmer 20 to 30 minutes or until meat is tender, stirring occasionally. Add 1-1/2 cups fresh mushrooms sliced, sprinkle with 1/3 cup bread crumbs, 1/3 cup Romano cheese, grated. Simmer a few minutes.

Serve with cooked polenta or rice.

Baked Ham With
Orange and Lemon Pesto Sauce

Serves 8 to 10

1-9 to 10 pound fully cooked (bone in) ham
2   cups any sweet white wine
1   cup pomegranate syrup or orange juice
8 to 10 spiced crab apples (or kumquats for garnish)
1/2   cup pomegranate seeds (for garnish)
orange and/or lemon leaves (for garnish)
orange and lemon pesto sauce, for dipping

Line a large roasting pan with double layers of foil. Place ham into prepared pan. Pour wine and pomegranate syrup over ham. Bake in a 350 degrees oven until heated through, about 45 minutes.

Transfer to serving platter, cover, keep warm until ready to serve.

Pour pan juices into gravy boat.

Serve ham with orange and lemon pesto sauce (and pan juices if desired).

Garnish with spiced crab apples, pomegranate seeds, orange and lemon leaves.

Orange and Lemon Pesto Sauce

Makes about 3-1/2 cups

1/2   medium orange
2   lemons
1/4   cups pure maple syrup (or to taste)
1/2   cup Marsala Olive Oil
1/2   cup basil leaves
1/4   cup pistachios (or nuts of your choice)
       salt and pepper to taste

Quarter orange and lemons, remove seeds, chop coarsely.

Place fruit in container of food processor with remaining ingredients, blend until smooth and thick.

Pour into serving bowl.

Note:

Pomegranate syrup maybe purchased in specialty stores.

It's **_so_** good for you
Oranges are rich in terpenes, a compound that reduces serum cholesterol levels, preventing heart disease.

Veal Piccata

Serves 4

2	pounds veal cutlets
1/2	cup parsley, basil or mint, minced
	flour
1/4	cup Marsala Olive Oil
	Salt, pepper and paprika to taste
1/3	cup lemon juice (or lime)
2	lemons or limes, cut into wedges
1	teaspoon Dijion mustard
1/4	cup white wine or broth

Pound cutlets between waxed paper to about 1/4 inch thick. Coat with flour on both sides, remove excess.

Heat olive oil in large non stick skillet over medium heat. Add veal with out crowding, brown quickly (about 40 seconds) on each side.

Place on warm platter. To skillet add lemon juice, mustard and wine, heat one minute.

Pour over meat, sprinkle with salt, pepper and paprika.

Garnish with lemon wedges, sprinkle with parsley.

Variation:

2	lemons sliced thin, add to skillet, cook 1 minute
	mushrooms, sliced
	sun chokes, sliced
	capers
	artichoke hearts
	garlic

Note:

One of the best gifts I received is an instant read thermometer.

Olive Oil

The Greek poet Homer called olive oil "liquid gold" because of its brilliant color, superb flavor and extraordinary versatility. Numerous studies show the mono-unsaturated fats in olive oil help the body both reduce its "bad," or LDL, cholesterol levels and lower the risk of heart disease.

Pot Stickers

Makes 25

1/2	pound turkey, pork or beef, lean, ground
1/4	cup Marsala Olive Oil
3/4	cup cabbage, shredded
1/2	cup mushroom, chopped
1/3	cup green onions, minced
1/4	cup carrots, shredded
2	teaspoons ginger, fresh, grated
1/4	cup soy sauce
25	squares won ton wrappers
1/2	cup chicken broth

In non-stick skillet brown meat in olive oil until no longer pink. Add cabbage, mushrooms, onions, carrots and ginger. Cook stirring about 5 minutes or until liquid has evaporated.

Stir in soy sauce. Place heaping teaspoon filing in center of each won ton wrapper. Brush edges with water, bring up edges to enclose filling. Twist firmly to form small pouches.

Heat 2 tablespoons olive oil in large skillet. Place half of the pot stickers in skillet, cook over medium heat until bottom is golden brown, about 5 minutes.

Add half the broth in skillet, cover, cook over low heat for about 5 minutes.

Repeat with remaining filled won tons. Serve with desired sauce.

Variation for sauces:

teriyaki sauce

sweet and sour sauce

hot chili oil

Health benefit

Perk up with pork. The other white meat is high in vitamin B_{12}, also called "the energy vitamin" because it fights fatigue.

Beef Rib Roast

Serves 6

1	(3-1/2 pound) boneless rib eye roast
2	onions, quartered
2	carrots, cut into 1 inch pieces
1/4	cup Marsala Olive Oil

Dry Rub:

2	garic cloves (or to taste) minced
1	teaspoon pepper, black
1	teaspoon dry mustard
1	teaspoon paprika
1	teaspoon chili powder
1/2	teaspoon thyme or sage
1/2	teaspoon salt
1/2	teaspoon cayenne

> **Health benefit**
>
> Keep your colon healthy with onions. These flavor bulbs contain quercetin, an antioxidant that may halt tumor growth.

Remove as much fat as possible from meat. Brush roast with olive oil. In small bowl combine dry rub ingredients.

Place roast on plastic wrap, rub the marinade all around meat. Wrap tightly and refrigerate several hours or up to 24 hours.

Place roast on rack, fat side up, place in roasting pan.

Arrange onions and carrots on rack around roast. Brush with olive oil. Bake in a 325 degrees oven for 1-1/2 hours or until instant read thermometer registers 160 degrees, for medium.

Place roast on serving platter, slice thin, serve with vegetables and Yorkshire pudding.

Yorkshire Pudding

Serves 6

1	teaspoon sugar
2	tablespoons Marsala Olive Oil
2	eggs
1	cup milk
1	cup flour
1/2	teaspoon salt
1/2	teaspoon white pepper

Preheat oven to 425 degrees. Pour olive oil into a 10 inch pie plate, tilt to coat surface.

Continued

In medium bowl, beat eggs, milk, sugar, flour, salt and pepper to make a smooth batter. Pour into prepared pie plate, bake 20 to 25 minutes or until golden brown. Serve immediately with roast beef.

Note:

Batter may be baked in 6 popover cups. Coat cups with cooking spray. Divide batter evenly among prepared cups. Bake in a 400 degrees oven for 10 minutes. Lower temperature to 325, bake another 25 minutes or until golden. Serve immediately.

Baked Orange Glazed Ham

Serves 8 to 10

5 to 6	pounds ham
1/4	cup pure maple syrup or honey
1/4	cup brown sugar
1/4	cup Sciabica orange olive oil
	whole cloves

Place ham, fat side up in an uncovered roaster. Bake in a 300 degree oven 25 to 30 minutes per pound. 45 minutes before ham is done remove rind and pour off fat. With sharp knife score the surface in diagonal lines. Decorate with cloves. Blend syrup, sugar and orange olive oil, spread mixture over surface of ham. Return to oven, baste frequently with mixture in pan Serve garnished with orange slices, crab apples, canned or fruit of your choice. Serving per person – 1/4 tp 1/3 pound.

Veal Pouches With Sage

Serves 4

8	veal scallops, pounded thin
8	fresh sage leaves
3	slices prosciutto, cut into thirds
8	strips mozzarella or fontina cheese
1/4	cup Marsala Olive Oil
1/2	cup white wine
1	cup grapes, seedless or cherries, pitted

On each scallop, place one sage leaf, one piece prosciutto and one strip mozzarella. Tuck in two sides of scallop and roll into a pouch, secure with toothpicks.

Heat oil in large non stick skillet, sauté pouches, turning to brown on all sides. Place on serving plate, keep warm.

Add wine into skillet, heat, stir in grapes. Pour over veal.

Chicken With Rice

Serves 4

1	cup rice
1-1/2	cups water or broth
1/2	cup whole wheat or white flour
4	chicken breast, boneless, skinless (or meat of your choice)
2	onions sliced or chopped
4	garlic cloves, chopped
1-1/2	cups tomatoes, fresh or canned, chopped
1	bell pepper, chopped
1/4	cup Marsala or Sciabica olive oil
1/2	cup olives, sliced (or raisins)
2	cups spinach leaves
1	jalapeno or 1/2 habanero, diced
1/2	cup basil, parsley, mint or cilantro, chopped
1	cup mushrooms, sliced
	salted pepper to taste
1/2	cup red wine
	pinch of saffron

Pound chicken pieces to about 1/2 inch thick. Place flour, salt and pepper on waxed paper. Dust both sides of chicken pieces, remove excess flour.

In a large non stick skillet add olive oil, heat over medium heat. Brown chicken on both sides until golden. Remove from pan onto plate cover to keep warm.

To skillet add a little olive oil if needed. Add onion, bell pepper, jalapeno and garlic cover cook until crisp tender.

Add wine, cook 1 minute. Add tomatoes and water, bring to a boil, stir in rice. Lower to simmer, place chicken back in pan, cover, cook until meat and rice are tender, about 25 to 30 minutes.

Add spinach, olive, mushrooms and remaining ingredients, stir gently. Cover and simmer 5 to 10 more minutes. Serve with green salad.

Variation:

2	tablespoons capers
	rosemary or oregano
	carrots, sliced
	brocoli flowerets
2	bay leaves, remove before serving
	apples or pears
	grated peel of 1 orange or lemon

> ### An apple a day lowers cholesterol
>
> Apples are rich in the soluble fiber, pectin, which helps eliminate unhealthy cholesterol from the blood. Pectin also binds to pollutants, like lead, and helps the body get rid of them.

Walnut Braid Pg 160 ~ Breadsticks Pg 141 ~ Carta da Musica Pg 142

Bagels Pg 164

All-Bran Muffins

Makes 12

1	cup all bran
3/4	cup milk, non fat
1	cup flour
1	teaspoon baking powder
1/2	teaspoon baking soda
1/2	teaspoon salt
1/2	cup molasses
1	egg (or 2 egg whites)
2	tablespoons Marsala Olive Fruit Oil
1/2	cup raisins, prunes, chopped or dried blueberries

Combine all bran and milk in mixing bowl.

Sift dry ingredients into same bowl.

Add remaining ingredients, stir only until combined.

Fill greased muffin cups 2/3 full. Bake in a 375 degrees oven for about 20 to 25 minutes.

To bake batter in a greased 9 inch square pan, bake slightly longer. Cut into squares.

Variation:

1/2	teaspoon cinnamon
1/4	cup wheat germ

Applesauce Muffins

Makes 12

1	egg or 2 egg whites
1	cup all bran
1/2	cup chunky applesauce or banana, mashed
1/2	cup raisins
1-1/2	cup flour
4	teaspoons baking powder
1/2	teaspoon salt
1/4	cup sugar
3	tablespoons Marsala Olive Fruit Oil

Grease muffin cups. Preheat oven to 375 degrees.

In mixing bowl add egg, milk, oil, all bran, applesauce and raisins.

Sift dry ingredients into same bowl, stir only until combined.

Fill muffin cups 2/3 full. Bake 25 to 30 minute.

Variation:

1	teaspoon cinnamon
1/2	teaspoon nutmeg or cardamom
1/4	teaspoon cloves

Olive You!

Bread Sticks

Makes 20 to 30

1	tablespoons sugar or honey
1	egg white
1	cup water (110 degrees)
1	package dry yeast
3-1/4	cups flour
1/4	cup Marsala Olive Fruit Oil
3/4	teaspoon salt (or to taste)
1	egg white lightly beaten (to brush on top)
1/2	cup sesame seeds (to sprinkle tops)

In mixing bowl add yeast, water and sugar, let stand about 10 minutes.

Add remaining ingredients, stir until dough holds together.

Turn out onto lightly floured board, knead until smooth.

Oil mixing bowl, place dough in, turning to coat.

Cover, put in a warm place to rise until doubled in bulk, about 1 hour.

Turn dough out onto lightly floured board. Pat dough down to about 14x14 inches.

Cut into 20 stripes, roll and stretch to 12 or 14 inches long.

Arrange sticks on lightly greased baking pans placed 1 inch apart.

Brush with egg white, sprinkle with sesame seeds.

Let rest covered until puffy, about 20 minutes. Bake in a 375 degrees oven for 15 to 20 minutes or until golden brown.

Variation for dough:

1/4	cup currants, raisins or dried fruit of your choice, chopped small
1	teaspoon curry, rosemary, turmeric, cayenne, thyme or oregano
1/2	cup fresh basil, parsley or cilantro, chopped
1/2	teaspoon ginger or chili powder
1/2	teaspoon black pepper
1/2	cup walnuts, or nuts of your choice, chopped fine
	Grated peel of 1 orange or lemon
4	garlic cloves, minced
2	green onions (white part) minced

Variation for top:

1/3	cup black sesame or poppy seeds
1/3	cup Romano cheese
1/3	cup fennel, anise, caraway or cumin seeds
1	tablespoon cinnamon sugar

Substitute 1 cup cornmeal, rye, whole wheat flour for white flour.

Bread sticks may be twisted or shaped as desired.

Carta Da Musica
(Sheet Music Bread)

Makes 10 to 12

1-1/2	cups semolina
2	cups flour
1/2	teaspoon salt
1	cup warm water
2	tablespoons Marsala Olive Fruit Oil
1	egg or 2 egg whites

In mixing bowl combine all ingredients, stir until dough holds together. Depending on flour and weather, less water may be needed.

On lightly floured board, knead dough until smooth and not sticky. Cover, let rest about 20 minutes. Cut dough into 10 or 12 pieces. Roll each piece into a ball, flatten slightly. Let rest about 15 minutes.

On floured board, roll each piece very, very thin, to about 1/16 of an inch and to about 10 inches rounds. Add a little flour as needed when rolling out, to keep from sticking.

Place round on very lightly greased baking sheet. Bake at 400 degrees fro 5 to 6 minutes, about 2 to 2-1/2 minutes on each side, or until crisp and lightly golden. Watch carefully as not to over brown.

Cool on wire rack, brush with a little olive oil and sprinkle with salt or Romano cheese, grated.

Sweet Carta Da Musica
Add 1/2 cup confectioners' sugar to dough

Whole Wheat Carta Da Musica
Substitute 1 cup whole wheat pastry flour for white flour

Carta Da Musica With Sesame Seeds
Add 1/2 cup black or regular sesame seeds.

After dough is rolled out, sprinkle rounds evenly with seeds. With rolling pin, press seeds in lightly.

Variation:
	grated peel of 1 lemon
1/2	cup anise, fennel, caraway or seeds of your choice.
1/4	cup fresh rosemary, tarragon or sage chopped fine.

Note: 2 round pizza pans (about 12 inches) will work well when baking the sheets.

Corn Muffins
Makes 12

1	cup corn meal
1-1/4	cups flour
1/2	cup sugar
3	teaspoons baking powder
1/4	teaspoon baking soda
1	egg (or 2 egg whites)
1/2	cup milk non fat
1/4	cup Marsala Olive Fruit Oil
1/3	cup pistachios, chopped (or nuts of your choice)
1	tablespoon orange peel, grated
1	teaspoon vanilla
1/2	teaspoon salt
1/2	cup orange juice

> **Perk up with pistachios**
> These tasty green nuts contain boron, a trace mineral that boosts brain activity to keep you alert and on your toes.

Topping

	Grated peel of 1 orange
1/4	cup sugar
1	tablespoon flour
1	tablespoon Marsala Olive Fruit Oil
1	tablespoon pistachios, ground

Stir altogether, set aside.

In mixing bowl combine dry ingredients. Make well in center add milk, orange juice, egg and olive oil.

Stir, add nuts. Fill greased muffin cups 3/4 full, sprinkle topping on each evenly.

Bake in a 400 degrees oven for 18 to 20 minutes or until golden. Good served right from the oven with honey or jam.

Variation for topping:

1	teaspoon cinnamon or nutmeg

Variation for muffins:

Substitute

	raisins, dried blueberries or dates, chopped, for nuts
	dried fruits of your choice, chopped small
2	cups raspberries or blueberries
1/2	teaspoon raspberry jam in each muffin
2	jalapeno chilies, minced
1/4	cup cream-style corn
1/3	cup pine nuts

Date Scones

Makes 16

2   **cups flour**
1/2   **cup sugar**
2   **teaspoons cream of tartar**
1   **teaspoon baking soda**
3/4   **teaspoon salt**
1/3   **cup Marsala Olive Fruit Oil**
2   **eggs (or 4 egg whites)**
1   **egg white slightly beaten (to brush tops)**
1/2   **cup dates, chopped**
       Grated peel of 1 orange

In mixing bowl, sift in dry ingredients, make well in center.

Add eggs and olive oil, stir just until dough holds together.

Add dates, place on lightly floured board. Pat dough down to about 2/3 inch thick.

Cut into rounds with a 2 inch fluted cookie cutter. Flour cutter each time with flour.

Brush tops with egg white, place on greased baking sheet.

Bake in a 375 degrees oven for about 15 minutes or until golden.

Cool on wire rack, serve warm.

Note: Dough may be patted down to a 7 inch round, cut into 8 wedges.

Variation:

substitute 1/2 cup mixed candied fruits, prunes, raisins, dried apricots, cranberries, cherries or blueberries for dates.
add coconut or ginger, shredded

Sprinkle with cinnamon sugar

Variation for flour:

substitute 1/2 cup whole wheat pastry flour or cornmeal for white flour.

Health benefit

Sidestep sniffles with berries. These red gems contain compounds that reduce histamine release and fend off allergies.

Fig Bread

Makes 1 loaf

1	package dry yeast
1	teaspoon sugar
1/2	cup water, lukewarm
1/2	cup orange juice, room temperature
1	egg white
2-1/2	cups flour
3	tablespoons Marsala Olive Oil
1/2	cup pine nuts (or nuts of your choice, chopped)
1/2	teaspoon salt (or to taste)
	grated peel of 1 orange
3/4	cup dried figs, chopped
4	tablespoons honey
1/4	teaspoon fiori di Sicilia (or 1 teaspoon orange extract)

In mixing bowl add water, orange juice, yeast, 1/2 cup flour and sugar, stir. Let stand about 15 minutes.

Stir in remaining flour, olive oil, honey, fiori di Sicilia, egg white and salt. Turn onto floured board, knead until smooth.

Return to bowl, cover, let rise in a warm place until doubled.

Place dough on floured board, pat down, cover with figs and grated orange peel.

Work figs into dough. At this point the dough may be made into a round loaf or into a braid.

Place on oiled baking pan. Let rise covered, until doubled. Drizzle top with oil.

May be baked in the pan or on a baking stone placed in oven. Slide risen dough onto stone.

Bake in a 375 degrees oven for 25 to 35 minutes or until golden brown.

Cover with foil loosely if browning too quickly.

Remove from oven, cool on wire rack.

Serve with meals or for a snack.

Top slices with a drizzle of olive oil or spread with ricotta and honey.

Variation:

Substitute dates, dried apricots, pitted prunes, raisins, dried pineapple chopped, or dried fruit of your choice for figs.

Note: For braid, cut dough into 3 even pieces. Roll each piece to about 14 inches long.

Place rolls side by side on greased baking sheet. Braid rolls, pinch each end together, tuck under braid.

To form a wreath, bring ends together, seal both ends.

Focaccia

Makes about 20 pieces

Dough:

1	package dry yeast
1	teaspoon sugar
1-1/4	cups water (110 to 115 degrees)
1/4	cup Marsala Olive Fruit Oil
1	teaspoon salt (or to taste)
1	egg white
2	garlic cloves, minced
2	tablespoons Marsala Olive Fruit Oil for bottom of pan
2	tablespoons cornmeal for bottom of pan
	About 4-1/4 cups flour

In large mixing bowl, sprinkle yeast and sugar over water. Stir in 1/2 cup flour, let stand about 10 minutes.

Add remaining flour, salt, garlic, egg white and olive oil, stir until dough holds together.

Turn dough out onto floured board, knead until smooth, adding more flour to keep from sticking to fingers.

Place dough back in lightly oiled bowl, cover, let rest in a warm place until doubled in bulk.

Lightly grease a 10 x 16 inch baking pan, sprinkle with cornmeal. Drizzle with olive oil evenly over bottom of pan.

Spread dough to edges of pan, cover, let rise about 20 minutes. Dimple top with finger tips every inch or so over entire surface.

Cover focaccia evenly with fresh chopped rosemary, 1/4 cup Romano cheese, grated and black pepper to taste. Drizzle with Olive Oil.

Bake in a 400 degrees oven for 20 to 25 minutes or until crust is golden brown.

Variation:

1	cup provolone, shredded (or dried ricotta)
1	teaspoon oregano (or rosemary)
1/2	cup fresh basil or parsley, chopped
4	garlic cloves (or to taste) minced
1-1/2	cup mozzarella, shredded
1	cup olives, sliced
1/4	pound lean beef, ground, cooked, well drained
2	tablespoons sage leaves, fresh, chopped
	anchovy to taste, rinsed

Continued

1	cup mushrooms, sliced
1	cup raisins, golden
2	onions, sliced, sauteed in 2 tablespoons olive oil
1-1/2	cups red Swiss chard, cooked, well drained, chopped

Substitute 1 cup whole wheat flour for white

Substitute 1/2 cup semolina or cornmeal for white flour

Dough may be baked in 2 - 13x9 inch greased baking pans.

To serve: cut focaccia into squares. Cut squares in half, fill sandwiches with chopped arugula, olive oil, lemon juice, salt and pepper to taste.

Variation:

Fill sandwiches with grilled eggplant, Italian sausage (cooked, well drained, sliced) onions and bell pepper mixture.

Another combination of prosciutto, mozzarella, olives, tomatoes, basil, olive oil and capers.

Tuna, roasted bell peppers, lemon juice, olive oil, onions, sliced thin, and capers is a nice filling also.

Sweet Focaccia

Add 1/4 cup sugar to focaccia dough, and 1 small potato, shredded.

Topping

3	cups grapes, seedless
1/2	cup brown sugar
1	teaspoon cinnamon
3/4	cup pine nuts, pistachio, or pecans, chopped
2	tablespoons rum or Irish Cream Liqueur
2	tablespoons Marsala Olive Oil

In mixing bowl combine topping ingredients, toss gently.

Dimple top of dough with finger tips at 2 inch intervals, drizzle with olive oil.

Spread topping evenly over dough. Bake in a 375 degrees oven for 25 to 35 minutes.

Variation:

2	cups dried blueberries, cranberries or cherries
1	cup raisins, golden
3/4	cup hazelnuts, cashew or macadamia nuts, chopped

apples, pears, peaches or fruits of your choice

Golden Corn Bread

Makes 16 Squares

1-1/2	cups flour
1-1/2	cups cornmeal
4	tablespoons baking powder
1-2/3	cups milk (non fat)
3/4	teaspoons salt (or to taste)
1/3	cup Marsala Olive Fruit Oil
1/4	cup sugar
2	eggs (or 4 egg whites)

> **Burn more fat calories with chili peppers.**
> Capsaicin, the compound that gives jalapeños their heat, has been shown to speed up metabolism, which can help you shed those pesky extra pounds.

Grease a 9 inch square baking pan. Preheat oven to 375 degrees.

In mixing bowl add dry ingredients, make well in center. Stir in remaining ingredients.

Batter should be lumpy, pour into prepared pan, spread evenly.

Bake about 30 minutes or until golden.

When cool, cut into 16 squares. Serve with honey, jam, pure maple syrup or peanut butter.

Variation:

1	cup apple diced or pineapple, crushed, drained
1/2	cup pecans, pistachio or walnuts, chopped
1	cup corn or asparagus tips
1	cup blueberries, raspberries or berries of your choice
2	garlic cloves, minced
1/2	cup olives, sliced
1/2	teaspoon cumin, paprika or thyme
1/2	cup fresh basil, parsley or cilantro, chopped
1	zucchini or carrot, shredded
1/3	cup dried tomatoes, chopped
3/4	pumpkin or butternut squash, shredded
2	green onions (white part), chopped
1	bell pepper, minced
1/2	cup Cheddar, provolone or Swiss cheese, shredded
1	jalapeño pepper, minced
1/2	teaspoon cinnamon, nutmeg or ginger
1/2	cup dried fruits of your choice, chopped
1/2	cup raisins or dates, chopped
1/2	cup raspberry jam (or jam of your choice)

Drop 1/2 teaspoon of jam in dollops over top of batter.

Substitute low fat evaporated milk or plain yogurt for non fat milk.

Jumbo Popovers

Makes 8 to 10

4	tablespoons Marsala Olive Fruit Oil
6	eggs
2	cups flour
1/2	teaspoon salt (or to taste)
2	cups milk
	Pinch of white pepper

Grease 8 or 10 – 2-1/2 inches deep, seven ounce custard cups, place on cookie sheet for easier handling.

In bowl of electric mixer, beat eggs until frothy. Add milk and oil, beat until blended.

Add flour and salt, mix until batter is smooth. Fill each custard cup 3/4 full with batter.

Bake in a 375 degrees oven for 50 to 60 minutes or until golden.

While still in oven, cut a small slit in side of each popover, with tip of knife, to let steam out.

Bake another 5 to 10 minutes until crisp and golden brown. Serve with honey, soft cheese or jam.

Note: Batter may be made in jar of blender.

Variation:

1/2	teaspoon chives, basil, thyme, anise seeds
1/3	cup spinach, drained, finely chopped, lightly packed
1/3	cup olives, minced
1/3	cup Monterey Jack, shredded, Romano, grated or Cheddar cheese, shredded
1/2	teaspoon cinnamon or allspice
1	teaspoon sugar
1/4	cup nuts of your choice ground
1/4	cup green onion (white part) minced
1	garlic clove, minced
	Grated peel of 1 orange

Regular Popovers

Cut the amount of ingredients in half. Bake in greased twelve 2-1/2 inch muffin pan cups.

Bake in a 375 degrees oven for 40 to 50 minutes or until golden brown.

Olive You!

Muffuletta Sandwich

Serves 6 to 8

1	10 inch muffuletta bread, a ring or 1 large French bread loaf
1/4	pound provolone or mozzarella, sliced
3	ounces prosciutto, sliced thin (or roast beef)
3	ounces mortadella, salami or coppa, sliced thin
1-1/2	cups olive salad

Olive Salad

Makes 6 to 8 cups

2	celery stalks, sliced thin
1	cup marinated onions
	Salt and white pepper to taste
4	garlic cloves, minced
3	cups pitted olives of your choice, chopped
2	bell peppers, roasted, sliced
1/2	cup Marsala Olive Fruit Oil
1/4	cup fresh basil, parsley, mint or cilantro, chopped
1	teaspoon Dijon mustard
1/3	cup white wine vinegar or lemon juice
2	tomatoes, chopped
1	cup artichoke hearts (fresh cooked or canned), chopped
1/2	teaspoon oregano or rosemary, crumbled
6	anchovies rinsed, chopped

Combine all ingredients in glass bowl, cover, keep refrigerated until ready to use.

Cut bread in half crosswise. Scoop out a little of soft bread in center of each half. (Save to make bread crumbs.) Drizzle with 1 tablespoon olive oil over each half if desired.

Spoon as much olive salad as desired on one half. Top with cheese and cold cuts. Sandwich together with top of loaf, pressing to compact.

Wrap tightly in plastic wrap, refrigerate 6 to 8 hours, slice in wedges.

Variation for filling:

3	ounces smoked salmon, sliced
3	ounces beef or meats of your choice, roasted, sliced thin
1	cucumber, sliced thin
1/4	cup capers
1/4	cup pesto sauce

Continued

2	cups cauliflower, cooked crisp tender, chopped
2	cups spinach or lettuce leaves, shredded
1	cup clams, shrimp or scallops, cooked, chopped
4 to 6	eggplant or zucchini slices, grilled
3	ounces chicken, turkey or duck, cooked, sliced
1	sweet red onion, sliced thin
2	hard cooked eggs, yolks removed if desired, chopped
2 to 4	sweet pickles, chopped

Muffuletta Bread

Makes 1 Loaf

1-1/4	cups milk, (non fat) or water (110°)
1	egg yolk
1	package dry yeast
1	tablespoon sugar
3/4	teaspoon salt (or to taste)
4	tablespoons Marsala Olive Fruit Oil
3	cups flour
1	tablespoon lemon juice
2	tablespoons sesame or poppy seeds
1	egg white slightly beaten
1	tablespoon cornmeal

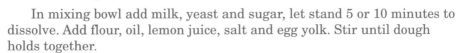

In mixing bowl add milk, yeast and sugar, let stand 5 or 10 minutes to dissolve. Add flour, oil, lemon juice, salt and egg yolk. Stir until dough holds together.

Turn onto a lightly floured board, knead until smooth. Return to lightly oiled bowl, cover, let rise in a warm place until doubled, about 45 minutes.

Place on lightly floured board, form dough into a round loaf, pat to about 10 inches in diameter.

Grease baking sheet, sprinkle with cornmeal, place dough on. Brush with egg white, sprinkle with seeds, let rest until doubled in bulk.

Bake at 425 degrees for 10 minutes, reduce heat to 375 degrees. Bake about 25 more minutes, or until golden brown.

Whole Wheat Muffuletta

Substitute 1 cup of whole wheat flour for 1 cup white flour.

Cheese Muffuletta

Add 1 cup cheddar, Swiss or provolone cubed 1/4 inch or shredded. Pat cheese into dough when forming the round loaf.

Pizza Dough

Makes 1 - 15x10 or 2 - 12 inch

3-1/2 to 4 cups flour
3/4   teaspoon salt
1   package dry yeast
1-1/4   cups water (110 degrees)
1/4   cup Marsala Olive Fruit Oil
1   egg white

In mixing bowl add 1/4 cup water and dry yeast. Let stay about 10 minutes.

In another bowl add dry ingredients. Make well in center, pour in yeast mixture, oil, remaining water and egg white.

Stir to mix into a smooth pliable dough. On lightly floured board, knead for several minutes.

Place dough back in lightly oiled bowl, cover, put in a warm place for about 1 hour or until doubled.

Turn dough out on floured board, cut into desired sizes.

Place toppings of your choice, leave to rise about 20 minutes or until dough is puffy. Drizzle with olive oil.

Bake in a 375 degrees oven for 20 to 30 minutes or until crust is golden.

Variation:

Substitute 1 cup whole wheat, semolina or cornmeal flour for white flour.
Add 1/4 cup wheat germ.

Topping Combinations:

Fresh tomatoes, fresh garlic, grilled vegetables, fresh herbs, Feta or Gorgongola, crumbled.

Pesto brushed crust, provolone, ricotta, Romano, fresh tomatoes, roasted garlic and grilled mushroom slices.

Olive oil brushed crust, garlic, mozzarella, (fresh spinach, cooked, well drained, chopped) mushrooms, roasted peppers and Canadian bacon.

Grilled lemon herb chicken, roasted potatoes, dried ricotta shredded or provolone.

Fresh tomatoes, fresh or canned clams, garlic, parsley, basil, oregano, black and red hot pepper flakes, Romano cheese.

Shrimp, pineapple tidbits, Canadian bacon, mozzarella, Romano cheese, tomato, olives.

Our Lady of Mount Carmel Pizzetti

Makes 10 to 12

Recipe for pizza dough
Marsala Olive Fruit Oil for cooking pizzetti

Pat dough down to 1/4 inch thick. Cut dough into 4 or 5 inch rounds. Let rest 10 minutes.

Heat 2 inches olive oil in medium skillet. Cook pizzetti on both sides until golden, on medium heat.

Spoon on pizza sauce, cover with cheese.

Pizza Sauce

1	onion, chopped
1	bell pepper, chopped
2	cups fresh or canned tomatoes, chopped
1/2	teaspoon oregano
2	tablespoons tomato paste
	Salt, pepper and cayenne to taste
1	teaspoon fennel seeds
2	tablespoons Marsala Olive Fruit Oil
2	cups mozzarella, shredded
1/2	cup fresh basil, chopped

Lower "bad" cholesterol levels with olive oil.

Research shows that regular consumption of olive oil reduces the amount of bad (LDL) cholesterol in the body.

Cook onions in oil over medium heat until tender. Add remaining ingredients, except mozzarella, cook simmering about 15 minutes.

Variation:

1	cup Romano cheese, grated
1	cup fresh mushrooms, chopped
1	cup fontina, shredded

These mini pizzas are very, very popular at the Feast of Our Lady of Mount Carmel in Waterbury, Connecticut.

Every year many of the ladies of the parish make the pizza dough and sauce working long hours.

Many stand in line waiting patiently to pick up their order. Seems like this is the longest line of all the booths at the feast.

Other popular foods are Italian sausage with peppers and soffritto.

Note: Pizzelle may be baked on greased cookie sheet in a 400 degrees oven for 10 to 12 minutes.

Grilled Pizzas

Makes 8

Dough may be cut into 6 to 8 pieces. Roll or pat each piece into about 6 inch round.

Brush lightly with olive oil, let rest about 15 minutes. Grill on both sides.

Cover with topping choices, return to grill.

Variation of toppings:

caramelized onions
tomatoes cut into 1/4 inch thick slices
mozzarella, Monterey Jack, or provolone, shredded
4   **garlic cloves minced**
basil, parsley or cilantro
roasted peppers
pesto sauce
chicken, turkey or meat of your choice, cooked, chopped
mini meatballs
goat cheese crumbled

Cover grill with lid, open vents, cook until topping is hot, 3 to 4 minutes.

Remove from grill.

Deep Dish Pizza

2 - 8 inch

Pizza dough

The sides of pan for making deep dish pizza should be about 1-3/4 inches high.

Ease the pizza dough into a lightly greased pan; across the bottom and up the sides.

Leave the dough a little thicker on sides than bottom.

Place slices of mozzarella cheese over dough, add garlic, oregano, fresh basil, tomatoes and olive oil.

Bake in a 400 degrees oven for 25 to 30 minutes or until crust is golden brown.

Note:

Substitute 1 cup semolina for 1 cup white flour for a tender crust.

Use any combination of ingredients for pizza filling desired.

The pizza crust may be baked about 12 to 15 minutes before adding filling. This will alter the texture of the crust.

Green Tomato Pizza

| 1 | recipe for pizza dough |
| 2 | tablespoons cornmeal |

Topping

4	large green tomatoes (with a pink blush)
6	large fresh mushrooms, sliced
1/2	cup fresh basil or parsley, chopped
	white pepper to taste
1/2	teaspoon oregano
1	cup provolone, shredded
4	garlic cloves, minced
1	bell pepper, sliced thin
1	onion, chopped
1/3	cup Marsala Olive Oil
1/4	cup Romano cheese, grated

> **Breathe easy with oregano**
> This aromatic herb contains carvacrol, an oil that soothes the respiratory tract and helps suppress coughs.

Over medium heat, in a large non stick skillet add oil, pepper, garlic and mushrooms.

Cook until vegetables are crisp tender, cool, drain.

Lightly greased 12 or 14 inch pizza pan, drizzle with a little olive oil. Sprinkle with corn meal.

Turn dough onto pan, pat evenly to edges. Brush with olive oil.

Sprinkle provolone evenly over dough, spread with basil, pepper and oregano.

Cover with sauteed vegetables and top with tomato slices. Drizzle with a little olive oil, sprinkle with grated cheese.

Bake in a 375 degree oven for 20 to 30 minutes or until crust is deep golden.

Variation:

1	cup mozzarella, shredded
1	cup Monterey Jack, shredded
1/2	cup olives, sliced
1	small eggplant sliced 1/4 inch thick, grilled or baked
1	cup artichoke hearts, sliced
3/4	cup dried ricotta, shredded
2	anchovies rinsed, minced
1	cup pepperoni, sliced, degreased

Note: To degrease pepperoni, place in a small saucepan, cover with water, boil 10 minutes.

Remove from water with slotted spoon, drain on clean paper towels.

By boiling the pepperoni it should remove some of the grease.

Pizza Rounds

Makes 8 to 10

1   cup warm water (110 degrees)
1   tablespoon lemon juice
1   package dry yeast
1/4   cup water, lukewarm
1/4   cup Marsala Olive Fruit Oil
1/2   cup semolina or cornmeal
3   cups unbleached flour
3/4   teaspoon salt
2   garlic cloves, minced
1   egg white

In mixing bowl combine 1/4 cup water and yeast. Let stand about 5 minutes.

Stir in oil, lemon juice, 1 cup water and remaining ingredients.

Turn out onto lightly floured board. Knead until no longer sticky, adding a little more flour if needed.

Place back in lightly oiled bowl, cover, let rise until doubled in a warm place, about 1 hour.

Turn dough out on lightly floured board, cut into 8 pieces. Pat each piece into a 5 or 6 inch round.

Place on greased baking sheets about 2 inches apart. Place topping ingredients on evenly. Drizzle with oil, bake in a 400 degrees oven for 15 to 20 minutes or until golden.

Topping

4   garlic cloves, chopped
8 to 10 slices of red, yellow or (green tomatoes with pink blush)
6 to 8   green onions, minced
1   bell pepper cut into strips
1/2   cup fresh basil or parsley, chopped
1-1/2   cups provolone or Cheddar cheese, shredded
       Rosemary to taste (or oregano)
1/4   cup Marsala Olive Fruit Oil
1-1/2   cups mozzarella, shredded or Monterey Jack cheese
       Pepper and red pepper flakes to taste

In skillet add oil, peppers, onions and garlic, cook over medium heat until crisp tender.

Spread provolone over rounds evenly. Sprinkle with basil, rosemary and onion mixture.

Continued

Cover with tomato slices, bake. Sprinkle with mozzarella, return to oven, just until cheese melts.

Note: Dough may be made in container of food processor according to manufacturers directions.

Variation:

	smoked salmon
1/2	cup ham, tuna, shrimp, crab or mussels
1/2	cup olives, sliced
1/2	cup feta, fontina or Gorgongola, crumbled
1	cup fresh mushrooms, sliced
	Italian sausage, cooked, well drained, sliced
	jalapeno peppers, minced
	roast beef cut into strips
	dried tomatoes, chopped
	sage, tarragon or mint
	dried ricotta, shredded
1	teaspoon oregano or rosemary
4	anchovies, rinsed, chopped

Stuffed Pizza Turnover
(Calzone)
Makes 8

1	recipe for pizza rounds
1-1/2	cups radicchio, spinach or broccoli, cooked, drained, chopped
1	cup ricotta or goat cheese crumbled
1/2	cup olives, chopped
1/2	cup dried tomatoes, chopped
	pepper and red pepper flakes to taste
1/2	cup fresh basil, chopped
1/3	cup Romano cheese, grated
1/2	cup ham, chopped or sausage, cooked, drained
3/4	cup mozzarella, shredded
2	green onions, chopped
4	garlic cloves, chopped
1/4	cup sesame seeds for top

In mixing bowl combine all ingredients.

Cut dough into 8 pieces. Pat into 6 inch rounds.

Brush surface lightly with olive oil, leaving a 1/2 inch unoiled edge around disc.

Continued

Continued

Place about 1/2 cup filling on dough rounds, slightly off center. Brush border with water, fold top half dough over bottom.

With tines of fork, press to seal so it resembles a half moon.

Brush tops with olive oil, make a small slit on center top. Place on greased baking sheets, sprinkle with seeds.

Bake in a 375 degrees oven for 15 to 20 minutes or until deep golden.

Brush again with olive oil, cool before serving.

Variation:

1	**cup prosciutto, chopped**
1	**cup kale, tough stems removed, cooked, chopped**
1	**teaspoon cumin, curry or ginger**
	eggplant, grilled
2	**anchovies, rinsed**
1/2	**cup raisins**
2	**bell peppers, roasted, chopped**
1	**teaspoon sage, rosemary or thyme**
1	**cup clams or sardines**
1	**cup potatoes, cooked, diced**

Mom's Onion Calzone

1	**recipe for pizza rounds**
4	**onions, sliced**
4	**tomatoes, plum, peeled, chopped**
	Salt, pepper and cayenne to taste
1/4	**cup Marsala Olive Fruit Oil**
1/2	**cup fresh basil, chopped**

Cook onions with oil in a non stick large skillet until crisp tender, stirring occasionally.

Squeeze as much moisture out of the tomatoes as possible.

Combine onions, tomatoes, salt, pepper and basil in mixing bowl.

Cut dough into 8 or 10 pieces, pat into 6 inch rounds.

Place about 1/2 cup filling on dough rounds. Brush border with water, fold top half dough over bottom.

With tines of fork, press to seal forming a large turnover.

Bake in a 375 degrees oven for 15 to 20 minutes or until deep golden.

Variation:

1	**cup Gorgonzola or cheese of your choice**
1/2	**cup olives, chopped**

Grilled Italian Bread

Makes 4

1-1/4	cups water (110 degrees)
2	package dry yeast
1-1/4	cups whole wheat flour
1	teaspoons salt
1/4	cup Marsala Olive Fruit Oil
2-1/2	cups flour
1/2	cup fresh basil, parsley or rosemary
2	tablespoons lemon juice
1	teaspoon oregano

> **Health benefit**
>
> Keep your colon healthy with almonds. These crunchy morsels are high in fiber, which reduces the risk of some cancers.

In mixing bowl add water and yeast, let stand about 10 minutes.

Stir in 1 cup of whole wheat flour, cover, let stand in a warm place 3 or 4 hours.

Add remaining flour, salt, lemon juice and olive oil, stir just until dough holds together.

Turn dough out onto floured board, knead until smooth. If too sticky to knead, add 1 tablespoon of flour at a time as needed.

Place dough back in lightly oiled bowl, cover, let rise until doubled in a warm place.

Turn out onto lightly floured board, cut into 4 pieces. Shape each piece into a ball, let stand about 5 minutes.

Flatten each piece to about an 8 or 10 inch round.

Brush lightly with olive oil, sprinkle with 1 tablespoon of herbs, press in lightly.

Place on floured baking pans, or foil. Let rise about 10 minutes.

On prepared barbecue grill, about 4 to 6 inches above coals, slide rounds on 2 at a time.

Cook on both sides until golden. If barbecue grill has a hood, cover, grill and cook turning once, 7 to 10 minutes total.

Each round serves 2 to 3.

Continued

Walnut Braid

Makes 1 loaf

2-1/2	cups flour
1	cup whole wheat flour
1-1/4	cups milk, non fat
2	tablespoons Marsala Olive Fruit Oil
2	tablespoons sugar
3/4	teaspoon salt (or to taste)
2	teaspoons dry yeast
2	egg whites

Add all ingredients to container of bread machine. Set machine on dough cycle according to manufacturer's directions.

Remove dough from machine container when cycle is completed.

Place on lightly floured board, cover, let rest about 10 minutes.

Filling

1-2 to 3/4 cup onion chopped, cooked crisp tender in 2 tablespoons olive oil

1/4 to 1/3 cup walnuts, chopped

1/2   cup provolone cut into 3x1/2 inch strips

Roll or pat dough into 15x9 inch rectangle. Cut into 3 - 15x3 inch strips.

Spread walnuts down center of one strip. Brush one side with water. Fold dough over walnuts from each side, pinch to seal.

Repeat with second and third strips filling one with cheese, the other with onion.

Place rolls seam side down, side by side on greased baking pan. Braid rolls, pinch ends together, tuck under braid.

Brush with egg white, sprinkle with black or regular sesame seeds.

Cover let rise in a warm place until doubled.

Bake in a 350 degrees oven for about 25 minutes or until golden.

Cool on rack, serve at room temperature. Store bread in plastic bag in refrigerator. Slice with serrated knife.

Topping

1   egg white, slightly beaten

2 or 3 tablespoons black or regular sesame seeds

Health benefit
Keep eyes healthy with eggs. Lutein, a compound abundant in eggs, reduces the risk of macular degeneration.

Continued

Variation for filling:

Gouda or Cheddar cheese, shredded
Canadian bacon, chopped
pesto sauce
2   teaspoons garlic, minced
1/2   cup dried tomatoes, chopped
1/2   cup olives, sliced
1   jalapeno pepper, minced
3/4   cup Monterey Jack cheese, shredded
1   6 inch Italian sausage, cooked, well drained, crumbled
1/4   cup pine nuts
1/3   cup fresh basil, parsley or cilantro, chopped
3   plum tomatoes, chopped
1/3   cup red bell pepper, roasted, chopped

> ## Health benefit
> Stay heart healthy with peanuts. These nuts contain resveratrol, an antioxidant that's been found to lower LDL cholesterol.

Any filling left over may be served in taco shells.

My friend Lillian likes this bread.

Date Nut Bread

Makes 1 Loaf

1   cup dates, or apricots, chopped
2   cups flour
1/2   cup walnuts, chopped
1   cup brown sugar, packed
1   teaspoon salt
1   teaspoon baking soda
1   egg (or 2 egg whites)
3   tablespoons Marsala Olive Fruit Oil
3/4   cup orange or apple juice
grated peel of 1 orange or 1 lemon

In mixing bowl add dry ingredients. Make well in center, add egg, olive oil and juice, stir until blended.

Add dates and nuts, pour into a greased 9x5 loaf pan.

Bake in a 350 degrees oven for 55 to 60 minutes or until cake tester comes out clean when inserted in center.

Variation:

1   teaspoon cinnamon
1   cup carrots, shredded
1   teaspoon vanilla
substitute raisins, dried figs or prunes, chopped for dates
substitute applesauce or banana, mashed, for juice

Yellow Tomato Pizza

4 - 6 inch rounds

Serves 4 to 6

1   recipe for pizza dough

Topping

1   cup mozzarella, shredded (for top)
1   onion, sliced thin
3 to 4   yellow tomatoes, (firm) sliced
1   yellow bell pepper, sliced into thin rings
1   medium yellow zucchini, sliced thin
1/2   cup fresh basil, chopped
3/4   cup Monterey Jack or provolone cheese, shredded
1/2   cup feta, goat or Gorgonzola cheese, crumbled
1 or 2   hot yellow chili peppers, minced
2   tablespoons Marsala Olive Fruit Oil
4   garlic cloves (or to taste) chopped
         Pepper to taste

In large skillet cook onion, garlic, pepper, zucchini and chili in oil until crisp tender, cool.

Lightly grease 2 cookie sheets.

Cut dough into 4 pieces, roll into balls, cover, let rest about 15 minutes.

Pat dough down to a 6 inch round. Place 2 rounds on each sheet.

Brush each round lightly with olive oil. Cover with cheese, top with basil and onion mixture.

Arrange tomato slices over vegetables, sprinkle with pepper, drizzle with a little olive oil.

Bake in a 400 degrees oven for 15 to 20 minutes or until crust is deep golden.

Sprinkle with mozzarella, place back in oven just until cheese melts, about 1 minutes.

Variation:

1   cup pineapple tidbits
1-1/2   cups pumpkin, sliced thin, cooked crisp tender
4 or 5   tomatillos, sliced
3/4   cup yellow lentils or peas, cooked, drained
1   cup water chestnuts, sliced

Mini Olive Oil Crackers

Makes about 40

2   **cups self-rising flour (not cake flour)**
1/2   **cup milk**
1/2   **cup Marsala Olive Oil**

Preheat oven to 375 degrees. Lightly grease large cookie sheet.

In mixing bowl add flour, make well in center. Pour in milk and olive oil. Stir until dough holds together. Add 1 or 2 more tablespoons milk if needed. Do not overwork dough.

On lightly floured board, roll dough out to 1/4 inch thickness.

Cut into 1-1/2 inch rounds with plain or fluted cookie cutter.

Place on prepared cookie sheet. Bake for 10 to 12 minutes or just until crackers turn golden.

Cool, brush lightly with olive oil.

Note:

Dough may be cut into 1-1/2 or 2 inch squares with fluted pastry wheel or 2 inch mini cookie cutters (leaf, fish, cactus, star, tree, etc.)

Mini Olive Oil Biscuits

Makes about 20

Roll dough out to 1/3 inch thickness, follow directions for mini oil crackers.

Variation:

Brush tops of crackers with lightly beaten egg white or water, sprinkle with sesame, poppy or seeds of your choice.

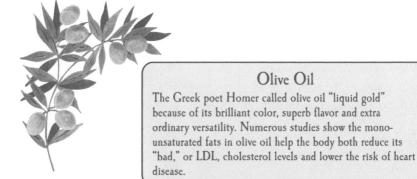

Olive Oil

The Greek poet Homer called olive oil "liquid gold" because of its brilliant color, superb flavor and extra ordinary versatility. Numerous studies show the mono-unsaturated fats in olive oil help the body both reduce its "bad," or LDL, cholesterol levels and lower the risk of heart disease.

Bagels

Makes 6

1	package dry yeast
1	cup water (about 110 degrees)
1	tablespoon sugar
1	tablespoon Marsala Olive Oil
3/4	teaspoon salt (or to taste)
2	cups flour
1	tablespoon diastatic malt powder
1	tablespoon sugar for water
1	tablespoon malt powder for water
1	egg yolk with 1 tablespoon water (to brush tops)
	sesame or poppy seeds to sprinkle tops
	cornmeal

In mixing bowl add 1/4 cups water, yeast, malt powder and sugar. Let stand about 5 minutes.

Stir in remaining water, olive oil, flour and salt. Stir until dough holds together.

Turn dough out onto a lightly floured board, knead until smooth 2 or 3 minutes.

Return to lightly oiled mixing bowl, let rest covered in a warm place until doubled in bulk.

Turn dough out onto lightly flowered board, cut into 6 equal pieces. Roll into smooth balls, let rest covered 10 minutes.

Holding balls with both hands, poke your thumb through the center. With one thumb in the hole, work around perimeter, shaping like a doughnut.

Place bagels on a greased, cornmeal dusted baking sheet, cover, let stay until puffy, about 20 minutes.

Bring 2 or 3 quarts of water (in large pan) to a boil. Add sugar and malt.

Lower 3 bagels in water for 30 seconds on each side, turning once.

With slotted spatula lift bagels out, place on lightly greased and dusted with cornmeal baking sheet.

Brush bagels with yolk mixture, sprinkle with seeds. Bake in a 375 degree oven for 14 to 15 minutes or until golden.

Note:

Recipe may be doubled.

For smaller bagels, cut dough into 8 pieces. *Continued*

Another way to shape bagels; roll each ball into a thick 11 inch long rope.

Form the bagels by overlapping ends of each rope, moisten with a little water, press ends together. Let rest covered about 15 minutes or until puffy.

Variation:

Substitute honey or molasses for sugar and half of the flour with whole wheat or rye flour.

Add 1/2 cup instant toasted onions.

Sprinkle with onion or caraway seeds.

Add 1 egg to dough plus 1/4 cup flour.

Diastatic malt powder may be purchased from King Arthur Flour in the bakers catalogue. Call 1-800-827-6836 or write to P.O. Box 876, Norwich, Vermont 05055-0876

Cinnamon Raisin Bagels

Increase yeast in bagel dough to 1 more teaspoon. Add 1 tablespoon cinnamon and 5 tablespoons sugar in with the flour.

Add 1 cup raisins, rinsed and well dried at start of mixing.

For cinnamon crust, after baking brush bagel with a little olive oil. Sprinkle with cinnamon sugar while still hot.

Beat the blues with sesame seeds

Sesame seeds are rich in calcium. The brain uses this vital nutrient to synthesize serotonin, a neurotransmitter that's responsible for producing feelings of well-being.

Pizza Margherita

1- 12 to 14 inch pizza

1	pizza dough recipe
1-1/2	cup pear tomatoes sliced 1/4 inch thick
4	ounces mozzarella, sliced
1/4	cup Marsala Olive Oil
	salt and pepper to taste
1/2	cup basil, fresh, chopped

Pat or roll out dough to a 12 or 14 inch round. Place on greased baking sheet or pizza pan. Sprinkle with basil, cover evenly with tomato slices.

Sprinkle with salt and pepper, drizzle with olive oil. Bake in a 400 degrees oven for about 15 minutes or until edges are golden brown.

Cover with mozzarella, return to oven to melt cheese (about 30 seconds)

Remove from oven, brush edges with olive oil.

Many years ago, Mom only made this pizza topping. To-day pizza toppings are made with many, many different ingredients.

Yellow Tomato Grilled Pizza

Makes 8 to 10 wedges

1	12 inch pizza dough
1/4	cup Marsala Olive Oil
1/4	cup pesto
1	cup tomatoes, yellow, chopped
4 to 5	slices Monterey Jack, fontina or mozzarella
1	onion sliced, caramelized
	white pepper to taste
4 to 5	scallops, large, sliced in half across

Lightly oil pizza pan, place in dough, press to edges. Spread with pesto evenly; cover with cheese slices, onions and pepper. Sprinkle with tomato and place scallops on top. Drizzle with olive oil. Leave to rise about 15 minutes or until dough is puffy. Place on grill, cover with lid, open vents, cook until crust is golden. Serve with green salad if desired.

Variation:

Substitute large prawns for scallops (or seafood of your choice)

Joseph's Mom Bread Balls

Serves 6

	milk or chicken broth
4 to 5	cups Italian or french bread, several days old, cubed
1	onion, chopped
2	celery stalks, chopped
1/2	cup raisins or currants
2 or 3	eggs
1/3	cup pine nuts, walnuts or pecans, shopped small
1/2	cup Romano cheese, grated
	salt, peppers and cyenne to taste
1	cup basil leaves or parsley, chopped
1	cup provolone, shredded
4	garlic cloves, minced
1	teaspoon dry Italian herbs (or herbs of your choice)
1/4	cup Marsala Olive Oil

In non stick skillet add olive oil, onions and celery. Cook over medium heat until crisp tender.

In mixing bowl add remaining ingredients with onion mixture. Add just enough milk to moisten so mixture will hold together when pressed in hands.

Shape into 2 inch balls, place on greased baking sheet, drizzle each with a little olive oil.

Bake in a 375 degrees oven for 20 to 25 minutes or until crisp and golden brown.

During difficult times, many years ago, bread balls were substituted for meat balls in the tomato gravy. The bread balls were added to the gravy 5 to 10 minutes at the end of cooking time.

Bread balls are also called stuffing balls. These may be substituted for the bread, potatoes or rice with barbecued turkey or chicken.

It's twice as easy to roast a chicken or turkey without stuffing them.

It's twice as good if you bake these elegant stuffing balls after the bird comes out of the oven.

Variation:

tomatoes, roasted, peeled, chopped
zucchini, shredded
olives, chopped small
Dijon mustard
fennel bulb, chopped
spinach, cooked, drained well, chopped

> **Pine nuts fight the common cold**
> Pine nuts contain high levels of the nutrients folate (or folic acid) and zinc, which bolster immunity, preventing colds and the flu and lowering the risk for several types of cancer.

Continued

Continued

green onions, white part, chopped
dried tomatoes, chopped
chestnuts, cooked, peeled, chopped
jalapeno, minced
dried cherries or apricots chopped
apple, pear or peach diced
mushrooms, chopped
bell pepper, roasted, peeled, chopped

This recipe is one of the family's favorite.

Potato Egg Bread

Makes 1 Loaf

1 to 2	**tablespoons of mixed seeds of your choice**
1	**potato, medium, shredded**
3	**eggs or (6 egg whites)**
1/4	**cup Marsala Olive Oil**
3	**cups flour**
1	**teaspoon salt (or to taste)**
1	**package dry yeast**
1/4	**cup water, lukewarm**
1	**tablespoon sugar**
1/2	**teaspoon pepper, white**

> ### Health benefit
> Slim down with eggs. This breakfast food is high in biotin, which revs the body's metabolism to burn fat faster.

In mixing bowl add yeast, water and sugar. Let stand about 5 minutes.

Add eggs, olive oil and potato. Stir in flour, salt and pepper.

Turn out onto floured surface, knead until smooth. Place back in lightly oiled mixing bowl, cover, let rise in a warm place until doubled, about 50 to 60 minutes.

Turn out onto lightly floured surface, shape into a round loaf. Spray with water, sprinkle with mixed seeds. Let rise in a warm place until doubled.

Bake in a 375 degrees oven on lightly greased baking sheet for 25 to 30 minutes or until golden brown.

This dough may be used for pizza, focaccia, bread sticks, rolls, calzone or what ever shape desired.

Note: Olive Potato Egg Bread

Add 1/2 cup chopped olives, 1/2 cup pecans, walnuts or nuts of your choice, chopped, 1/2 cup provolone, shredded and rosemary or herb of your choice.

Suggested seeds: poppy, sesame, anise, caraway, fennel, pumpkin

Lemon Blueberry Bread

Makes 8 to 10 slices

1-1/2	cups flour
1-1/2	teaspoon baking powder
1/2	teaspoon salt
5	tablespoons Marsala Olive Oil
1/2	cup sugar
2	eggs
1/3	cup milk or orange juice
3	tablespoons lemon juice
1	teaspoon vanilla
1/2	teaspoon baking soda
	grated peel of 1 lemon and 1 orange
2	cups blueberries
1/2	cup brown sugar

Preheat oven to 350 degrees. Lightly grease an 8-1/2 x 4-1/2 inch loaf pan. In measuring cup combine lemon juice and milk. Let stand 5 minutes.

In mixing bowl combine dry ingredients, make well in center. Pour in milk mixture, vanilla, eggs and olive oil, stir to blend.

Stir in berries an peels. Spoon into prepared pan. Bake for 60 to 70 minutes or until cake tester comes out clean from center.

Cool in pan on wire rack about 30 minutes. Turn bread out of pan and cool completely on rack.

Cover with lemon glaze.

Variation:

3/4	cup pecans, minced

Lemon Glaze

2	tablespoons lemon juice
1/4	cup sugar
1	tablespoon limoncello liqueur

In small saucepan, bring sugar and juice to a boil, stirring until sugar dissolves. Stir in limoncello.

Pierce top of loaf with tines of fork or tooth pick several places, pour lemon mixture evenly over loaf.

Walnut Cheddar Crackers

Makes about 40 - 1-1/2 x 1-1/2 inch crackers

1	cup flour
1/2	cup pecans or walnuts, ground
2	tablespoons Marsala Olive Oil
1-1/4	cups Cheddar cheese, shredded (about 3-1/2 ounces)
1/2	teaspoon salt
1/2	teaspoon white pepper
1/4	cup water
1/4	teaspoon baking powder

In mixing bowl combine dry ingredients, make well in center: Pour in water and olive oil, stir until blended. Form dough into ball.

Flatten slightly, wrap dough in waxed paper, chill refrigerator about 15 minutes.

On flouted surface, roll dough out to about 1/4 inch thickness. Using a 1-1/2 inch cookie cutter, cut as many crackers as possible.

Gather scraps, reroll dough, cut out more crackers until all dough is used.

Place crackers on cookie sheets lines with non-stick aluminum foil.

(Reynolds Release)

Bake in a 350 degrees oven until crisp, 15 to 18 minutes or until golden.

Dough may be rolled out to 1/4 inch thick on lightly floured surface. Cut with pastry cutter into 2 x 1 inch strips.

Mini Buttermilk Biscuits

Makes 12

1	cup flour
1	teaspoon baking powder
1/2	teaspoon baking soda
1/2	teaspoon salt
3	tablespoons Marsala or Sciabica olive oil
1/4	cup buttermilk

In mixing bowl add dry ingredients. Make well in center add buttermilk and olive oil.

Stir until dough holds together. Turn dough onto a lightly floured surface, pat down to 1/2 inch thick. Cut out 12 biscuits with a 1 inch cutter, place on greased baking sheet.

Bake in a 375 degree oven for 14 to 16 minutes or until golden. Serve warm.

May be baked in mini muffin pan.

Fougasse
(Pull apart Bread)

Serves 8 to 10

3 to 3-1/2 cups flour
1   package dry yeast
1/4   cup water lukewarm
1   teaspoon sugar or honey
1   egg
1/2   cup milk, nonfat
2   tablespoons Marsala or Sciabica olive oil
1   teaspoon salt (or to taste)
1/2   teaspoon pepper
2   garlic cloves, minced
1/2   medium onion minced
1/2   cup parsley, chopped
1   teaspoon anise seeds
1/2   cup cheese of your choice, shredded
1   small potato, shredded
1/3   cup sesame seeds for top

> **Health benefit**
> Boost bone health with raisins. These fruits contain boron, which enhances the body's use of vitamin D to prevent osteoporosis.

In mixing bowl add yeast water and sugar, let stand 5 minutes. Stir in milk, egg and olive oil.

Add flour, work with wooden spoon until dough holds together. Add remaining ingredients, knead on floured surface until well blended.

Place back in lightly oiled bowl, let rest until puffy, about 1 hour.

Place dough onto a lightly greased baking sheet. Shape dough into an oval 3./4 inch thick.

Cut slits in center and decorative slits on sides all the way through to bottom. Pull the dough apart widely (at least 2 inches) at the slits.

Spray dough with water, sprinkle with sesame seeds. Cover, let rest about 30 minutes or until puffy.

Bake in a 375 degrees oven for 18 to 20 minutes or until golden. Remove from oven, cool on rack.

Serve with proscuito, ham, Cheddar or goat cheese, smoked salmon, grilled eggplant or zucchini, roasted peppers, marinated artichoke hearts, grilled meats sliced, salads, fruits and nuts or whatever desired.

Variation:

Substitute 1 cup corn meal for 1 cup flour.

Easy Asparagus Pie

Serves 8

3 to 4 slices white, whole wheat, egg or challa bread
1   cup mushrooms, chopped
1   onion, chopped
1/2   cup prosciutto, ham or sausage, cooked well drained, crumbled
4   eggs
1/2   cup provolone, fontina or Cheddar cheese, shredded
2   cups asparagus, cooked crisp tender, chopped
1/3   cup Romano cheese, grated
1/2   cup basil, parsley or cilantro, chopped
        salt, pepper, nutmeg or cinnamon to taste
1/3   cup ricotta
1/3   cup Marsala or Sciabica olive oil
8 to 10 asparagus spears about 3 inches long, cooked crisp tender

Lightly grease a 10 inch pyrex pie plate. Line bottom with bread slices, cutting slices to fit. In skillet cook onion with olive oil over medium heat until crisp tender.

In mixing bowl combine cooked onion with olive oil and remaining ingredients except asparagus spears. Gently mix and spoon onto bread lined pie plate.

Arrange asparagus spears on top in spoke fashion. Bake in a 350 degrees oven for 40 to 50 minutes or until center is fairly firm and golden.

If desired place a tomato rose on center of pie. Peel tomato in about a 3/4 inch strip, roll in a spiral.

Variation:

1/2   cup raisins or pinenuts
substitute spinach, zucchini, broccoli, tomatoes or vegetable of your choice for asparagus.

If using broccoli, place with heads outward. Press stems in on top a little gently, in pinwheel fashion.

If using tomatoes, firm ones are best. Green tomatoes with a pink blush works well also.

> ## Health benefit
> Slim down with asparagus. These succulent stalks are high in potassium and asparagine, two compounds that help reduce water retention and bloat.

Zucchini Flowers Pg 217 ~ Cavatelli Pg 177 ~ Figs with Mascarpone Pg 30

Bite Size Gourmet Tidbits Pg 278

Bucatini With Tuna Sauce

Serves 4 to 6

1	carrot, diced
1/2	cup olives, sliced
2	garlic cloves, minced
1/4	cup pine nuts or pistachio
1	cup mozzarella, shredded
1/2	pound fresh mushrooms, sliced
1	onion, chopped
1/3	cup Marsala Olive Fruit Oil
4	cups fresh or canned tomatoes, chopped
1/2	cup fresh basil or parsley, chopped
	salt, pepper and cayenne to taste
1	can tuna (6-1/2 ounce) water packed
4	ounces tomato paste
1/4	cup white wine
2	bay leaves
1	pound bucatini, fettuccine or spaghetti

> ### Health benefit
> Shiitake mushrooms contain eritadenine, an amino acid that studies suggest may help lower cholesterol. Research also indicates that shiitakes may boost immunity.

In sauce pan, over medium heat, add oil, garlic and onion, cook until tender.

Add tomatoes, wine, bay leaves, tomato paste, salt, pepper and cayenne.

Cook about 20 minutes, add basil olives and mushrooms.

Cook another 5 minutes, add tuna, heat through.

Cook pasta according to package directions. Drain, place in serving dish, spoon gravy over pasta.

Remove bay leaves, toss gently. Sprinkle with mozzarella and nuts.

Variation:

Substitute 1/4 pound fresh tuna or swordfish steak 1 inch thick, cut into 1 inch pieces, for canned tuna.

In skillet add 2 tablespoons olive oil and cook tuna over medium heat until golden, flake.

Proceed with recipe for bucatini with tuna sauce.

Variation:

1	tablespoon fresh sage
1-1/2	cups celery, chopped or peas
	grated peel of 1 lemon
1	medium lobster tail, chopped

Cannelloni

Serves 4 to 6

1	recipe pasta dough cut into 5 inch squares
3 or 4	cups chunky tomato gravy
2	cups white sauce

Filling

1/2	pound lean turkey, veal or beef, ground
1/2	cup Romano cheese
1/3	cup fresh basil or parsley, chopped
1	cup mozzarella, shredded or teleme cheese
	pepper and cayenne to taste
1/4	teaspoon cardamom or nutmeg
1-1/2	cups spinach cooked, drained and chopped
1	egg (or 2 egg whites)
1/3	cup Marsala Olive Fruit Oil
1	cup ricotta

Prepare tomato gravy and white sauce. In skillet add oil and turkey.

Cook on medium until golden brown, cool.

In mixing bowl combine turkey, egg, cheeses, spinach, basil, pepper and cardamom.

Cook pasta in boiling water until tender, drain.

Place a heaping tablespoon filling spread evenly along center on each square. Roll jelly roll fashion.

Spoon half tomato gravy in greased baking dish. Place filled cannelloni seam side down on gravy.

Top with remaining gravy, cover with white sauce. Sprinkle with mozzarella, cover with foil.

Bake in a 350 degrees oven for about 25 to 30 minutes.

White Sauce (Bechamel)

3	tablespoons flour
3	tablespoons Marsala Olive Fruit Oil
2	cups milk, non fat
	salt, white pepper and nutmeg to taste

In saucepan add flour and oil, cook stirring over medium heat until light golden.

Remove from heat, gradually blend in milk, salt, pepper and nutmeg.

Return pan to heat, cook, stirring until sauce is smooth and thick.

Continued

Continued

Variation for filling:

1	cup cod, bass or any firm fish, cooked, flaked
1	cup fontina cheese, crumbled
1	cup crab or bay scallops, cooked
1	cup chicken or sausage, cooked, chopped
	sage to taste
1/4	cup pine nuts or raisins
1	cup eggplant, cubed, cooked
1	cup carrots or zucchini, shredded
1	onion, chopped
1	cup mushrooms, chopped
1/2	cup proscuitto, chopped

Variation:

Use store bought cannelloni shells.

Filling Combinations:

Veal, mushrooms, escarole, egg white
Grilled chicken, spinach, red pepper flakes
Beef, veal, chicken, broccoli and ricotta
Sausage, artichokes, ricotta, mushrooms

Pasta Aglio e Olio
(Garlic and Oil)

Serves 4

6	garlic cloves (or to taste) minced
1	cup fresh parsley, chopped
	salt, white pepper and red hot pepper flakes to taste
12	ounces linguine, thin spaghetti or pasta of your choice
1/2	cup Romano cheese (or to taste) grated
1/3	cup Marsala Olive Oil

Cook pasta as label directs, adding parsley to water.

In non stick skillet add olive oil, garlic and red pepper flakes. Cook only a few seconds, do not burn garlic or it will become bitter.

Drain pasta, place in shallow serving bowl or platter. Spoon oil mixture over pasta, add white pepper, toss gently. Sprinkle with cheese.

Variation:

1-1/2 cups escargot or mushrooms (cook along with oil and garlic)

This is such a good recipe for something fast. When ever I get unexpected company this is just great. It seems everyone likes it.

Cavatelli

Serves 4

1   cup semolina
1   cup flour
1   large egg (or 2 egg whites)
1/4   cup water
2   tablespoons Marsala Olive Fruit Oil
        salt to taste

In mixing bowl add flour, salt and semolina, make well in center. Add water, egg and oil, stir until dough holds together. Add a little more water if needed.

Knead dough on lightly floured board until smooth. Cover, let stay about 30 minutes. Cut dough in half, knead into 2 balls, flatten a little.

Let stay covered about 15 minutes. Roll each ball out to about 1/8 inch thick. Cut into 1 inch strips.

Place 3 strips on top of one another, sprinkle flour in between to prevent sticking.

Cut through 3 strips into between 1/4 and 1/8 inch pieces. With index and middle finger, press fingers firmly in center, curl toward you to form a shell.

Lightly flour as needed when curling cavatelli.

Cook cavatelli in boiling water for 8 to 10 minutes or until tender.

Serve with tomato gravy, pesto sauce, walnut sauce or with vegetables.

Sprinkle with Romano cheese or with ricotta cheese mashed and spread over pasta.

When I was little I had to help Mom curl these very small pieces of dough. She would put a mound in front of me to curl; it seemed like a mountain!

When Mom would get up to stir the gravy, I would throw some in without curling them.

When I got older I told Mom what I used to do and she answered, "Did you think I didn't see them uncurled?"

I would rather be out playing with my friends. What play? We had no toys.

It was hopscotch, hide and seek, jump rope, jacks, or learn how to crochet, embroider, sew or cook. Take your pick.

Eggplant Pasta

Serves 4 to 6

1	large eggplant, cubed
1/2	cup Marsala Olive Fruit Oil
1	onion, chopped
4	cups fresh or canned tomatoes, chopped
1	teaspoon fennel or anise seeds
	salt, pepper and red hot pepper flakes to taste
1/2	cup wine or vermouth
1-1/2	cups mushrooms, quartered or sliced
3	ounces tomato paste
6	garlic cloves, chopped
2	carrots, diced or zucchini
1-1/2	cups mozzarella, cubed or diced
1/2	cup Romano cheese, grated
1	pound rolette, penne, fusilli or pasta of your choice
1/2	cup fresh basil or parsley, chopped

In large skillet cook eggplant with oil on medium heat until golden and tender.

With slotted spoon, lift eggplant out onto a shallow serving bowl.

In same skillet with remaining olive oil add onions, carrots and garlic, cook until soft.

Add wine, cook 1 minute, add tomatoes, tomato paste, fennel seeds, salt, pepper and pepper flakes.

Cook about 20 minutes on medium heat. Add basil and mushrooms, cook another 5 minutes. Stir in eggplant.

Cook pasta according to label directions (al dente) Drain, place in serving bowl.

Spoon eggplant sauce over pasta, toss gently. Sprinkle with grated cheese and mozzarella cubes.

Variation:

1/2	pound sweet or hot Italian sausage
1/2	cup water

In skillet add water and sausage. Cook until browned, turning frequently. Remove, drain well on clean paper towels.

Cut into 1/2 inch slices, add to pasta.

Variation:

1-1/2	cups ricotta, low fat
1/2	cup olives, sliced (or capers)
1/4	cup raisins and/or pinenuts (or currants)
1	cup artichoke hearts, sliced
1	red bell pepper, chopped

Lasagna

Serves 8

1   **recipe for mini meatball gravy**
12   **ounces lasagna noodles, cooked**
3   **cups ricotta, low fat**
2   **eggs (or 4 egg whites)**
1/2   **cup fresh basil or parsley, chopped**
         salt, pepper and cayenne to taste
3/4   **cup Romano cheese, grated**
1-1/2 **cups mozzarella or Swiss cheese, shredded**
1-1/2 **cups spinach, cooked, drained, chopped**

In mixing bowl combine ricotta, Romano cheese, spinach, eggs, basil, salt, peppers.

Grease a 13x9 inch baking pan. Spread evenly 1/2 cup gravy on bottom.

Place a layer of cooked noodles over gravy, spread with 1/3 of cheese mixture, 1/3 of mozzarella and 1/3 of meatball gravy.

Repeat layers ending with gravy. Sprinkle with mozzarella, cover with foil.

Bake in a 350 degrees oven for 30 to 40 minutes or until bubbly.

Variation:

Substitute broccoli, eggplant, zucchini, peas or vegetable of your choice for spinach, cooked crisp tender.

      olives of your choice
      mushrooms
      goat cheese
      seafood
      chicken or turkey

Note: Substitute bow tie pasta, cooked, for lasagna noodles.

Health benefit

The FDA now requires enriched grain products like lasagna noodles to contain folic acid, which may protect against coronary artery disease.

Manicotti

Serves 6

1 recipe for chunky tomato gravy

Crepe

3   eggs (or 6 egg whites)
1-1/2   cups milk, non fat
         salt to taste
         pinch of nutmeg or cardamom
2   cups flour
2   tablespoons Marsala Olive Oil

Add above ingredients in jar of blender, whirl until smooth.

Brush a 6 or 8 inch non stick skillet with olive oil

Pour in 2 or 3 tablespoons of batter, cook until light golden on both sides, over medium heat.

Filling

1   egg (or 2 egg whites)
2   cups ricotta
3/4   cup Romano cheese, grated
1   cup mozzarella or fontina, shredded
1/2   cup parsley, minced
1-1/2   cups asparagus tips, cooked crisp tender

In mixing bowl combine all ingredients, blend.

Pour about 1/2 cup gravy evenly over bottom of greased baking pan.

Spoon heaping tablespoon of filling on each crepe to 1/2 inch of edge. Roll jelly roll fashion.

Place seam side down over gravy in pan. Cover with remaining gravy, sprinkle with cheese.

Cover with foil, bake in a 350 degrees oven for 35 to 40 minutes.

Garnish with chopped parsley.

Variation:

Turkey Filling

1/2   pound lean turkey, veal or chicken, ground
1/4   pound lean pork, ground (or Italian sausage)
1   onion, chopped
1-1/2   cups spinach or broccoli, cooked, drained, chopped

Continued

2	**eggs (or 4 egg whites)**
1	**cup cheddar or Swiss cheese, shredded**
1/2	**cup mozzarella, shredded (or Gorgonzola, crumbled)**
	pepper to taste
1/4	**cup Marsala Olive Fruit Oil**
1/2	**cup fresh basil or parsley, chopped**
1	**cup fresh mushrooms, chopped**

In non stick skillet, over medium heat cook meat and onion in oil, cool.

Combine in mixing bowl with remaining ingredients.

Variation:

Substitute shrimp, sea scallops or salmon, cooked and flaked, for meat.

Monterey Jack or Swiss Cheese for mozzarella.

Eggplant, olives, yellow squash, zucchini, shredded or carrots for asparagus.

Ham or prosciutto.

Filling Combinations:

Goat cheese, spinach, dried tomatoes, chopped and pesto.

Gorgonzola, pesto, pine nuts, grilled chicken, chopped.

Feta cheese, lamb, eggplant, mint.

Zucchini Manicotti

Add 1 cup zucchini or carrots, shredded, to crepe batter and add 1 cup shredded zucchini to ricotta filling.

Zucchini keeps your eyes healthy

The green skin of the zucchini contains beta-carotene, a carotenoid and antioxidant known to prevent many diseases, including cataracts and macular degeneration.

Broccoli and Pasta

Serves 4 to 6

2	bunches broccoli (2 to 2-1/2 pounds)
2	cups short pasta (penne, rolette or shells)
6	garlic cloves (or to taste) chopped
1/2	cup Marsala Olive Fruit Oil
1/2	cup Romano cheese, grated
	Salt, pepper and red hot pepper flakes to taste

Cut broccoli into flowerets.

In large pot bring water to a boil. Add pasta and broccoli. When water comes to a boil again, cook 2 minutes.

Turn off heat, let stay in water 10 to 12 minutes or until broccoli is crisp tender.

Drain well, place in a shallow serving bowl.

In small skillet add olive oil and garlic, cook until light golden. Watch carefully, do not burn.

Pour olive oil and garlic over pasta, sprinkle with peppers and cheese, toss gently.

This method should keep broccoli nice and green.

Note: Use a good brand of pasta that holds its shape and does not get mushy when cooked. (if using spinach, add a few minutes before pasta is cooked)

Of all the recipes in this book, this one is a favorite of all the family, from the oldest to the youngest, including guests.

When my Mom and Dad were first married in Italy, Mom made broccoli with hand made cavatelli.

My Dad ate so much of it that he had to get up during the night to walk the floor; he was so uncomfortable.

Grandson Jonathan said he could eat broccoli made this way everyday.

Grandson Joseph phoned from the air base where he was stationed to ask, "Grandmom how do you make broccoli and pasta?"

There are many variations of this recipe but the original one is it!

Variation:

Add 1 or 2 of the following:

1	onion, chopped, cooked along with garlic and oil
1/3	cup golden raisins
2 or 3	tomatoes, chopped, cooked
1/4	cup pine nuts or pistachio, chopped
1/2	cup fresh basil, chopped or 2 tablespoons pesto sauce
1	cup fresh mushrooms, sliced
1	potato diced, cooked in with broccoli and pasta
2	carrots, sliced, cooked in with broccoli and pasta
4	anchovies rinsed, chopped, 6 ounces crabmeat or shrimp
1	bell pepper, diced
1	cup dried beans cooked (or garbanzo)

Pasta and Beans
(*Pasta e Fagioli*)

Serves 6

1/2	pound ground meat (lean)
1/2	pound dried beans or garbanzo, cooked
2	carrots, diced
1-1/2	cups celery, diced
1	onion, chopped
4	cups fresh or canned tomatoes, chopped
3	tablespoons tomato paste
1	teaspoon fennel or anise seeds
1/2	cup fresh basil or parsley, chopped
1/2	cup wine
1/3	cup Marsala Olive Oil
1	teaspoon rosemary of sage
1	pound escarole or spinach, chopped
	salt, pepper and hot pepper flakes to taste
2	cups tubetti, ditalini or any small pasta
6	garlic cloves, chopped

Form ground meat into mini meatballs. Cook in non-stick skillet with 2 tablespoons olive oil until brown on all sides.

In saucepan add oil, onion, garlic, celery and carrots. Cook over medium heat, covered, until vegetables are tender.

Add wine, salt, peppers, tomatoes, tomato paste and rosemary, cook about 15 minutes covered.

Add escarole, cover, cook until wilted.

Cook pasta according to package directions, drain. Add to vegetables along with meatballs, cooked beans and basil.

Simmer one minute. Serve with grated Romano cheese or dried ricotta, shredded.

Variation:

1	red bell pepper, diced
	rice, cooked
	potatoes, cooked
	greens of your choice
	ham or sausage, cooked, chopped
	turkey or chicken, grilled or baked, chopped
	fusilli or orecchiette pasta
2	cups broccoli flowerets

Pasta Dough

Serves 4 to 6

1-1/2   cups flour
1-1/2   cups semolina
1/3 to 1/2 cup water
3   tablespoons Marsala Olive Fruit Oil
1   egg and 2 egg whites
         salt to taste

In mixing bowl add flour, semolina and salt, make well in center. Add remaining ingredients.

Stir until dough holds together, adding a little more water if needed.

Dough should be a little firmer than pie crust dough.

On lightly floured board, knead dough until smooth. Let rest 20 to 30 minutes.

Follow directions of pasta machine, roll and cut dough to desired size.

Cook pasta in boiling water 5 to 8 minutes or until desired doneness.

Serve with your favorite sauce.

Note: This dough works well for manicotti, ravioli, tortellini or cannelloni.

Variation for pasta dough:

Substitute one of the following cooked and strained for 1/3 cup of water.

May be blended in jar of blender or passed through a food mill.

       spinach or carrots
       beets or pumpkin
       tomato or zucchini
       red, green or yellow bell pepper
       broccoli or peas
1   **square unsweetened chocolate melted with 1/3 cup hot water**
1/2   **cup fresh basil blended with 1/3 cup water**
2   **garlic cloves, cooked**
       substitute orange, lemon or pineapple juice for water
       saffron

Variation for flour:

Substitute 1/2 cup whole wheat, chestnut or chi chi flour for semolina.

Another way to flavor pasta dough is to add a tablespoon or so of tomato, spinach, Cheddar, blue cheese or orange powder.

Pasta With Pesto Sauce and Ricotta

Serves 4 to 6

Award Winning Recipe at Riverbank Cheese and Wine Exposition.

1	pound fettuccine, linguine or rotelli
2	cups fresh basil leaves
4	garlic cloves (or to taste)
	salt and pepper to taste
3/4	cup Marsala Olive Oil
1/4	cup pine nuts
1	cup ricotta (low fat)
1/3	cup cooking pasta water
1/2	cup Romano cheese, grated

Traditionally one mashes basil and garlic in a mortar and pestle, gradually blending in remaining ingredients.

OR

Add garlic and 1/4 cup olive oil in jar of blender, whirl until garlic is liquefied.

Add remaining oil and basil leaves, whirl just until combined, do not over puree.

When coarse and thick, pour pesto in a mixing bowl, stir in ricotta, salt, pepper and cheese.

Cook pasta as label directs, drain, place in large serving bowl.

Spoon on as much pesto mixture as desired, pour in cooking water, toss gently.

Sprinkle with Romano grated cheese and pine nuts. Garnish with basil sprigs.

To freeze pesto sauce, omit cheeses. When thawed and ready to use, stir in cheeses.

Variation:

1-1/2	cups fava beans, cooked, peel outer skin of each bean
1	c up green beans or peas, cooked
1	potato, cooked, diced
	substitute mozzarella, cubed for ricotta
	substitute tortellini for fettuccine

For plain pesto, omit ricotta.

This recipe may be served cold as a salad.

Potato Gnocchi

Serves 4

1/4	cup Romano cheese, grated
	white pepper to taste
4	medium potatoes (dry mealy type) 1 pound

1 to 1-1/2 cups flour

3	egg yolks (or 1 egg yolk and 2 egg whites)
	salt and white pepper to taste
1/4	teaspoon nutmeg
1	tablespoon Marsala Olive Fruit Oil
1	recipe for chunky tomato gravy

Bake or boil potatoes until tender, cool, peel. Press potatoes in a potato ricer or food mill, let fall on lightly floured board or in mixing bowl.

Sprinkle with salt, pepper and nutmeg, make well in center. (Potatoes should be cold.)

Add oil, cheese, egg and 1 cup flour. Mix, knead lightly, (adding more flour if needed) until smooth.

Dough should be soft and slightly sticky. Divide dough into 6 pieces, shape each into a roll about 1/2 inch in diameter.

Cut rolls into about 1/2 inch pieces. Press each gnocchi against back of grater with thumb. May be pressed along the length of tines of fork.

May also be made with a little hand cranked gnocchi machine. Spread out onto floured surface.

Fill a large pot with water, bring to a boil. Add gnocchi, cook until they come to the surface of water.

Cook 15 to 20 seconds, any longer they will absorb too much water.

Remove gnocchi with a large slotted spoon onto a serving platter or shallow bowl.

Pour gravy over gnocchi, toss gently, sprinkle with grated cheese.

Variation:

Substitute mini meatball gravy for chunky tomato gravy.

Serve with your favorite cheese, drizzle with olive oil, sprinkle with white pepper.

Pesto sauce goes well with gnocchi.

Notes: Gnocchi may be pressed on a special wooden paddle with groves.

Baked potatoes work a little better then boiled as they contain less water.

Potatoes cooked in microwave is also ideal.

Continued

Variation for sauce:

Gorgonzola Sauce

	white pepper to taste
1/2	cup green onion (white part) minced
1/4	cup muscatel or vermouth
2	tablespoons Marsala Olive Fruit Oil
2	cups milk, non fat
1/3	cup Gorgonzola or blue cheese, crumbled
1/4	cup parsley, minced
2	tablespoons flour
1/4	cup pine nuts

Cook onions in oil over medium heat until tender. Stir in flour, cook until golden.

Add wine, cook 1 minute. Pour in milk, cook stirring until thickened and bubbly, cook 1 minute.

Remove from heat, stir in pepper and cheese. Pour sauce over gnocchi, sprinkle with parsley and pine nuts.

Pappardelle with Basil Leaves

Serves 4

1 recipe for pasta dough
16 to 20 large basil or edible leaves of your choice

With pasta machine roll dough out to about 1/8 inch thick and 4 inches wide by 12 inches long.

Arrange basil leaves flat on sheet, about 1 inch apart. Brush edges lightly with water or lightly beaten egg white.

Place another sheet, same size on top, press edges together.

Roll the strip of dough filled with basil, through rollers of pasta machine. Pasta will stretch thin, considerably.

Repeat with remaining pasta, let set on floured board to dry, about 20 minutes.

Using pastry cutter or knife, cut sheets into about 1 inch wide strips.

Cook in boiling water for 4 to 5 minutes. Drain, place in shallow serving bowl or platter.

Spoon sauce of your choice over pappardelle, toss gently.

Variation:

Substitute unsprayed edible flower petals, such as rose, nasturtium or petals of your choice for basil.

Cut sheets into 4 inch pieces if desired.

Ravioli

Serves 4 to 6

1   recipe for chunky tomato gravy
1   recipe for pasta dough
1   egg white slightly beaten

Ricotta Filling

1   egg (or 2 egg whites)
1   pound ricotta (low fat)
1/3   cup Romano cheese, grated
1/2   cup mozzarella, shredded
       pepper to taste
1/2   cup parsley chopped, small

Combine above ingredients in mixing bowl.

Cut dough into 2 pieces. Roll out to about 1/8 inch thick with rolling pin, (very thin) or use a pasta machine.

Cut dough into 4 inch wide strips. Place heaping teaspoon of filling on long edge of strip, two inches apart.

Brush dough on long edge and in between filling with egg white. Fold dough over filling, press firmly along long edge and in between fillings to seal.

Cut ravioli with fluted pastry wheel. Press all around edges with tines of fork to seal well.

Meat Filling

2-1/2 cups turkey, chicken, veal, rabbit or beef, ground
1   egg and 1 egg white
1-1/2 cups spinach, cooked, well drained, chopped
1   onion, chopped fine
       pepper to taste
1/2   cup fresh basil or parsley, chopped
3/4   cup bread crumbs
1   cup Romano cheese, grated
       pinch of rosemary or sage
1/4   cup Marsala Olive Oil

In skillet over medium heat add oil, onion and meat. Cook until meat is browned, cool.

Add meat and remaining ingredients in mixing bowl, stir until blended.

Ravioli may be stamped out with a wooden ravioli rolling pin, then cut in between each one with pastry wheel.

Continued

Continued

In large pot, bring water to a boil, cook ravioli 7 to 10 minutes or until tender.

Drain, place in shallow serving bowl, spoon on gravy, toss gently, sprinkle with cheese.

> ### Health benefit
> Beat the PMS blues with chicken. This mealtime favorite is high in vitamin B_6, a nutrient that alleviates mood swings.

Variation:

Filling combinations:

> **chicken, zucchini, pesto, garlic, feta cheese**
> **goat cheese, red swiss chard, pork (lean)**
> **sausage, arugula, ricotta, mashed potatoes**
> **beet, shrimp, mushrooms, lemon peel, grated**
> **eggplant, ricotta, Romano cheese, mozzarella**
> **artichoke bottoms, onion, garlic, Romano cheese, ricotta**

Gus's Spaghetti With Ricotta and Chocolate

Serves 3 to 4

8   **ounces spaghetti**
1-1/2   **cups ricotta, whole milk**
1   **cup milk chocolate, chopped very small**

Cook spaghetti according to package directions, drain.

Place in serving platter. In mixing bowl add ricotta, mash with fork.

Stir in chopped chocolate.

Spoon ricotta mixture on pasta, toss gently until well distributed.

Garnish with chocolate curls.

Note: To make chocolate curls, have chocolate at room temperature. Shave chocolate with vegetable peeler.

If using low fat ricotta, add 1/3 cup milk to ricotta, mash, blend, add chocolate.

A very dear friend gave me this recipe. It sounded so good and it really is, we think.

Rigatoni With Pork Sauce

Serves 4

1	cup carrot, diced
1/2	cup red wine
1	red bell pepper, chopped
1/2	pound pork, lean, ground coarsely
1	teaspoon anise or fennel seeds
1/4	cup Marsala Olive Fruit Oil
	salt, pepper and cayenne to taste
2	cups swiss chard, arugula or radicchio, chopped
1/2	fennel bulb, chopped (or celery)
1	large onion, chopped
1/2	cup fresh basil or parsley, chopped
2	tablespoons flour
6	tomatoes, fresh or canned, chopped
3	ounces tomato paste
1-1/2	cups mushrooms, sliced
1	cup olives, sliced or peas
12	ounces rigatoni or pasta of your choice
	Romano cheese, grated, to taste
1	teaspoon paprika

In sauce pan, brown pork in oil over medium heat. Add onions, pepper, fennel, carrot and greens. Cook until crisp tender.

Add tomatoes, tomato paste, wine and anise seeds, cook about 15 minutes.

Sprinkle flour in sauce, stir until well blended. Add remaining ingredients, stir.

Cook pasta according to package directions. Drain, place in large shallow serving bowl. Cover with meat sauce, toss gently, sprinkle with cheese.

Variation:

1-1/2	cups mozzarella, cubed
1-1/2	cups ricotta
1-1/2	cups Monterey Jack, shredded (or dried ricotta)

Drop ricotta by teaspoon over pasta evenly or sprinkle with mozzarella or Jack cheese.

Stuffed Jumbo Pasta Shells

Serves 6

1/2	cup Gorgonzola, crumbled
1	pound jumbo pasta shells
1	recipe for chunky or mini meatball tomato gravy
2	cups ricotta, low fat
1-1/2	cups spinach, cooked, drained, chopped
1/2	cup mushrooms, chopped small
	salt and pepper to taste
1/3	cup Romano cheese, grated
2	egg whites
1-1/2	cups mozzarella, shredded
1/2	cup parsley, chopped
1/2	cup walnuts, ground

Cook pasta according to package directions. In mixing bowl combine ricotta, spinach, mushrooms, salt, pepper, walnuts, parsley, grated cheese and egg whites, stir.

Preheat oven to 350 degrees. Fill shells with ricotta mixture. Arrange in large greased baking dish.

Spoon gravy over shells, cover loosely with foil. Bake for 25 to 30 minutes or until bubbly.

Sprinkle with mozzarella, return to oven, bake until cheese melts.

Variation:

Salmon Filling

1	egg (or 2 egg whites)
1	pound ricotta, low fat
1-1/2	cups salmon, crab (or fish of your choice) canned
1/4	teaspoon nutmeg
1	cup broccoli or asparagus, cooked, chopped
4	cups white sauce
1/2	cup Romano cheese, grated
1/3	cup parsley, minced

Flake salmon, place in mixing bowl with ricotta, broccoli, egg whites, nutmeg and cheese.

Fill shells, place in greased baking dish, pour white sauce over, sprinkle with grated cheese.

Bake in a 350 degrees oven for 30 to 35 minutes. Garnish with parsley.

Continued

Eggplant Filling

	paprika to taste
1	medium onion, diced
1/4	cup Marsala Olive Fruit Oil
4	garlic cloves, minced
1	small eggplant, cubed small
1	bell pepper, diced
1	small zucchini, shredded
1	cup ricotta
1	cup mozzarella or fontina cheese, shredded
	salt and pepper to taste

> ### Health benefit
> Stay an egghead with eggplant. It's one of the few veggies that contains anthocyanins, purple plant compounds that reduce the risk of agerelated memory loss.

In large non stick skillet add oil, onion, garlic, pepper, eggplant and zucchini. Cook covered until soft, add salt, pepper and paprika.

In mixing bowl combine eggplant mixture with remaining ingredients.

Proceed with recipe for filled pasta shells.

Variation:

1/2	pound chicken or turkey, ground
2	tablespoons olive oil

Brown chicken in large non stick skillet in olive oil over medium heat until browned, about 10 minutes, stirring frequently.

Pasta, Tomato Gravy With Ricotta

Serves 4 to 6

4	cups chunky or mini meatball tomato gravy
1-1/2	cups ricotta, low fat (or 1/2 cup Gorgonzola)
3/4	pound pasta, elbow, tubette, shell or wagon wheels
1	cup Romano cheese, grated
1	cup mozzarella, cubed
1-1/2	cups fresh mushrooms, chopped

Combine gravy, mushrooms, heat and keep warm.

Cook pasta according to package directions. Drain, place in shallow serving bowl.

Stir ricotta into gravy, pour over pasta, toss gently. Sprinkle with grated cheese and mozzarella.

Variation:

1	cup artichoke hearts, chopped

Tagliarini
(Egg Noodles)

Serves 4 to 6

1-1/2	**cups flour**
1-1/2	**cups semolina**
3	**eggs (or 1 egg and 4 egg whites)**
	salt to taste
3	**tablespoons Marsala Olive Fruit Oil**

In mixing bowl combine dry ingredients, make well in center, add eggs and oil.

Stir until dough holds together, adding a little water if needed. (Dough should be a little firmer than pie dough.)

On lightly floured board, knead dough until smooth. Cover, let rest 20 to 30 minutes.

Using rolling pin or pasta machine, shape pasta into thin sheets.

Cut on small cutter of pasta machine for fine noodles.

If cutting by hand, flour sheets lightly, roll jelly roll fashion, cut as fine as possible.

Cook in boiling water 5 to 8 minutes or until tender. Serve with tomato gravy.

Tagliarini With Chicken Soup

Serves 4 to 6

1	**recipe for tagliarini**
2 to 3	**quarts chicken soup (homemade preferably)**
1/2	**cup parsley, chopped fine**
	Romano cheese, grated (to taste)
	salt and pepper (to taste)

Make chicken soup, strain, remove all fat which comes to top.

Bring soup to a boil, add noodles and parsley, Cook on medium boil for 5 to 8 minutes or until tender, add salt and pepper.

Serve in soup dishes, sprinkle with cheese.

Tagliarini With Milk

Serves 4 to 6

1	recipe for tagliarini
6	cups milk
1/4	cup sugar (or to taste)
1/2	teaspoon cinnamon (or to taste)
	pinch of salt

Cook noodles in boiling water until tender, 5 to 8 minutes.

Heat milk, sugar, salt and cinnamon. Drain noodles, place in a large serving bowl, stir in milk mixture.

Add more milk if desired.

This was a favorite of ours growing up.

Tigliarini With Ricotta

Serves 4 to 6

1	recipe for tagliarini
1-1/2	cups ricotta
1/3	cup Marsala Olive Fruit Oil
	salt, pepper and cayenne to taste
1/2	cup fresh basil or parsley, minced
4	garlic cloves, minced
1/4	cup Romano cheese, grated
1/2	cup pasta cooking water

Cook tagliarini in boiling water for 5 to 8 minutes or until tender.

In mixing bowl combine remaining ingredients.

Drain noodles, place in serving bowl, spoon on ricotta mixture, toss gently.

Serve with a bowl of Romano cheese, grated and freshly ground black pepper.

Note: Garlic may be sauteed in a little olive oil a few seconds. Careful not to burn.

Variation:

1	cup spinach, cooked, drained, chopped
1	cup olives, chopped
1	cup artichoke hearts, sliced

Mom's Christmas Eve

Tagliarini With Walnuts

Serves 4 to 5

1	recipe for tagliarini or 12 ounces spaghetti
1/2	cup fresh parsley
3/4	cup bread crumbs
3/4	cup walnuts, ground
	salt, pepper and red pepper flakes to taste
1/2	cup Marsala Olive Fruit Oil
4	garlic cloves, minced
1/2	cup Romano cheese, grated
1/2	cup water in which pasta was cooked

In non stick large skillet on medium heat add oil, garlic, walnuts and bread crumbs.

Cook stirring until toasted and golden brown.

Cook pasta with parsley until tender, drain.

Place in large serving shallow bowl, cover with walnut mixture. Add water, salt, peppers, sprinkle with cheese.

Variation:

1/2   cup olives and 2 anchovies chopped

Mom made this recipe every Christmas eve. She would always say legend has it that Mary made this pasta with walnuts on that evening.

Tagliarini With Wine

Serves 1

1	cup homemade wine (room temperature)
1	fork full of noodles

Pour wine into soup bowl. Remove 1 heaping fork full of noodles from boiling water, when cooked.

Place into bowl with wine. The heat of the noodles will warm up the wine.

This was one of my Father's favorite ways to have homemade pasta.

I could still picture him with the little soup bowl containing his homemade wine, waiting for Mom to put a forkful of noodles in it.

Tagliarini and Beans

Serves 4 to 6

1	recipe for tagliarini
1	onion
2	garlic cloves, chopped
1/4	cup Marsala Olive Fruit Oil
4	cups fresh or canned tomatoes, chopped
3	ounces tomato paste
	salt, pepper and red pepper flakes to taste
1	teaspoon fennel seeds
1/2	cup fresh basil, chopped
2	cups dried beans, cooked (garbanzo or fava beans)
1/2	teaspoon sage

In saucepan add onion, garlic and oil. Cook over medium heat until soft.

Add tomatoes, tomato paste, salt, pepper, pepper flakes and fennel seeds.

Cook on low heat about 20 minutes. Add sage and basil, cook about 5 more minutes.

Cook tagliarini, 5 to 8 minutes or until tender, drain.

Place pasta in a large shallow serving bowl, cover with sauce and beans, toss gently. (Serve with Romano cheese if desired.)

Note: There are several names for handmade noodles, tagliarini, tagliatelle, tagliolini.

Meatballs and Spaghetti

Serves 4

1	pound spaghetti (or pasta of your choice)
1	recipe for chunky tomato gravy
1	recipe for Italian meatballs
	grated Romano cheese
1	cup mozzarella, cubed

Make meatballs according to recipe directions, cook, add to tomato gravy.

Cook for about 20 minutes or until meatballs are well done.

Cook pasta according to package directions, drain, place in serving platter.

Add gravy, toss gently, arrange meatballs around pasta.

Sprinkle with grated cheese, top with mozzarella.

Variation:

Serve with ricotta on the side, if desired.

Tortellini

Serves 4 to 6

1   **recipe for pasta dough**
1   **egg white slightly beaten**

Roll out pasta about 1/8 inch thick, using a pasta machine. Cut dough into 2-1/2 inch circles.

Place 1/2 teaspoon filling in center of dough round. Brush edge with egg white.

Fold dough over filling, pinch outside edges firmly to seal. Press edges with tines of fork if desired.

Brush end of half circle with egg white. Wrap around finger, overlap ends and press to seal.

Place on lightly floured board.

Filling

2   **cups lean meat, (turkey, beef, veal, rabbit or chicken, ground)**
1   **egg and 1 egg white**
1-1/2 **cups spinach, cooked, well drained, chopped**
1   **onion, chopped fine**
          pepper to taste
1/2   **cup fresh basil or parsley, chopped fine**
1   **cup chanterelle mushrooms, chopped**
3/4   **cup bread crumbs**
1   **cup Romano cheese, grated**
          pinch of rosemary (or to taste)
          pinch of sage (or to taste)
1/4   **cup Marsala Olive Fruit Oil**

In non stick skillet, over medium heat add oil onion and meat.

Cook until meat is browned. Cool, add remaining ingredients, stir to blend.

White Sauce

3   **tablespoons flour**
3   **tablespoons Marsala Olive Fruit Oil**
1   **cup onion, chopped fine**
4   **cups milk, non fat**
1/4   **cup fresh basil or parsley, minced**
1/2   **pound fresh mushrooms, chopped**
          salt and pepper to taste

Continued

Continued

1/2   **cup Romano cheese, grated**
1/4   **teaspoon nutmeg or thyme**

In saucepan, over medium heat add oil and onion, cook until tender.

Add flour, stirring until well blended. Add milk, stir until thickened.
Stir in cheese and nutmeg.

In large pot, cook tortellini in boiling water until tender, 5 to 8 minutes.

Drain, place on serving platter, cover with sauce, toss gently.

Serve sprinkled with cheese and basil.

Variation:

Substitute chunky tomato gravy for white sauce.

Also may be cooked in clear chicken broth.

Pappardella with Garbanzo

Serves 4

1   **cup mozzarella, cubed**
1   **cup celery sliced thin**
1   **teaspoon rosemary**
1   **onion chopped, small**
4   **garlic cloves, minced**
      salt, pepper and red hot pepper flakes
3 to 4 **cups fresh or canned tomatoes chopped**
2   **ounces tomato paste**
2 to 3 **cups garbanzo, cooked (or fava beans)**
1/4   **cup Marsala Olive Fruit Oil**
1/2   **cup fresh basil or parsley, chopped**
3/4   **cup Romano cheese, grated**
8   **ounce pappardella or homemade noodles**
1   **teaspoon grated lemon peel**

In saucepan add onions, garlic, celery and oil. Cook over medium heat until soft.

Add salt, peppers, tomato, tomato paste and rosemary. Cook about 15 minutes, stir in lemon peel.

Add cooked garbanzo and basil, simmer another 8 to 10 minutes.

Cook pasta according to package directions (al dente, not to mushy).

Place in serving platter, spoon garbanzo sauce over pasta, toss gently. Sprinkle with mozzarella and Romano grated cheese.

Buckwheat Pasta Lamb and Peas

Serves 4

12	ounces buckwheat or whole-wheat spaghetti
1/2	pounds lamb, lean, ground
1	cup mushrooms, chopped
1	onion, chopped
2	cups peas, fresh or frozen and/or zucchini diced
3	ounces tomato paste
1/2	cup wine, red
	salt, pepper and cayenne to taste
1/2	cup basil, chopped
1/4	cup Marsala Olive Oil

In sauce pan add olive oil and onions, cook until crisp tender. Add lamb, cook until no longer pink. Stir in tomatoes, salt, pepper and cayenne, cook about 15 minutes. Add remaining ingredients, cook about 20 more minutes. Serve over cooked pasta.

Gnocchi alla Romana

Serves 4 to 6

4	cups milk
1/2	teaspoon salt (or to taste)
	white pepper to taste
1/4	teaspoon nutmeg
1	cup semolina
1	egg, lightly beaten
1/2	cup Romano cheese, grated
1/2	cup provolone, shredded
1/4	cup Marsala Olive Oil
3/4	cup proscuitto or ham chopped
4	green onions, white part, minced

> **It's _so_ good for you**
> Onions contain quercetin. This flavonoid prevents heart disease by inhibiting bodily changes that can lead to blocked arteries.

In sauce pan add milk, stir in semolina. Cook over medium heat stirring frequently until thick.

Stir in remaining ingredients. Pour mixture onto 15 by 10 – 1 inch baking pan, lined with foil and greased. Smooth top, refrigerate uncovered for 1 hour.

Turn mixture out of pan onto flat surface, peel off foil. Cut mixture into squares or 4 inch round cookie cutter.

Arrange gnocchi overlapping in a 10 inch greased shallow oven proof baking dish. Drizzle with olive oil, sprinkle with cheese. Bake in a 350 degrees oven until golden, 15 to 20 minutes.

Midnight Spaghetti

Serves 4 to 6

2	cups fresh bread crumbs
1/3	cup Marsala Olive Oil
6	anchovies, rinsed (or to taste) chopped
1	onion, minced
4	garlic cloves, minced
1	cup olives, sliced
4	tablespoon tomato paste
4	cups tomatoes, fresh or canned, chopped
1/2	cup red wine
1/2	cup basil, chopped
	salt, pepper and red hot pepper flakes to taste
1	pound spaghetti or pasta of your choice
	Romano cheese and toasted bread crumbs to taste

Work bread in food processor until coarsely chopped. In a large non-stick skillet add 2 tablespoons olive oil and crumbs.

Stir crumbs until golden brown over medium heat, remove to a bowl, set aside, keep warm.

In same skillet add remaining olive oil, garlic and onions. Cook until tender, add anchovies, stir to mix.

Add wine, cook about 2 minutes. Stir in tomatoes, tomato paste, salt, pepper and red pepper flakes.

Cook about 20 minutes, add remaining ingredients, simmer while pasta is cooking.

Cook pasta al dente (not too soft), drain, place in large shallow serving bowl.

Pour gravy, over pasta, toss gently.

Sprinkle top with toasted bread crumbs and grated Romano cheese if desired.

Variation:

> ### Health benefit
> Shrimp help scrapes heal faster. These shellfish are a significant source of zinc, which speeds skin repair after injuries.

capers
artichoke hearts, sliced
fennel seeds
walnuts, ground or pine nuts
roasted eggplant, peppers or zucchini, chopped
Italian sausage, cooked, well drained, crumbled
ricotta or mozzarella cubed
shrimp or crab
clams or mussels

Continued

Continued

mushrooms of your choice

1/2 pound squid cut into rings, lightly floured, cooked until golden in olive oil

1 can (6 or 7 ounce) water packed tuna

After family and friends played cards at night, many times they would decide to have spaghetti around midnight.

Pasta with Fresh Tomato

Serves 4

8 ounces gemelli or pasta of your choice
2 pounds tomatoes, plum, peeled and chopped
8 ounces (bocconcini) mozzarella
1/2 cup Romano shaved (or ricotta salata)
1/3 cup Marsala Olive Oil (or to taste)
1/2 cup basil (or to taste) chopped fine
 salt, pepper and cayenne to taste

Combine all ingredients (except pasta) into a mixing bowl. Leave at room temperature for about 1 hour.

Cook pasta (al dente) not to mushy. Drain, place into a shallow serving bowl.

Spoon tomato mixture onto pasta, toss gently.

Variation:

2 garlic cloves, minced
3/4 cup ricotta, low fat or goat cheese
1/4 cup pine nuts
2 cups arugula or spinach leaves, chopped
1/2 cup olives, sliced or grapes seedless
1/3 cup provolone, shredded
1-1/2 cups asparagus tips, steamed crisp tender
1 cup snow peas, cooked crisp tender (or green beans)
1 cup fava beans, cooked tender
1 avocado, diced
 cherry tomatoes

> ### Health benefit
> Just one medium-sized tomato supplies almost half the RDA of vitamin C, which boosts immunity. Tomatoes are also an excellent source of folate, which may help prevent heart disease.

Anatreciana Sauce "ala Piconi"

Serves 4 to 6

1	pound spaghetti
1/2	pound pancetta, cut into strips
1	onion, chopped
1/4	cup Marsala olive Oil
1	cup wine, red
2	garlic cloves, minced
1/2	cup milk
	salt and pepper to taste
2	teaspoons hot pepper flake
4	cups fresh or canned tomatoes
1-6	ounce can tomato paste
1	cup Romano cheese, grated

In sauce pot saute pancetta until golden brown. Pour off the fat. Add olive oil and onion, cook until tender.

Add wine, when bottom is deglazed, stir in tomatoes, tomato paste, garlic cloves, salt and pepper. Cook simmering 30 to 40 minutes, Add milk last 5 minutes of cooking.

Cook pasta in boiling water until "al dente" (not to soft). Drain, place in serving platter, sprinkle with cheese, add sauce. Toss gently to coat pasta. "Bon Appetit" by Dr. John

This sauce is also excellent served over hand made pappardelle pasta. We had this last evening. Dr. John made the sauce. A young friend visiting Nick and Terese from Italy made the pappardelle, what a treat!

Note:

Pancetta is a non smoked Italian bacon.

Variation:

Add 1/2 pound beef or pork ribs (or meat of your choice) to sauce. Cook sauce longer, about 1 hour or until meat is well done

Pasta With Black Olive Sauce

Serves 4

In container, process until blended 6 ounces black olives, 4 anchovy fillets, 2 ounces capers, juice of 1 lemon, 3/4 cup Marsala Olive Oil, salt, pepper to taste, 2 garlic cloves, 1/2 cup parsley, 2 tablespoons cognac or brandy and 1/4 cup pistachios. Serve desired amount over 12 ounces of cooked pasta of your choice. Sprinkle with Romano cheese, grated. (Sauce is good on toasted slices of Italian bread also)

Stuffed Artichokes with Potatoes

Serves 4

4	large artichokes
1-1/2	cups bread crumbs
1/2	cup Romano cheese grated
1/2	cup fresh basil or parsley chopped
1/2	teaspoon white pepper to taste
1/2	cup raisins or dried cranberries
1/4	cup pine nuts or pistachio chopped
1/3	cup Marsala Olive Fruit Oil
4	slices tomatoes 1/4 inch thick (or canned)
4	peeled whole potatoes
	salt to taste

> **Health benefit**
>
> Keep arteries clear with artichokes. Cynarin, an antioxidant in this vegetable, may lower levels of blood cholesterol.

Wash artichokes, trim stems. Cut off 1 inch from tops. Snip off sharp leaf tips with shears.

In mixing bowl stir together crumbs, basil, cheese, pepper, olive oil and raisins.

Starting with lower leaves and working up, put about a teaspoon of stuffing on each leaf 3/4 of way up.

Place in deep pan with potatoes in between. Place a slice of tomato on each artichoke.

Add 2 inches of water or enough to come half way up artichokes, add salt.

Bring to a boil, lower to simmer. Cook about 30 to 40 minutes or until tender and leaves pull out easily.

Remove from water, let drain, place on shallow serving bowl with potatoes. Drizzle a little olive oil over artichokes and potatoes if desired.

Variation:

crab, shrimp or seafood at your choice

Artichokes With Lemon Olive Oil

Serves 6

6	artichokes, cooked
10 to 12 tablespoons Marsala Lemon Olive Oil (or to taste)	
6	individual mini cups (for dipping)

To serve, place one artichoke on each serving plate. Pour a little lemon oil in each mini cup, set on plate with artichoke.

Dip soft edible bottom of leaves in lemon oil. Quarter or slice artichoke heart, dip in olive oil.

Catch dripping with toasted Italian bread.

Add salt and pepper to oil if desired. *Continued*

Continued
Lemon Olive Oil
Makes 2 Cups

1	**lemon**
2	**cups Marsala Olive Fruit Oil**

Peel lemon with vegetable peeler. Place peel and olive oil in glass container, cover.

Keep refrigerated for several days. Bring to room temperature before serving.

Variation:

1   **fresh sprig of mint or rosemary**

Anita's Cabbage Patch Stew
Serves 4 to 6

2	**onions, chopped**
1	**cup celery chopped**
1/3	**cup Marsala Olive Oil**
1/2	**head of cabbage, shredded or chopped**
1	**pound turkey or lean meat of your choice, ground**
	salt and pepper to taste
2	**cups dried kidney beans, cooked (or canned)**
1	**can (12 ounces) Italian style stewed tomatoes**
1	**cup water**
1/2	**cup fresh basil (or to taste) chopped**
1	**teaspoon chili powder**
4	**garlic cloves (or to taste) chopped**
1	**recipe for dumplings**

In Dutch oven, over medium heat add onions, garlic, celery and olive oil.

Cook until vegetables are tender.

Add meat, cook until browned, stirring occasionally.

Add water and cabbage, cook until wilted. Stir in tomatoes, salt, pepper, chili powder and basil. Simmer about 10 minutes.

Gently stir in cooked beans. Combine dumpling dough ingredients. Using heaping teaspoon, shape dough into small dumplings. Gently poach dumplings covered over low heat. When dumplings come to the top, cook about 2 to 3 minutes.

Continued

Dumplings
Makes about 8

2	tablespoons olive oil
1	egg (or 2 egg whites)
1	cup fresh bread crumbs
	salt, pepper and paprika to taste
1/4	cup fresh basil, parsley or herb of your choice
	pinch of nutmeg
1	garlic clove, minced
2	tablespoons Romano cheese, grated
1/4	teaspoon baking powder
2	tablespoons semolina

Combine all ingredients in mixing bowl until well blended.

Using heaping teaspoon shapes dough into small dumplings. Gently poach dumplings over low heat, about 3 minutes in stew.

Variation:
Substitute Veggie "Just Like Ground" original, fat free, crumbled for ground meat. Yves Brand may be found in the refrigerated section of health food stores.

My friend Anita had this stew at "7 Lazy P Guest Ranch" in Montana. The guests like this stew very much.

Crumb Topping for Vegetables
Serves 4

3 to 4	cups vegetables of your choice, cooked crisp tender (zucchini, eggplant, green beans, broccoli, cauliflower, etc.)
1/3	cup bread crumbs
2	tablespoons Romano cheese, grated or shaved
1/4	cup Marsala Olive Oil
	salt, pepper and cayenne to taste
1/3	cup fresh basil (or herb of your choice, chopped)
1/3	cup walnuts (or nuts of your choice, ground)
	garlic to taste, minced

Combine all ingredients in mixing bowl, sprinkle over vegetables evenly.

Potato Pancakes
Serves 2 to 4

In large non stick skillet heat 1/4 cup Marsala Olive Oil. In mixing bowl have ready 2 cups potatoes and 1 onion, shredded. Add 2 eggs, salt, pepper and paprika to taste, mix.

Drop potato mixture by heaping tablespoonful into skillet. Flatten to form pancakes. Cook on both sides over medium heat until golden brown.

Black Olives Cured in Salt

4   quarts black olives
          coarse salt

Dressing

8   garlic cloves (or to taste) chopped
          Marsala Olive Fruit Oil
          red wine vinegar
          cumin
          paprika
          basil, parsley and mint
          oregano
          orange and lemon peel
          bay leaves

Pierce olives with a fork. In a clean basket, cover bottom with 1/4 inch coarse salt. Top with 2 or 3 inches of olives, sprinkle with 1 or 2 cups salt. Repeat with olives and salt, ending with a thick layer of salt.

Place the basket over a container to catch the liquid from the olives. Turn olives weekly, adding more salt, making sure olives do not get moldy.

Leave olives 3 to 4 weeks or until they look wrinkled and shrivelled. Remove olives to another container, pour boiling water over olives, let soak overnight.

Drain olives, rinse in cold water. Drain well, add dressing ingredients to taste. Keep olives refrigerated covered with a little olive oil.

May be made in smaller or larger quantities.

Oven Fried Potatoes

Serves 4

4   potatoes, peeled or unpeeled
          salt and pepper to taste
1/4   cup Marsala Olive Oil

Cut potatoes into desired sizes. Place on a lightly greased cookie sheet.

Sprinkle with salt and pepper.

Drizzle with olive oil, toss to coat potatoes.

Bake in a 400 degrees oven for 20 to 30 minutes or until golden brown and fork tender. Stir several times during baking.

Variation:

          paprika, cayenne, parsley, Romano cheese, garlic powder
          rosemary or bread crumbs to taste

Cactus Leaves or Pads
(Nopalitos)

Serves 4 to 6

1/2	cup fresh basil, parsley or cilantro, chopped
4	small tender cactus leaves (new shoots)
1	each red, yellow and green bell pepper
1/4	pound pork loin, cut into 2 inch strips
1	onion, sliced lengthwise
	salt, pepper and cayenne to taste
1/4	cup Marsala Olive Fruit Oil
4	garlic cloves (or to taste) chopped
1-1/2	cups fresh mushrooms, sliced
1	teaspoon fennel seeds

Remove spines (or stickers) from cactus leaves.

Cut each leaf into size of green beans.

Slice peppers and onion about 1/2 inch thick, lengthwise.

In non stick skillet, over medium heat, brown pork in olive oil.

Add onions, peppers, salt, pepper, cayenne and garlic. Cook until crisp tender.

Add nopalitos, mushrooms, basil and fennel seeds. Cook until crisp tender.

Serve with meat or fish.

Grilled Cactus Leaves and Eggplant
(Nopalitos)

Serves 4

1/2	cup fresh cilantro or parsley, minced
4	garlic cloves, minced
1/3	cup lemon juice
	salt, pepper and cayenne to taste
2	medium zucchini, sliced 1/4 inch thick
4	small tender cactus leaves (new shoots)
1/4	cup Marsala Olive Oil
1	small eggplant, sliced 1/4 inch thick
2	red or yellow bell peppers, quartered
1	teaspoon Italian seasoning

Brush nopalitos and vegetables with olive oil on both sides.

Grill until tender, sprinkle with salt, peppers, Italian seasoning and cilantro.

Drizzle with a mixture of lemon juice, garlic and olive oil before serving.

Variation:

4	slices fresh pineapple, cut into about 3/4 inch thick
1-1/2	cups mushrooms or onions, sliced

Caponata

Makes about 6 cups

2	bell peppers (red, yellow or green) cubed
1	large eggplant, cubed
1	onion, chopped
1-1/2	cups fennel bulb or celery, sliced
1/3	cup Marsala Olive Fruit Oil
1/2	pound yellow or green zucchini, cubed
3	tomatoes, chopped (or to taste)
1/2	cup olives of your choice, pitted
1/3	cup white wine vinegar or lemon juice
1/3	cup golden raisins
1/3	cup pine nuts, almonds, sliced or walnuts, chopped
	salt, pepper and cayenne to taste
6	garlic cloves (or to taste) chopped
1	cup mushrooms, sliced (or button mushrooms)
1/2	cup fresh basil, parsley or mint, chopped
1/2	cup white wine
1	teaspoon sage or tarragon
3	tablespoons cocoa (or 1 square unsweetened chocolate, melted)
1	tablespoon fresh ginger, grated

> **Health benefit**
> Smooth out those smile lines with eggplant. Deep purple eggplant contains phenolic compounds, which strengthen the skin's collagen and reduce wrinkles.

Heat oil in Dutch oven or large sauce pot over medium high heat. Add onions, fennel and peppers, cook about 2 or 3 minutes stirring occasionally. Add eggplant, tomatoes, zucchini and garlic. Cover, cook on medium heat until crisp tender.

Add mushrooms, vinegar, wine, olives, ginger, raisins, sage, salt, pepper, cayenne and basil. Cook over low heat, stirring occasionally until slightly thickened, stir in cocoa. Sprinkle with nuts.

Serve hot as a vegetable side dish or cold as a relish in center of an antipasto tray.

May also be used as pizza topping.

Variation:

Add one or two of the following:

1	cup carrots, sliced, cooked crisp tender
4	bay leaves (remove before serving)
1	cup mozzarella or dried ricotta, shredded
1	tablespoon Dijon mustard
1	cup prosciutto, chopped
1/4	cup capers
1-1/2	cups chicken, boneless, skinless, cooked, chopped
8	ounces rotelle or penne pasta, cooked

Cucuzzi
(Italian Heirloom Squash)

This unusual Italian heirloom squash is in a class by itself. At maturity, it grows into a long hard shelled gourd on a long, trailing vine.

Normally harvested when 10 to 12 inches long. It is used like a regular summer squash. Enjoy baked, grilled, raw, frozen and pickled.

Mom would peel the squash with a vegetable peeler. Then cut it into about 2 to 2-1/2 inch pieces, crosswise.

She would then scoop out the seeds from the center and fill with stuffing.

Grease a 9 by 13 baking dish. Place cucuzzi pieces in a single layer, cut side down.

Fill with your favorite stuffing, place a slice of tomato on top, drizzle with oil.

Cover with foil, bake in a 350 degrees oven for 20 to 30 minutes or until squash is fork tender.

Note: Stuffing recipe for eggplant or bell peppers will go well in the cucuzzi.

Breaded Cauliflowerets
Serves 4 to 6

1	cauliflower, separated into flowerets, cooked crisp tender
1/2	cup provolone or Romano cheese, shredded
1/2	cup bread crumbs
4	garlic cloves, minced
1/2	cup fresh basil or parsley, chopped
	salt, pepper and cayenne to taste
1/3	cup Marsala Olive Oil
2	tablespoons ground pecans, almonds, or walnuts
1	egg lightly beaten

In pie plate add egg. In another pie plate combine cheese, bread crumbs, garlic, basil, salt, pepper, cayenne and nuts.

Dip flowerets in egg, coating all around, then roll in bread crumb mixture.

In large non stick skillet add oil, heat. Cook flowerets on all sides until golden brown.

Note: This method works well with many vegetables. A friend serves the cauliflowerets over cooked pasta.

Variation:

broccoflower, brussels sprouts or broccoli, cooked crisp tender
mushrooms
asparagus

Eggplant Parmigiana

Serves 4

4	tablespoons tomato paste
1/4	cup white wine or water
1/4	cup Marsala Olive Fruit Oil
1	eggplant cut into about 1/4 inch slices
1	onion, chopped
4	cups fresh or canned tomatoes, chopped
	salt, pepper and cayenne to taste
1/2	cup fresh basil or parsley, chopped
1/4	cup bread crumbs
2	eggs, small
1	cup mozzarella, shredded
1	cup ricotta, low fat

Grease lightly, large cookie sheet. Drizzle with a little olive oil evenly on bottom of sheet.

Arrange eggplant slices slightly overlapping in pan; drizzle with remaining olive oil.

Add wine, cover with foil. Bake in a 400 degrees oven for 30 to 40 minutes or until eggplant is tender.

In saucepan add onion and 2 tablespoons olive oil. Cook covered until tender.

Add tomatoes, tomato paste, salt, pepper, cayenne and basil, simmer about 15 minutes.

Combine in mixing bowl cheeses and eggs.

Lightly grease a large baking dish. Arrange half of the eggplant slices in, slightly overlapping.

Spoon half cheese mixture over evenly. Spoon tomato sauce over cheese.

Repeat with eggplant, cheese mixture and tomato sauce. Sprinkle with bread crumbs.

Cover with foil, bake in a 350 degrees oven for about 35 minutes or until bubbly in center.

Variation:

1-1/2	cups mini meatballs
1-1/2	cups fresh mushrooms, sliced

Variation:

Eggplant slices may be dusted with flour then dipped in beaten egg on both sides. Coat with dry bread crumbs.

Our grandson Jonathan likes this eggplant Parmigiana so much that after we have our dessert, he goes back for another serving of eggplant.

Grampa Nicola's Sicilian Olives

4   quarts fresh green olives

Seasonings

fresh hot chilies
2   **lemons, sliced**
8   **garlic cloves (or to taste) chopped**
      oregano
      fennel seeds
      salt

Gently crack olives with a stone or hammer, remove pits. Place in a stainless container crock or plastic bucket, cover with water.

Place a dish on top, weight it down with a stone to keep all olives completely under water. Change water everyday for 12 to 15 days or until bitterness is removed.

Taste as you go along, it may take less time. When ready, drain off water. Place in brine with seasonings.

Brine

For correct proportions of salt for brine, continue adding salt to water in a bucket, stirring, until a raw egg will come to the surface and floats. Remove egg, pour brine into olives, add seasonings.

Dressing

celery, leaves included, sliced
orange and lemon peel in strips
bay leaves
garlic
oregano
mint, basil and parsley, chopped
jalapeno peppers, minced
Marsala Olive Fruit Oil
vinegar

Health benefit
Scientists at NASA have found that poinsettias actually filter headache-causing pollutants from indoor air.

To serve, remove as many olives as desired, rinse, drain, place in serving dish. Add dressing ingredients to taste.

Notes: Remaining olives may be placed in glass jars with brine and seasonings, covered with a little olive oil. Keep refrigerated.

May be made in smaller or larger quantities.

Swiss Chard With Tomatoes

Serves 4 to 6

2	pounds Swiss chard, parboiled, chopped
1	small onion, chopped
1/4	cup Marsala Olive Fruit Oil
2 or 3	cups fresh or canned tomatoes, chopped
3	tablespoons tomato paste
4	garlic cloves, chopped
2	cups Italian bread cubed, toasted
1/2	cup fresh basil, chopped

In saucepan add oil, onions and garlic, cook over medium heat until tender.

Add tomatoes, tomato paste, basil, salt, pepper and hot pepper flakes, simmer about 15 minutes.

Add Swiss chard to tomato mixture, cook another 5 to 8 minutes.

Add bread cubes, stir, cover, turn off heat. Let stand 5 or 10 minutes before serving.

Variation:

Substitute red Swiss chard for green chard.

Several day old hard Italian bread works well in the above recipe.

Boiled Potatoes

Serves 4

2	tablespoons lemon juice
1-1/2	pounds tiny potatoes, peeled or unpeeled
1/4	cup Marsala Olive Fruit Oil
1/4	cup fresh basil or parsley, chopped
	Salt, pepper and cayenne to taste
4	garlic cloves, minced

Cook potatoes, in boiling water until tender, drain.

In saucepan add oil, garlic, basil, lemon juice, salt, pepper and cayenne.

Heat slightly, pour over hot potatoes in serving plate, toss gently.

Variation:

Sprinkle with Romano grated cheese or cheese of your choice.

Mom's Potato Fans

Serves 6

6	potatoes, peeled
6	tablespoons Marsala Olive Oil
	salt, pepper and red hot pepper flakes to taste
1/3	cup Romano cheese, grated
1/4	cup bread crumbs
1/3	cup white wine or water

Preheat oven to 375 degrees. Grease baking pan, drizzle with a little oil evenly.

Cut potatoes crosswise into 1/4 inch slices, almost to bottom, about 3/4 of the way through.

Combine salt, peppers, bread crumbs and cheese in mixing bowl. Place about 1/2 teaspoon filling between each slice.

Place potatoes cut side up in pan, add wine. Drizzle with olive oil evenly.

Cover with foil, bake about 1 hour or until fanned out and fork tender.

For browned potatoes, remove foil last 10 minutes of baking.

Variation:

1	teaspoon fresh rosemary, chopped

Notes:

Each potato may be wrapped in foil and placed in baking pan to bake.

Potatoes may be cut by placing in a large serving spoon.

Cut crosswise in 1/4 inch thick sliced, only to edge of spoon.

Hashed Brown Potatoes

Serves 4

4	potatoes, cooked, shredded
3/4	cup onion, grated
	Salt and pepper to taste
1/4	cup Marsala Olive Fruit Oil

In large non-stick skillet over medium heat add oil, potatoes, salt, pepper and onion.

Leave 1/2 inch space around edge, brown mixture on both sides until golden.

Italian Mashed Potatoes

Serves 4 to 6

1-1/2	pounds red or new potatoes
1/3	cup Marsala Olive Oil
6	garlic cloves (or to taste) minced
	Salt, pepper and paprika to taste
1/2 tp 3/4	cup hot milk (non fat) or broth
1/3	cup fresh basil or herb of your choice, minced
1/3	cup Romano cheese, grated
1	cup olives for garnish
2	tablespoons capers for garnish
1/3	cup fresh parsley or mint leaves for garnish

Cook potatoes in boiling water until fork tender.

Drain, peel, place in mixing bowl, mash smooth or lumpy.

Add remaining ingredients, stir until well blended.

Spoon into serving dish, garnish with olives, capers and parsley.

Variation: add 1 or 2 of the following –

1-1/2	cups cooked noodles
1/2	cup dried tomatoes, crumbled
1/2	cup prosciutto or lean ham, chopped
1-1/2	cups spinach or greens of your choice, cooked, chopped
1	tablespoon rosemary, chives or sage, chopped
1/2	teaspoon nutmeg, cinnamon or cloves
1/2	cup dried ricotta, Gorgonzola or goat cheese, crumbled
1	cup green onions, broccoli or peas, cooked crisp tender
1	avocado, mashed
1/2	fennel bulb, cooked crisp tender, chopped
1	pound turnip greens, cooked, chopped
1	cup garbanzo, cooked, mashed smooth
1	cup tuna, water packed, flaked
	cayenne or red pepper flakes to taste
	substitute half yams for white potatoes

Note: Potatoes will become gummy if electric mixer is used.

Get a whiff of energy with rosemary
The volatile oils that give this pungent herb its
scent act as mild stimulants to make you feel
more energized and alert.

Italian Spinach

Serves 4 to 6

2	green onions, sliced thin
1/4	cup Marsala Olive Oil
6	garlic cloves (or to taste) minced
	salt, pepper and red hot pepper flakes to taste
1/4	cup white wine
2 to 3	pounds spinach, cleaned, chopped
1/3	cup raisins, golden
1/4	cup pine nuts, hazelnuts or pistachios, chopped
1/2	cup fresh basil, parsley, mint or cilantro, chopped

In large non-stick skillet or Dutch oven, cook onions and garlic in oil over medium heat until soft. Careful not to burn.

Add spinach with water that clings when washed and drained. Add wine, salt and peppers.

Cook covered on medium low heat until spinach wilts. Add basil, raisins and nuts.

Serve with mashed potatoes, couscous, orzo pasta or rice cooked.

Variation:

2	cups seafood (shrimp, crab, scallops etc.)
1/2	cup bread crumbs or cheese of your choice
1-1/2	cups mushrooms, sliced
1/2	cup prosciutto or ham, chopped
1-1/2	cups peas or dried beans, cooked
1	cup garbanzo or fava beans, cooked
1/4	teaspoon cinnamon, nutmeg or cloves
1/2	cup chestnuts, cooked, chopped
1/4	cup lemon or lime juice
1/2	cup Italian sausage, cooked, well drained, crumbled
1/3	cup dried cherries, blueberries or cranberries
1/3	cup Romano cheese, shaved

> ### Health benefit
> A half-cup serving of spinach provides 30% of the RDA for iron. A lack of this mineral can cause fatigue, especially in women.

Substitute: radicchio, escarole, curly or regular endive, cabbage, flowering kale, lettuce, turnip greens or greens of your choice.

Quince with Italian Spinach

Serves 4 to 6

4	quince, peeled or unpeeled, quartered

Remove seeds, place in lightly greased baking pan, drizzle with 2 tablespoons olive oil and 1/4 cup white wine.

Bake covered in a 350 degrees oven until tender, about 30 minutes. Arrange prepared spinach over quince evenly, bake until heated through, about 5 minutes. Garnish with olives.

Lillian's Eggplant Stew with Rice

Serves 5 to 6

1-1/2	pounds beef, lean, cut into bite size pieces
1	large onion, chopped
4	garlic cloves (or to taste) chopped
1/3	cup Marsala Olive Oil
3	cups tomatoes, fresh or canned, chopped
3	ounces tomato paste
1	cup celery, chopped
2	eggplants, small, cut into 2 inch cubes
1/2	cup fresh basil or parsley, chopped
1	cup mushrooms, fresh, sliced
	salt, pepper and cayenne to taste
2	cups green beans, cooked crisp tender (or peas)
2	bell peppers, cubed
3	cups rice, cooked

In large Dutch oven, cook beef in oil with onions, garlic, celery and peppers, until meat is no longer pink.

Add eggplant, cover, cook on medium heat about 10 minutes. Add tomatoes, tomato paste and basil.

Cook about 20 minutes, covered, or until meat and vegetables are tender.

Add salt, pepper, cayenne, green beans and mushrooms, cook a few minutes.

Serve over cooked rice, sprinkle with Romano cheese if desired.

Variation:

Substitute lamb, chicken, pork, veal or meat of your choice for beef.

Substitute cooked whole wheat, couscous, polenta or pasta for rice.

Lillian uses long grain rice for baking, medium grain (or California blue rose) for stuffing vegetables and pearl short grain for puddings, (creamy texture).

Mike's Vinegar Peppers With Meat

Serves 4

1   recipe for chunky tomato gravy
1   pound pork, veal, beef or meat of your choice
4 to 6   vinegar peppers (homemade or store bought)
1/4   cup Marsala Olive Fruit Oil

Cook meat until browned all around. Add to chunky tomato gravy. Cook on low heat 20 to 30 minutes or until meat is well done.

In large skillet add olive oil and sliced vinegar peppers. Cook over medium heat a few minutes.

Remove meat from gravy, cut into bite size cubes, add to peppers.

Cook together 2 or 3 minutes. Spoon into serving plate.

Serve with crusty Italian or French bread and a green salad.

This was a Sunday evening meal for our cousin Mike.

For the noon meal he served the tomato gravy over pasta.

The leftover meat would be served with the peppers for supper.

Zucchini Flowers
(Fiori di Zucca)
Serves 4

12 to 14 zucchini flowers
1   egg (or 2 egg whites)
2   tablespoons pancake flour
2   tablespoons milk
         salt, pepper and paprika to taste
1/3   cup Marsala Olive Oil
         Romano grated cheese to taste

Gently open blossoms, remove pistils, check for insects. Wash gently to avoid damaging them.

Drain, place on clean towel to dry.

In shallow bowl, combine flour, egg, paprika, pepper and milk.

Batter should be consistency of heavy cream. Gently dip each blossom into batter, let excess drip back into bowl.

Add oil to non stick skillet, heat. Cook blossoms a few at a time until golden on each side.

Remove with slotted spoon, sprinkle with Romano grated cheese.

Flowers may also be stuffed with precooked ground meat and vegetable filling, and cooked in the same way.

Mom's Spezzato
(Escarole With Veal)

Serves 4

1/3	cup white wine
2	tablespoons flour
1/2	pound veal cut into 1/2 inch cubes
6	garlic cloves (or to taste) chopped
1	onion, chopped
1/3	cup Marsala Olive Fruit Oil
3	cups escarole par boiled or steamed
3	eggs (or 1 egg and 4 egg whites)
1/2	cup Romano cheese, grated
1/3	cup provolone, shredded
	salt, pepper and red pepper flakes to taste
1/2	cup fresh basil or parsley, chopped

Coarsely chop well drained escarole.

Coat veal with flour. Brown veal in olive oil in a non stick skillet over medium heat.

Stir in wine, add onion and garlic, cook covered until onions are soft.

In mixing bowl add escarole, veal mixture, basil, eggs, cheeses, salt and peppers.

Stir and pour into greased baking casserole.

Bake in a 325 degrees oven for about 45 minutes or until fairly firm in center.

Cover with foil if browning too quickly.

Mom would serve this casserole before the main meal. It may be served as a side dish with meats or fish.

When first we met, my parents invited Joseph for supper, along with his cousin Tony and wife Florence.

At the time Joseph did not like greens. Mom placed a soup dish heaping full of (spezzato) in front of him.

Joseph and Tony looked at each other in disbelief. Tony knew Joseph did not care for greens. They got the giggles.

I guess Joseph did not want to hurt our feelings, so he ate the whole thing and liked it a lot.

Now he eats more greens and salads than the rest of us; says it is his dessert.

Onion Chrysanthemums

Serves 4 to 6

4 to 6   **medium sweet onions (about 8 ounces each) peeled**
1/4   **cup Marsala Olive Fruit Oil**
        salt, pepper and cayenne to taste
1/4   **cup lemon juice or white wine vinegar**
1/4   **cup pine nuts or pistachio, chopped**
1   **tablespoon fresh sage, rosemary or chives, chopped**

Stand onions on root end. Cut parallel vertical slices, 1/4 inch intervals, about 1/2 inch above root.

Turn onion and cut vertical slices in the same manner in crosshatch pattern, keeping onion in tact.

Place root side down in greased 9 by 13 inch pan, leaving space for onions to spread while baking.

Drizzle evenly with olive oil, salt, pepper and cayenne.

Bake, covered in a 375 degrees oven for 45 to 60 minutes or until tender when pierced in center.

Uncover, sprinkle onions evenly with lemon juice, pine nuts and sage.

Continue baking until onion tips are golden brown, about 10 minutes.

Serve hot or warm, spooning pan juices over onions.

Variation:

Sprinkle each onion with 1 teaspoon Romano cheese, grated
1/2   **cup fresh basil, mint or parsley, chopped**
1/2   **cup golden raisins (plump raisins in 1/2 cup port or sherry wine for about 1 hour, drain)**

> ## Health benefit
> Sage contains flavonoids, antioxidants which are more potent than vitamins A or C, promote heart health and protect the body from free radicals.

White Beans with Sage

Serves 4

In saucepan cook 1 onion, chopped, in 1/4 cup olive oil until tender, add 4 garlic cloves, chopped. Add 4 cups dried white beans, cooked, heat through.

Stir in 6 to 8 fresh sage leaves, chopped, 1/3 cup olive oil, salt, pepper and cayenne to taste.

Serve with crusty Italian or French bread.

Peas and Shells

Serves 4 to 6

1	teaspoon fennel seeds
1/3	cup wine
1/2	cup fresh basil or parsley, chopped
8	ounces shells or pasta of your choice
1	onion, chopped small
4	cups fresh or canned tomatoes, chopped
2	ounces tomato paste
2	cups fresh or frozen peas
1/4	cup Marsala Olive Fruit Oil
	Salt, pepper and hot pepper flakes

In saucepan add onion and oil, cook over medium heat until soft.

Add wine, cook one minute. Stir in tomatoes, tomato paste, fennel seeds and basil.

Cook about 10 minutes, add peas, simmer until tender, about 5 minutes.

Add remaining ingredients. Cook pasta according to package directions, drain.

In serving bowl add pasta, peas and tomato mixture. Stir gently, serve in soup dishes.

Variation:

1/2	cup Canadian bacon, chopped
1/2	cup salmon, smoked, chopped (or swordfish)
1-1/2	cups mozzarella cut into small cubes
1/2	pound shrimp, cleaned, cooked (or scallops)
1	cup celery, sliced or mushrooms
1	bell pepper, chopped or one small bunch arugula
1/2	cup prosciutto or ham, chopped
	Romano cheese, grated
1	carrot, or zucchini, diced

One of our friends never liked peas and pasta. There was a flood in the state one year. He landed in the hospital and food was scarce.

There was no electricity, his wife managed to cook on a wood stove; yes, pasta and peas.

She brought it to him in the hospital. Was he ever grateful. He now loves pasta and peas.

> ### Health benefit
> Eight ounces of peas has 20% of the RDA for vitamin C,
> an antioxidant that helps bolster the immune system.

Pasta and Potatoes

(Pasta con le patata)
Serves 4

8	ounces shells, bow tie or pappardelle pasta
2	potatoes peeled, diced
1/3	cup Marsala Olive Fruit Oil
1-1/2	cups mozzarella, cubed 1/2 inch
1/2	cup Romano cheese, grated
	Salt, pepper and paprika to taste
1	tablespoon fresh sage, chopped
2	garlic cloves (or to taste) minced
1/4	cup parsley, chopped small

> **Perk up with garlic**
> This bulb is a good source of scordinine, a compound that boosts stamina and helps the body fight fatigue.

In a large pot add water, bring to a boil. Add pasta and potatoes, cook until tender.

In small skillet heat oil, add garlic and sage. Cook a few seconds, do not burn.

Drain pasta, place in shallow serving bowl. Pour oil mixture, salt, pepper, paprika and Romano cheese, toss gently.

Sprinkle with mozzarella and parsley.

Variation:

1/3	cup Pesto sauce

Spinach and Rice Torte

Serves 8 to 10

4	garlic cloves, minced
2	cups rice, cooked
2	cups spinach, Swiss chard, cooked or zucchini, shredded
1	onion, chopped
1	bell pepper, roasted, chopped
4	eggs (or 8 egg whites)
	salt, pepper and paprika to taste
1	cup Cheddar, Swiss or Monterey Jack cheese, shredded
1/4	cup Marsala Olive Oil
1/2	cup fresh basil, parsley or cilantro, chopped

In non stick skillet add olive oil, onion and garlic, cook until tender. In mixing bowl combine all ingredients, mix.

Spoon into a square 9 inch greased baking pan. Bake in a 350 degrees oven for 25 to 30 minutes or until golden and firm in center. Cool, cut into squares.

Roasted Mixed Vegetables

Serves 6 to 8

2	carrots, cut into 2 inch pieces
6	baby red skin potatoes, quartered
1	large onion, sliced
1	chayote squash, cubed (or daikon)
1	fennel bulb, sliced thin
1	turnip or parsnip, peeled, cubed
2	celery stalks, chopped in 2 inch pieces
2 or 3	sprigs rosemary
1	eggplant, cubed
2	bell peppers, cubed
2	small zucchini, cut in 2 inch pieces
6	garlic cloves (or to taste) chopped
1/3	cup Marsala Olive Fruit Oil
1	cup wine or vermouth
1/2	cup fresh basil, parsley, cilantro or mint, chopped
	salt, pepper and cayenne to taste
1/2	teaspoon sage or thyme
1/2	cup lemon juice or soy sauce
1-1/2	cups fresh mushrooms, sliced (or button whole)
2	bay leaves

Health-smart solutions

Protect your eyes
A dash of olive oil on your spinach salad could save your sight. Spinach contains lutein, a compound that protects vision. Now a study shows that eating it with a little fat - a mere teaspoon of olive oil - improves benefits 88 percent.

Grease a large roasting pan. Drizzle with a little olive oil.

Add carrots, potatoes (peeled or unpeeled) onion, chayote, fennel, parsnip and celery.

Place rosemary sprigs in between vegetables.

Drizzle a little olive oil over all, add 1/2 of the wine, toss to coat, cover with foil.

Place in a 450 degrees oven for 25 to 30 minutes. Stir vegetables half way during cooking.

Next add peppers, eggplant, bay leaves, zucchini, garlic, basil, salt, pepper, cayenne, sage and remaining wine.

Drizzle with remaining olive oil, stir vegetables with large spoon.

Cover loosely with foil, bake another 30 to 40 minutes or until vegetables are fork tender.

Drizzle with lemon juice. Add mushrooms, cook about 2 minutes longer.

Serves as a side dish with fish, meat, cooked couscous, polenta or rice.

Remove bay leaves, garnish with mint sprigs.

Continued

Variation:

6	dried tomatoes
6	tomatoes, plum, chopped
4	cups fresh spinach, chopped
1-1/2	cups celery root or kohlrabi, sliced
1	inch fresh ginger, chopped
1/4	cup soy sauce
1	cup dried apricots, peaches, pears or prunes pitted
1-1/2	cups artichoke hearts
1 or 2	quince, quartered
2	yams or sweet potatoes, cubed
1	rutabaga, cubed
1	cup dried cherries, cranberries, blueberries or raisins
2	beets, cubed
2	ears of corn cut into 2 inch pieces
1-1/2	cups sugar peas or green beans
1/2	pound Jerusalem artichoke, peeled, sliced 1/4 inch thick

Add longer cooking ingredients first 30 minutes of baking and quicker cooking ingredients last 30 minutes.

Note: Vegetables and fruits may be grilled. Brush lightly with olive oil. Place on grill, careful not to let smaller ones slip through.

Remove quicker cooking vegetables to warm container, keep covered while longer cooking vegetables are still being grilled.

Note: Any leftover vegetables may be served in a salad or on top of pizza.

Mound roasted vegetables on mixed baby greens, sprinkle with macadamia nuts, chopped, crumbled Gorgonzola cheese, lemon juice and olive oil.

Tip: For quick roasting vegetables, slice vegetables about 1/2-inch thick.

Vegetables may be baked in two pans.

Note: Create your own combinations.

Health benefit
The skin of eggplant contains delphinidin, an antioxidant that is known to fight cancer-causing free radicals, as well as preventing the skin from aging.

Roasted Peppers

Serves 6 to 8

10 to 12 bell peppers red, green or yellow
1/2   cup fresh basil, chopped
1   cup celery, sliced thin (or tomatoes, chopped)
6   garlic cloves (or to taste) minced
        salt, pepper and red pepper flakes to taste
1/2   cup Marsala Olive Oil

Preheat oven to 400 degrees. Wash, drain peppers, place on foil lined cookie sheet.

Bake 30 to 40 minutes or until charred on all sides. Turn several times with tongs.

Remove from oven, cover with foil, cool. Peel off charred skin, remove seeds.

Cut peppers into fourths or strips, place in serving bowl.

Add remaining ingredients, toss gently.

Serve as an appetizer or in a cheese, ham, roast beef or tuna sandwich.

Note: Roasted peppers freeze well, add remaining ingredients after thawing.

Variation:

1/3   cup golden raisins
1   cup olives
1/4   cup pine nuts or pistachio, chopped

Note: Peppers may be charred under broiler. Place peppers about 4 inches from heat.

Turn with tongs, watch carefully as peppers will blister faster than baking.

Other ways to roast peppers may be done over an open flame or a grill.

Potatoes, Peppers and Onions

Serves 4

Place 4 peeled and quartered potatoes, 4 garlic cloves chopped, 2 bell peppers sliced, 2 onions sliced, salt, pepper, cayenne to taste and 1/2 cup fresh basil, parsley or rosemary in a lightly greased baking pan. Drizzle with 1/4 cup white wine and 1/3 cup Marsala Olive Oil, toss gently.

Cover with foil, bake in a 350 degrees oven for 35 to 45 minutes or until fork tender.

Stir Fry Vegetables and Beef

Serves 6

1-1/2	pounds beef flank steak
1	bell pepper cut in chunks
6	garlic cloves (or to taste) chopped
1/2	teaspoon ginger
1/3	cup soy sauce
1/4	cup cognac or brandy
1/4	cup broth
1	tablespoon corn starch
1/4	cup Marsala Olive Fruit Oil
1	large onion, sliced
1-1/2	cups celery cut diagonally
1-1/2	cups carrots cut diagonally
4	plum tomatoes, peeled, cut into wedges
1	cup water chestnuts, sliced
1	cup fresh or frozen peas or asparagus
	Black pepper to taste
1/2	cup fresh basil or parsley, chopped

> ### Health benefit
> Green olive oil will tone down a black-and-blue mark. Olive oil is an excellent source of vitamin K, which acts as a blood thinner and helps reduce bruising.

Cut steak diagonally across the grain into thin strips. In large skillet or wok, cook beef quickly over high heat in olive oil. When meat loses its red color, remove from pan with slotted spoon, onto a warm plate. (Do not overcook.)

In same skillet add onions, garlic, celery, carrots and peppers. Cover, cook on medium heat for about 2 or 3 minutes. Add basil, ginger, tomatoes, pepper and peas. Stir, cover and cook one minute, add chestnuts and beef, stir.

Combine in a small bowl soy sauce, cognac, broth and corn starch. Stir until blended.

Pour soy mixture on vegetables and meat, cook stirring gently until sauce clears and thickens.

Variation:

Substitute chicken, pork, or meat of your choice for beef.
Substitute shrimp or prawns for meat

2	pears or peaches, sliced
1/2	cup pear or peach nectar
1	cup green beans chopped
1/2	recipe for mini meatballs

Stuffed Bell Peppers

Serves 4 to 6

1	cup fresh mushrooms, chopped
1/2	cup bread crumbs, rice or barley, cooked
4 to 6	red, yellow or green bell peppers
1/2	pound lean beef, turkey, lamb or pork, ground
1/2	cup Romano cheese, grated (or Gorgonzola)
1/4	cup provolone or Monterey Jack cheese, shredded
1	egg (or 2 egg whites)
1/4	cup pistachio or pine nuts
1/4	cup olives, chopped
1	onion, chopped
2	garlic cloves, chopped
	Salt, pepper and paprika to taste
1/2	cup fresh basil or parsley, chopped
1/4	cup Marsala Olive Fruit Oil
1/2	cup raisins or currants

Slice tops of peppers, remove seeds, put aside tops. (Peppers may be cut in half lengthwise if desired.)

In large non stick skillet, over medium heat, add oil, onions, garlic and meat.

Cook until browned. In mixing bowl combine meat mixture and remaining ingredients.

Blend well, stuff peppers. Place pepper tops on peppers.

Place in greased baking dish or bake in a Bundt, tube, anglefood or muffin pan. Add 1/2 cup water in bottom.

Cover with foil, bake in a 350 degrees oven for 45 minutes or until cooked.

Serve sprinkled with additional grated cheese or topped with your favorite tomato sauce.

Variation:

1/2	cup corn or dried beans, cooked
2	tablespoons tomato paste
2	plum tomatoes, chopped or dried tomatoes, chopped
1/2	pound shrimp, scallops or crab
1/2	cup small pasta, cooked (or couscous)
2	tablespoons apricots or dates, chopped
2	tablespoons capers
2	anchovy rinsed, minced
1/4	cup peas, carrots or corn
1/2	cup wild or brown rice, cooked

Continued

Sauce

4	green tomatoes (with pink blush) chopped
1/2	cup onions, chopped
1/4	cup fresh basil, parsley or cilantro, chopped
2	tablespoons tomato paste
	Salt, pepper and cayenne to taste
2	tablespoons Marsala Olive Fruit Oil
2	tablespoons cognac or vermouth

In skillet cook onions in oil until tender. Add remaining ingredients, cook about 15 minutes.

Variation:

Peppers may be filled with chili con carne.

Green Beans Almondine

Serves 4 to 6

4	cups green beans or snow peas, cooked crisp tender
1/2	cup almonds slivered or sliced
	salt, pepper and paprika to taste
1/4	cup lime or lemon juice
1/3	cup Marsala Olive Fruit Oil
1/4	cup fresh basil, parsley or cilantro, minced
1/2	teaspoon Dijon mustard
2	garlic cloves, minced

In shallow serving salad bowl add beans, salt, pepper, paprika, lime juice, olive oil, basil, garlic and mustard.

Toss gently, sprinkle with almonds.

Variation:

1	cup red or yellow cherry tomatoes, whole or halved
1	cup corn
1-1/2	cups fresh mushrooms, sliced (or button) sauteed in a little olive oil
1	onion, sliced, sauteed in 2 tablespoons olive oil until lightly browned

Stuffed Eggplant

Serves 4

2	tablespoons fresh sage, chopped
2	medium eggplants cut in half lengthwise
1/4	cup prunes or dried apricots, chopped small
1/4	cup pine nuts, pecans or walnuts, chopped
1/2	cup Romano cheese, grated
1/2	cup lean lamb, chicken or beef, ground
1	onion, chopped
	salt, pepper and red pepper flakes to taste
2	fresh or canned tomatoes, chopped
2	tablespoons tomato paste
4	garlic cloves, minced
1/2	cup fresh basil, parsley or mint, chopped
1	cup fresh mushrooms, chopped
2	egg whites
1/3	cup mozzarella or Swiss cheese, shredded (for top)
1/4	cup Marsala Olive Fruit Oil
	scooped out eggplant, chopped

Scoop out center of halved eggplants, leaving a 1/2 inch shell. In large non stick skillet add oil, scooped out pulp, onion, lamb, sage and garlic.

Cook until meat is no longer pink over medium heat, place in mixing bowl.

Add remaining ingredients, stir to mix.

In greased baking pan, add about 3/4 cup water, place eggplant shells in, fill with meat mixture.

Cover with foil, bake in a 350 degrees oven for 45 minutes or until eggplant is tender. Sprinkle with cheese before serving.

Variation:

Substitute medium zucchini for eggplant.

Variation for filling:

4	portobello mushrooms, chopped
1/2	cup celery, diced
4	garlic cloves, minced
1	cup pasta, small shells, cooked
1	cup rice, cooked
1	cup Monterey Jack or goat cheese, crumbled
1	cup bell peppers or olives, chopped

Stuffed Mushrooms

Serves 4 to 6

First Place Award at Riverbank Cheese and Wine Exposition

2   tablespoons bread crumbs
1/4   pound Italian sausage cooked, drained, crumbled
8 to 12 large fresh mushrooms
1/2   onion, chopped
2   tablespoons fresh basil or parsley, chopped
1   egg white
1/2   cup ricotta
1/4   cup Marsala Olive Fruit Oil
1/3   cup provolone cheese, shredded
1/2   cup olives, chopped
1/2   cup wine

Preheat oven to 350 degrees. Remove stems from mushrooms and chop small. In skillet add oil, onion and mushroom stems.

Cook until tender, remove from heat, cool. Add remaining ingredients, blend.

Fill mushroom caps with stuffing, arrange in lightly greased baking dish, filled side up.

Drizzle with a little olive oil. Bake uncovered for 15 to 20 minutes in a 350 degrees oven.

Variation:

2   tablespoons currants or pine nuts
2   tablespoons macadamia nuts, finely chopped
6   cherry tomatoes, halved
1/2   cup Romano cheese
1/2   cup ham, chopped
1/4   cup dried tomatoes, chopped

Top each stuffed mushroom with 1 tomato half.

Succotosh

Serves 6

3	cups butternut squash cut into 1/2 inch pieces
2	cups green beans cut diagonally into 1 inch pieces
1/4	cup Marsala Olive Oil
1	onion chopped
4	garlic cloves, (or to taste) minced
1/2	cup beef or chicken broth
1	cup corn, fresh or frozen
1	cup edamame, fresh or frozen (green soy beans)
2	tablespoons parsley, basil thyme or fresh herb or your choice, chopped
1	cup sugar peas
1	cup fava beans
	salt and pepper to taste
	sliced almonds

In skillet add olive oil, onion and garlic, cook over medium heat until tender. Add broth and squash, cook about 5 minutes.

Add remaining vegetables, cook covered until all is tender, adding more broth if needed. Stir in salt and pepper, sprinkle with parsley. Top with almonds.

Fresh Peas and Lettuce

Serves 4

1/2	head iceberg or romaine lettuce coarsely shredded
4	cups peas, fresh
8	green onions, white part, chopped
1/4	cup Marsala or Sciabica Olive Oil
	salt, white pepper and paprika to taste
1/2	cup wine, white or water
1/4	cup parsley, chopped (or mint)

In large skillet add olive oil, lettuce and onios. Place peas on top, add wine, parsley, salt, pepper and paprika. Cover, cook over low heat about 25 minutes or until all is crisp tender.

> ### Health benefit
> Cut sugar cravings with almonds. They're a good source of manganese, an essential mineral that stabilizes blood glucose and insulin levels to suppress the craving for sweet treats.

Cassoulet

Serves 6 to 8

1/2	pound beans, dry, white
3	cups water
2	onions, chopped
4	garlic cloves, chopped
1	cup celery or fennel bulb chopped
2	bay leaves, remove before serving
1/2	teaspoon cloves
1/2	cup basil and or parsley
2	cups tomatoes, stewed
1/4	pound sausage, cooked, sliced thin
	salt, pepper and cayenne to taste
4	duck or chicken legs, boneless, skinless and fat removed
4	tablespoons tomato paste
1/2	cup Marsala or Sciabica's olive oil
2 or 3	slices Italian or French bread cubed

> **Health benefit**
>
> Boost your immunity with beans. Legumes are a good source of manganese, a mineral that keeps colds at bay.

Pick beans over, rinse, place in large pot with water. Cover, soak overnight. Next day cook beans simmering until tender.

In a nonstick skillet add olive oil, onions, garlic and celery, cook until crisp tender over medium heat.

Preheat oven to 350 degrees. In a 4 or 5 quart casserole add drained beans, sautéed vegetables, tomato paste, meats and remaining ingredients.

Bake covered with foil for about 30 minutes or until bubbly. Uncover, spread bread cubes over cassoulet evenly, bake another 5 minutes until croutons are golden. Garnish with fresh sage leaves if desired.

Variation:

2	ounce prosciutto or ham, chopped
1	cup carrot chopped
4 to 6	juniper berries
2	tablespoons thyme, fresh (or rosemary)
	lamb, cubed (or meat of your choice)
	loin of pork, cubed
1	teaspoon cinnamon
1/2	teaspoon nutmeg
1	cup beef or chicken stock
	substitute 2 (16 ounce) cans cannellini, beans, drained for dry beans

> **Rosemary improves memory**
>
> Rosemary is rich in the volatile oils borneol, camphor, limonene and rosemaricene, all of which help boost oxygen delivery to the brain, improving memory retention.

Steamed Corn

Serves 4

4	ears fresh corn
1	teaspoon garlic, minced (or to taste)
	basil, rosemary, parsley, mint or herb of your choice, chopped
2	tablespoons Marsala Olive Oil
	salt and pepper to taste
1/4	cup water
	Marsala Mayonnaise to taste

In a large skillet add olive oil, garlic, herbs, salt, pepper and water.

Cover skillet bring to a boil, lower to simmer. Cook corn about 6 to 8 minutes, depending on size.

Turn corn several times to cook evenly.

To serve – brush corn lightly with Marsala mayonnaise.

Diane likes to sprinkle hot pico powder (cut with salt) onto the mayonnaise.

Sarah's Zucchini

Serves 4

1	onion, chopped
3	cups zucchini, sliced (or any squash)
1-1/2	cups fresh or canned tomatoes, chopped
2	tablespoons tomato paste
1/2	cup fresh basil, chopped
	pepper to taste
1/4	cup Marsala Olive Fruit Oil
4	thin slices Velveeta cheese (or to taste)

In large skillet add oil and onion. Cook covered until tender over medium heat.

Add zucchini, cover, cook until crisp tender, 1 to 2 minutes, covered.

Stir in tomatoes, tomato paste and pepper, cook another 1 or 2 minutes, covered.

When vegetables are tender, turn off heat, place cheese slices on top evenly.

Cover again to allow cheese to melt through.

May be served over cooked pasta.

Variation:

1	cup mini meatballs
2	eggs lightly beaten; stir in before adding cheese.

One of grandsons Joseph and Jonathan's favorite vegetable.

Artichoke Pg 203 ~ Lemon Oil Pg 204 ~ Pesto Sauce with Pine Nuts Pg 244

Oil and Vinegar Dressing

Makes about 1-1/4 cups

1/3   **cup wine vinegar**
3/4   **cup Marsala Olive Oil**
         salt, pepper and paprika to taste

Stir all ingredients in mixing bowl, keep refrigerated in covered container until ready to use.

Variation in amount desired:

Add Blue, Gorgonzola or Roquefort cheese, crumbled
herbs of your choice
Dijon mustard
capers
grated peel of 1 lemon
garlic or shallots, minced
soy sauce
pomegranate, orange or pineapple juice

Bechamel Sauce

Makes about 4 cups

1/2	cup flour
1/2	cup Marsala Olive Fruit Oil
1/2	cup shallots, minced (or onions)
4	cups milk, non fat
1/4	teaspoon nutmeg or cardamom
2	bay leaves
	salt and white pepper to taste
4	tablespoons Romano cheese, grated

In saucepan add oil and shallots, cook until tender over medium heat.

Add flour, stir until smooth, cook about 1 minute.

Gradually stir in milk, bring to a boil stirring constantly. Add bay leaves, reduce heat.

Simmer until thickened, stirring often, about 2 or 3 minutes, add cheese, nutmeg, salt and pepper.

Remove bay leaves before serving.

Variation:

1/2	teaspoon prepared mustard
1/2	teaspoon Worcestershire sauce

For thinner sauce, use 1/3 cup flour and 1/3 cup olive oil.

Corn Salsa

Serves 4 to 6

3	cups fresh, frozen or canned corn, cooked
2	roasted red peppers, peeled, chopped
4	tomatoes, chopped
4	green onions (white part) chopped
4	garlic cloves, minced
1 or 2	jalapeno peppers, minced
1/2	cup lime or lemon juice
1/2	cup fresh basil, parsley or mint, chopped
	add salt, pepper and paprika to taste
1	cup olives, sliced
1/2	cup Marsala Olive Fruit Oil
1	tablespoon black or regular sesame seeds
1	cup tiny shrimp, cooked

In serving bowl combine all ingredients, toss gently.

Keep refrigerated until ready to serve.

Chunky Tomato Gravy

Makes about 1-1/2 quarts

1/4	cup wine or vermouth
1/4	cup Marsala Olive Fruit Oil
1	onion, chopped
5 to 6	cups fresh or canned tomato, chopped
3	ounces tomato paste
	salt, pepper and hot pepper flakes to taste
2	teaspoons fennel seeds
1/2	cup fresh basil or parsley, chopped

In saucepan add oil and onion, cook until soft, over medium heat.

Add wine, cook 2 minutes. Add remaining ingredients except basil.

Simmer 20 to 30 minutes, covered. *(Do not over cook tomatoes in order to keep as much nutrients in as possible.)*

Add basil, simmer about 5 minutes. (This gravy will not be like strained baby food.)

Variation:

1-1/2	cups mushrooms, quartered or sliced, add along with the basil
1	jalapeño pepper, minced
1/2	fresh fennel bulb, chopped, cooked along with onions
1-1/2	cups fresh or frozen artichoke hearts, chopped
1-1/2	cups asparagus cooked crisp tender, add last 5 minutes of cooking
1	6 or 7 ounce can of water packed tuna
3/4	cup red or yellow dried tomatoes, chopped or snipped with scissors

Note: 1/2 pound of lean pork, beef, veal or meat of your choice, cooked well, may be added to gravy. Cook simmering about 20 minutes.

Asparagus lowers heart-disease risk
Asparagus is a good source of folate, known for its ability to prevent birth defects and lower levels of the blood chemical homocysteine - a leading risk factor for heart disease.

Guacamole

Makes 3-1/2 Cups

1	tablespoon fresh coriander, basil or cilantro, chopped
4	avocados (ripe, soft)
1	tomato, chopped
1	jalapeno, minced
	juice of 1 lime or lemon
	salt, pepper and paprika to taste
1/4	cup Marsala Olive Fruit Oil
2	green onions (white part) minced
2	garlic gloves, minced
1/4	teaspoon cumin

With fork, coarsely mash avocado with lime juice and garlic.

Stir in remaining ingredients, blend.

Garnish as desired. Serve with slice toasted bread quartered or tortilla chips.

Serving suggestion:

Add a spoonful on individual servings of chili.

Spoon onto grilled mushroom caps, top on baked potatoes, grilled chicken or fish, top on omelets or cooked pasta dishes.

Variation:

1	teaspoon chile powder
	dash of tabasco
1/2	teaspoon Worcestershire Sauce
1/4	cup chili peppers, minced
2	hard cooked eggs (yolks removed if desired) chopped
1/2	teaspoon cayenne
1	anchovy, rinsed, minced
1/4	cup olives, pimiento stuffed, chopped small
1/4	cup cucumber, finely chopped
1/2	teaspoon oregano or ginger
1/2	cup nuts of your choice, finely chopped

Italian Dressing

Makes about 1-1/4 cups

2	drops hot pepper sauce
2	garlic cloves
1	teaspoon oregano
3/4	cup Marsala Olive Fruit Oil
1/2	cup vinegar or lemon juice
1	teaspoon paprika
2	green onions (white part)
	salt and pepper to taste

Place all ingredients in jar of blender. Cover and process to blend until well mixed.

Mango Salsa

Makes about 2-1/2 cups

2	mangos, diced
4	green onions (white part) sliced thin
2	kiwifruit, sliced
1	papaya, diced
1/4	cup fresh cilantro, basil or mint, minced
2	tablespoons lime or lemon juice
1	jalapeño pepper, minced
2	tablespoons pure maple syrup or honey
2	tablespoons Marsala Olive Fruit Oil
	salt to taste

Combine all above ingredients in mixing bowl, refrigerate until ready to serve.

Variation:

2	cups pineapple tidbits or crushed
2	tangerines, grapefruits or oranges in segments
1	avocado diced

It's **_so_** good for you
Mangoes are an excellent source of beta carotene, a compound that our bodies convert to vitamin A, which prevents vision problems.

Lena's Matarocco

Makes about 4-1/2 cups

4	garlic cloves, minced
4	cups tomatoes, peeled, chopped
	oregano to taste
1/3	cup Marsala Olive Fruit Oil
	salt and pepper to taste
1/2	cup fresh basil leaves, chopped fine

In mixing bowl, combine all ingredients. Serve as a sauce over grilled meats.

Several tablespoons of sauce may be spooned over meats, last few minutes of cooking.

This was a favorite in cousin Lena's family.

Salsa Verde

(Green Sauce)

Makes 2 to 3 cups

2	green tomatoes with pink blush, chopped
2	tablespoons honey
1	bell pepper, minced
1	tablespoon capers
1	cucumber, chopped small
3	hard cooked eggs (yolks removed if desired)
1/2	cup Marsala Olive Fruit Oil
1/4	cup lime, lemon juice or white vinegar
	salt, pepper and paprika to taste
2	garlic cloves (or to taste) minced
1	cup zucchini, shredded
1/2	cup green olives, chopped
2	green onions, chopped
1	jalapeño pepper, minced
1	avocado, diced
1	cup artichoke hearts, chopped
	dried dill, tarragon, parsley, mint, chives or rosemary to taste

Combine all ingredients, stir well, cover and refrigerate until ready to serve.

Serve with meats, poultry or fish.

Goes well with boiled meats.

Variation:

2	tomatillos, chopped

Loose Hamburger Gravy

Makes about 2 quarts

1	recipe for Chunky Tomato Gravy
2	bay leaves
1/2	pound lean lamb, turkey, veal or pork, ground
2	garlic cloves, chopped
1/4	cup Marsala Olive Fruit Oil
2	red bell peppers, chopped small

Crumble meat with fork.

In skillet over medium heat add olive oil and meat. Cook until browned.

Add peppers, garlic and bay leaves, cook until peppers are soft.

Add meat mixture to chunky tomato gravy, cook about 10 to 15 minutes.

Remove bay leaves before serving.

Serve over cooked rice, vegetables, pasta, couscous, polenta, semolina, whole wheat, toast or pizza dough.

Basil Mayonnaise Dressing

Makes about 1-1/3 cups

1/2	avocado
1	tablespoon lemon juice
1/4	cup parsley
1	cup fresh basil
1/4	cup Marsala Olive Fruit Oil
1	tablespoon vinegar
1	teaspoon honey
1	teaspoon dry mustard
	salt and pepper to taste
	pinch of cayenne
1	egg (or 2 egg whites)
3/4	cup Marsala Olive Fruit Oil

> ### Health benefit
> Give bad cholesterol the slip with olive oil. Research shows that regular consumption of olive oil reduces levels of bad cholesterol (LDL) in the body.

Blend all ingredients (except 3/4 cup olive oil) in jar of blender or food processor.

Slowly pour in 3/4 cup olive oil in a steady stream into mixture.

Continue blending until mixed and thickened.

Marsala Basil Mayonnaise

Makes about 2 cups

1	teaspoon dry mustard
1	tablespoon vinegar
2	egg yolks (or 1 egg)
1	tablespoon lemon juice
1	cup fresh basil leaves, packed
1-1/2	cups Marsala Olive Oil
3/4	teaspoon salt
1/4	teaspoon white pepper
1/4	teaspoon cayenne
1	garlic clove

> ### Health benefit
>
> Herbalists say basil soothes the lining of the digestive tract, making it a natural cure for nausea and stomach cramps. And, by stimulating the body to produce disease-fighting antibodies, basil boosts the immune system .

In jar of blender, add 2 tablespoons olive oil, yolks, vinegar, lemon juice, salt, pepper and cayenne.

Blend on high speed 5 seconds, add garlic, whirl another 5 seconds.

With motor running, add half the oil very slowly. Add basil leaves together with remaining oil slowly until thick and smooth.

If necessary turn blender occasionally, clean sides with rubber spatula.

Place in covered glass container, keep refrigerated.

Serve in sandwiches, with meats, vegetables, fish and in salads.

Caramelized Onions
(Marmellata di Cipolle)

1/2	cup raisins, golden
	grated peel of 1 lemon
4 to 6	onions, sliced lengthwise into 1/4 inch thick
	salt, pepper and cayenne to taste
1/3	cup white wine or left over champagne
1/4	cup Marsala Olive Oil
4 to 6	garlic cloves (or to taste) minced

In large non stick skillet, over medium heat cook onions and garlic in olive oil, covered, until softened and golden.

Stir often; add salt, peppers and wine. For golden brown color, cook uncovered until caramelized.

Add raisins and lemon peel, cook a few more seconds.

Serve on pizza, in sandwiches, salads, with meats or fish dished.

Variation:

1-1/2	cups mushrooms, sliced
1	bell pepper, sliced thin lengthwise
1	tablespoon fresh rosemary (or to taste) chopped
1/4	cup fresh basil or parsley, chopped
2	tablespoons capers

Marsala Mayonnaise

Makes about 1-1/2 cups

2   egg yolks (or 1 egg)
1/2   teaspoon dry mustard
1/2   teaspoon salt
1/8   teaspoon cayenne pepper or paprika
1   tablespoon fresh lemon juice
1   tablespoon white wine vinegar
1-1/2 cups Marsala Olive Fruit Oil

In jar of blender add egg, salt, vinegar, cayenne, egg, lemon juice and 1/4 cup olive oil. Cover, turn blender on low speed. Uncover, pour in remaining oil in a slow steady stream.

Blend until thickened, place in a covered glass container. Refrigerate until ready to use.

Mayonnaise

(no cholesterol)

Follow recipe for mayonnaise.

Substitute 2 egg whites for 1 egg.

Red Pepper Mayonnaise

Add 1/2 cup roasted red pepper, well drained before adding olive oil.

Orange Mayonnaise

Add 2 tablespoons frozen orange juice concentrate, thawed (or juice of your choice).

Variation:

2   tablespoons pineapple frozen juice concentrate or any juice desired

Mini Meatball Gravy

Makes about 8 cups

Mini Meatballs

1	cup milk (non fat) or water
1/4	cup pine nuts
1/2	cup wine
1/4	cup Marsala Olive Fruit Oil
3/4	pound lean turkey or veal, ground
3/4	pound lean beef or pork
1	cup provolone (or to taste) shredded
1	egg and 1 egg white
2 to 3	slices Italian or French bread
1/2	cup Romano cheese, grated
	pepper and red hot pepper flakes to taste
4 to 6	garlic cloves, minced
1/2	cup fresh basil, parsley or cilantro, chopped
2 to 4	green onions (white part) chopped small
2	teaspoons fennel seeds
1/2	cup currants, raisins or dried blueberries

1/2 to 3/4 cup flour to coat meatballs

In mixing bowl soak bread in milk for about 15 minutes. Squeeze bread, removing as much moisture as possible, crumble.

Combine bread and remaining ingredients in mixing bowl, working lightly.

Roll meatballs into size of a large olive, avoid pressing too tightly.

Place flour on cookie sheet evenly, drop meatballs on top. Roll meatballs in flour, coating all around, remove excess.

Cook meatballs in a non stick skillet with olive oil, over medium heat, until browned all around. Do not crowd; may have to be cooked in 2 batches.

Gravy

5 to 6	cups fresh or canned tomatoes, chopped
1/2	cup wine or vermouth
1	large onion, chopped
1	cup fresh fennel bulb, chopped
1/4	cup Marsala Olive Fruit Oil
	salt, pepper and red hot pepper flakes (to taste)
1	6-ounce can tomato paste
2	teaspoon fennel seeds
1/2	cup fresh basil or parsley, chopped
1-1/2	cups fresh mushrooms, sliced
1/2	cup dried tomatoes, chopped small

Continued

In saucepan add oil, onion and fennel, cook over medium heat until tender.

Add wine, cook 1 minutes. Add tomatoes, tomato paste, salt, peppers and fennel seeds. Cook about 25 minutes.

Add mushrooms, basil and cooked meatballs, simmer another 8 to 10 minutes.

Serve over cooked pasta, polenta, couscous or whole wheat.

Note: Meatballs may be baked in a 400 degrees oven on a lightly greased cookie sheet in a single layer.

Drizzle with 2 or 3 tablespoons oil. Bake for about 15 minutes or until browned.

To keep moist, cover loosely with foil.

Variation:

Substitute 1/2 pound Italian sausage, cooked, well drained and sliced for meatballs.

Meat Sauce

Makes about 6 to 8 cups

1	onion, chopped
4 to 6	garlic cloves, chopped
1/3	cup Marsala Olive Fruit Oil
1	carrot, diced
1	bell pepper, chopped
1	cup fresh fennel bulb or celery, diced
4 to 5	cups fresh tomatoes (or canned) chopped
4 to 5	tablespoons tomato paste
1/4	pound turkey or lean beef, ground
1/2	pound Italian sausage cooked, well drained, sliced
1/2	cup wine or vermouth
4 to 6	chicken livers, chopped fine
	salt, pepper and red hot pepper flakes to taste
1-1/2	cups fresh mushrooms, sliced
1/2	cup fresh basil or parsley, chopped
2	teaspoons fennel seeds
2	bay leaves
1/4	pound veal ground or lean pork

In large saucepan, over medium heat add oil and ground meats, cook until beginning to brown.

Add onion, garlic, carrots, fennel and pepper, cook covered until vegetables are tender. Stir occasionally.

Add cooked sausage, livers, wine, salt, peppers, pepper flakes and bay leaves. Cook 1 minute.

Add tomatoes, tomato paste and fennel seeds, simmer about 20 minutes. Add mushrooms and basil, cook another 6 to 8 minutes.

Remove bay leaves. Serve with cooked polenta, pasta, rice, whole wheat or couscous.

Pesto Sauce

Makes about 1-1/2 cups

3/4	cup Marsala Olive Fruit Oil
2	cups fresh basil leaves, packed (or arugula)
4	garlic cloves (or to taste)
1/2	cup fresh parsley, mint or cilantro
	salt, pepper and cayenne to taste
1/4	cup pine nuts, walnuts, macadamia or nuts of your choice
3/4	cup Romano cheese, grated

Combine olive oil, basil leaves, garlic, parsley, nuts, salt and pepper in container of a food processor.

Process until mixture is coarsely blended. Do not over blend.

Transfer mixture into a mixing bowl, stir in cheese.

Pesto may be refrigerated covered with a thin layer of olive oil for several days or when ready to use.

Pesto may be frozen very well but omit cheese. Stir cheese in when thawed.

Pasta with Pesto

Serves 4 to 6

1	pound linguini, tortellini, ravioli or pasta of your choice
1-1/2	cups pesto sauce
1/4	cup pine nuts
	Romano cheese, grated

Cook pasta according to package directions, drain.

Place in a serving platter. Spoon as much pesto sauce on pasta as desired.

Toss gently, sprinkle with additional cheese and pine nuts if desired.

Variation:

Stir into pesto sauce, 1 cup ricotta cheese, 1 cup cubed mozzarella or any soft cheese, and 1 tablespoon grated lime or lemon peel.

1   roasted bell pepper

Pesto Sauce with Tomato

Add 1 or 2 fresh tomatoes or 1/3 cup dried tomatoes when blending pesto mixture. Sunflower or pumpkin seeds if desired.

Pasta and Potatoes With Pesto

Serves 4 to 6

12	ounces fettuccine, fusilli or pasta of your choice
2	medium potatoes, peeled, diced in about 1/2 inch cubes

Cook pasta and potatoes until tender in boiling water, drain.

Transfer pasta and potatoes to large serving platter or bowl.

Add pesto, toss gently.

Roasted Tomatoes

Serves 4

1/4   **cup Marsala Olive Oil**
1   **onion, chopped**
6   **garlic cloves, sliced thin**
1/2   **cup fresh basil, chopped**
12 to 14 tomatoes, plum (peeled) sliced 1/2 inch thick
        salt and pepper to taste

Lightly grease a large nonreactive baking pan. Add olive oil, basil, onion and garlic.

Gently squeeze tomatoes to release excess juices, place over onion mixture in a single layer.

Drizzle with olive oil evenly, sprinkle with salt and pepper.

Bake in a 250 degrees oven for about 5 to 6 hours.

Serve hot or cold on grilled bread, in calzoni, pizza topping, grilled eggplant slices, or in sandwiches.

Variation:

2   **tablespoons fresh parsley, rosemary, mint, cilantro, chives or sage**

Yellow Tomato Salsa

Makes about 4 cups

4   **yellow tomatoes, chopped**
1   **yellow bell pepper, minced**
1   **yellow zucchini, shredded**
4   **garlic cloves, minced**
2   **green onions (white part) sliced thin**
1/4   **cup lime, lemon or grapefruit juice**
1/4   **cup fresh fennel bulb, sliced thin or diced**
1/3   **cup Marsala Olive Oil**
1   **chili pepper, minced**
1   **carrot, shredded**
1   **mango or papaya, diced**
1/3   **cup pineapple, tangerine or orange juice**
        salt to taste

Combine all ingredients in mixing bowl, toss gently, refrigerate until ready to serve.

Serve with meats, fish or cooked grains.

Spanish Omelet Sauce

Makes 3-1/2 to 4 cups

2	bell peppers, red, green or yellow
1	onion, sliced
1/4	cup Marsala Olive Fruit Oil
2	cups fresh or canned tomatoes, chopped
	salt, pepper and cayenne to taste
1/3	cup fresh basil or parsley, chopped
2	bay leaves
1/4	teaspoon cloves
1-1/2	cups mushrooms, sliced
3/4	cup olives, sliced
1/4	cup vermouth

In large skillet, over medium heat add onions and peppers. Cook until crisp tender.

Add vermouth and tomatoes, cook about 5 minutes.

Add remaining ingredients, simmer 10 to 12 minutes or until vegetables are tender.

Remove bay leaves before serving.

For omelet, place some sauce on one side, fold over, pour more sauce on top and around.

Sauce may be served on cooked rice, couscous, pasta or polenta.

Variation:

1	teaspoon Worcestershire sauce
1	cup Italian sausage, cooked, well drained, crumbled
1	cup potatoes, cooked, dried
1	cup mozzarella, shredded
1/3	cup Romano cheese, shredded
2	garlic cloves, minced

Taramasalata

Makes 2 cups dip

	milk or water
2	slices white bread, crusts removed
4	ounce jar tarma (carp roe)
1/4	cup lemon juice
1/4	cup onion, minced
1	cup Marsala Olive Oil
2	garlic cloves
	parsley, minced
	crackers bread or sesame crackers

Health benefit

The mono-unsaturated fat found in olives and olive oil increases blood levels of HDL (good) cholesterol, which helps reduce the levels of artery-clogging LDL (bad) cholesterol in the body.

In mixing bowl moisten bread in milk or water. Press out any excess moisture. Place bread, lemon juice, tarama, garlic and onion in jar of blender, whirl until smooth. Gradually pour in olive oil, blending until thick and creamy. Pour into serving bowl, chill.

To serve, sprinkle with parsley. Serve with cracker bread or sesame crackers. May also be served on meats, fish or vegetables.

Marinating Sauce

Makes about 2-1/2 cups

1	teaspoon fennel seeds, ground
1/3	cup lime or lemon juice
1/2	cup Marsala Olive Oil
1/2	cup orange juice
1/2	cup parsley, basil or cilantro chopped
4	garlic cloves (or to taste) minced
	grated peel each of 1 orange, lemon, and lime
1	teaspoon oregano and/or cumin
	salt, pepper and cayenne to taste
1/2	teaspoon turmeric, mustard or ginger
1/4	cup honey or pure maple syrup
1/4	cup peanut butter

Stir all ingredients in mixing bowl, blend well. Marinate meats, fish or vegetables for 1 hour or time desired.

Aioli Sauce

Makes about 1-1/4 Cups

6	garlic cloves
1	egg (or 2 egg whites)
3/4	cup Marsala Olive Fruit Oil
1/4	cup lime or lemon juice
	Salt and pepper to taste
1/4	cup almonds, ground
2	slices bread, crusts removed
1-1/2	teaspoon Dijon mustard
1/4	teaspoon ginger
1/2	cup fresh basil

> **Stave off headaches with ginger**
> This savory Asian staple may prevent migraines by blocking prostaglandins, compounds that cause blood vessel inflammation.

In blender or food processor add all ingredients except oil, process until smooth.

With blender running slowly pour in olive oil in a thin steady stream.

Pour into serving bowl, refrigerate until ready to serve.

Chunky Avocado Salsa

Makes about 3 cups

2	avocados, diced
1/4	cup Marsala Olive Oil
1/4	cup lime or lemon juice
2	tomatoes, chopped
1/4	cup fresh cilantro, parsley, mint or basil, chopped
1	jalapeno, minced
1	cup olives, pimiento, sliced
4	green onions (white part) sliced thin
1/4	cup dried tomatoes, crumbled
2	radishes, chopped
2	cilantro sprigs

> **Get a youthful glow by eating avocados.**
> Recent research shows this guacamole goody is the highest fruit source of vitamin E, an antioxidant that strengthens cells and may slow down the aging process.

In serving dish, combine all ingredients, keep refrigerated until ready to serve.

Garnish with sprigs of cilantro.

Food Pyramid

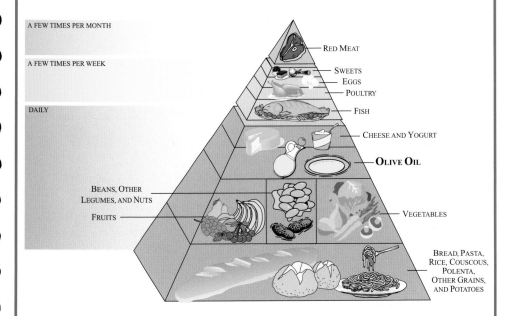

A FEW TIMES PER MONTH

A FEW TIMES PER WEEK

DAILY

RED MEAT

SWEETS
EGGS
POULTRY

FISH

CHEESE AND YOGURT

OLIVE OIL

BEANS, OTHER
LEGUMES, AND NUTS

FRUITS

VEGETABLES

BREAD, PASTA,
RICE, COUSCOUS,
POLENTA,
OTHER GRAINS,
AND POTATOES

Refried Beans
(Frijoles Refritos)
Serves 4

2	**cups dried beans of your choice, cooked, mashed**
1	**onion, chopped**
4	**garlic cloves, minced**
1/4	**cup Marsala Olive Oil**
	salt, pepper and cayenne to taste
1	**cup Monterey Jack, Cheddar or Swiss cheese, shredded**

Mash beans with potato masher.

In large non stick skillet, cook onion and garlic in olive oil until soft.

Add beans, salt, pepper and cayenne. Cook until desired consistency, adding more cooking liquid from beans, if needed.

Stir frequently. Serve with cheese and corn chips if desired.

Variation:

1/2	**cup fresh basil, cilantro or parsley, chopped**
	chili powder to taste
1/2	**teaspoon allspice, cinnamon, dry mustard or**

Worcestershire sauce

Chili Con Carne

Serves 6 to 8

1-1/2	cups dried beans or chick peas
4 to 6	cloves garlic, chopped
1	large onion, chopped
	salt, pepper and hot red pepper flakes (to taste)
1/3	cup Marsala Olive Fruit Oil
1/2	pound lean beef, ground or cut into small pieces
3	cups tomatoes, fresh or canned, chopped
4	tablespoons tomato paste
1/2	teaspoon dry mustard, cumin or paprika
1	teaspoon chili powder (or to taste)
1-1/2	cups cheddar cheese, shredded (or shaved)
3/4	cup red wine or beer
1/2	cup fresh basil, parsley or cilantro, chopped

Pick over beans and rinse. In Dutch oven, soak beans overnight covered with cold water.

Next morning bring beans and water to a boil, lower to simmer, cook until tender.

In large skillet add oil, onion, garlic and meat. Cook until meat is browned, add wine.

Add remaining ingredients (except cheese) and cook about 20 minutes. Pour into cooked beans, simmer about 10 minutes.

Serve with cheese.

Variation for Vegetable:

1	bell pepper, chopped (or carrots)
1	cup celery, chopped
1-1/2	cups lentils, cooked (or 2 potatoes, cubed)
1	cup corn

Variation for Meat:

Substitute veal, pork, turkey, chicken, ham, rabbit or meat of your choice for beef.

Mole Chili

Add 1/2 ounce unsweetened chocolate melted, 1/4 cup nuts, chopped, 2 tablespoons sesame seeds toasted, 1 teaspoon pumpkin pie spice and 1/3 cup golden raisins.

Variation for Dried Beans:

pinto
Great Northern
baby or large Lima
red kidney
pink

Corn Crepes

Makes about 20

1	cup milk, non fat
3	eggs (or 6 egg whites)
3/4	cup flour
3/4	cup corn meal
1/2	cup whole wheat flour
1/2	teaspoon salt
1	tablespoon Marsala Olive Fruit Oil

Place all ingredients in jar of blender or food processor, blend.

Lightly oil nonstick skillet, place over medium heat.

For each crepe, pour scant 1/4 cup batter into 7 inch skillet, tilting to coat bottom evenly.

Cook 1 to 2 minutes on each side or until golden.

Note: Stir batter occasionally, cornmeal has a tendency to sink.

Hope's Taco Shells

Makes 16

2	cups "Maseca" instant corn masa mix
1-1/2	cups water, lukewarm (more if needed)
1/2	teaspoon salt

In mixing bowl combine corn mix, water and salt, stir until dough holds together.

If dough feels too dry add 1 or 2 more tablespoons water, Knead until dough forms a firm ball. Cover, let rest 30 minutes.

Divide dough into 16 pieces, roll into balls. Cover with clean damp towel to keep dough moist.

Flatten dough between hands, place between two sheets of plastic wrap or waxed paper.

Roll out or press in a tortilla press until tacos measure 5 to 6 inches in diameter.

Carefully peel off paper. On medium heat in a non stick skillet or griddle, cook about 30 seconds, turn, cook second side for 30 seconds.

To keep tacos soft and pliable, keep in covered container. (If too dry tacos will crumble.)

To crisp tacos, heat shells on both sides in a little olive oil, in a non stick skillet.

Empanadas
(Meat Turnovers)
Makes about 20

1 recipe for pizza dough

Filling
(Picadillo)

1/2	cup bell pepper, chopped
1/4	teaspoon cinnamon or cumin
1/2	pound turkey, beef, pork or veal, ground
1	small onion
4	garlic cloves, minced
	salt, pepper and red hot pepper flakes to taste
1/3	cup raisins, golden
1/4	cup pine nuts or almonds, ground
1/3	cup olives, chopped
1	tomato, chopped
1/2	cup Cheddar cheese or provolone, shredded
2	tablespoons sherry
1/4	cup fresh basil or cilantro, chopped
1/4	cup Marsala Olive Oil
1	egg white lightly beaten (to brush tops)

In large non stick skillet add oil and onion, cook over medium heat until soft.

Add meat and garlic, cook until browned, remove from heat, cool.

In mixing bowl add meat mixture and remaining ingredients, stir to blend.

Preheat oven to 375 degrees, lightly grease 2 baking sheets.

Roll dough out to about 1/8 inch thick. Cut into 5 inch circles with cookie cutter.

Gather trimmings into a ball, reroll.

Place rounded teaspoon of filling on each half of dough round. Brush edges with egg white.

Fold dough over filling, press edges with tines of fork to seal well.

Place on baking sheets, brush with egg white, perforate tops with tines of fork.

Bake 15 to 20 minutes or until deep golden. Cool slightly, serve warm, with guacamole or salsa.

Variation:

Substitute roast beef, cooked and diced for ground meat

Substitute salmon, tuna (cubed), clams, mussels or scallops for meat

Continued

Empanadas
Variation for filling:
2	tablespoons Marsala Olive Oil
1-1/2	cups potatoes, cooked, mashed
1/2	cup ricotta
1	egg
1/4	cup Romano cheese, grated
	pepper, cumin or chili to taste
1/2	cup spinach, cooked, drained, chopped
1	cup mushrooms, chopped small
1/3	cup cilantro, basil or parsley, chopped
2	hard cooked eggs, minced

Cook mushrooms with olive oil in small skillet.

Combine all ingredients in mixing bowl, stir to mix well. Proceed with recipe.

Variation for dough:
Cornmeal Pastry
Makes about 12

1-1/4	cups flour
1/2	cup cornmeal
1-1/2	teaspoon baking powder
1/2	teaspoon salt
1/4	cup Marsala Olive Oil
1/2	cup milk
1	egg white
1	teaspoon cumin or caraway seeds
1	egg yolk beaten with 2 tablespoons water (for brushing)

In mixing bowl combine dry ingredients.

Make well in center, add remaining ingredients, except egg yolk.
Stir until dough holds together.

Gather dough into a ball, wrap in plastic, refrigerate for 1 hour.

Roll dough out onto floured board to about 1/8 inch thick.

Cut into 4 inch rounds (or desired size). Spoon 1 tablespoon filling slightly off center on dough.

Moisten edges with egg yolk mixture, fold over, seal with tines of fork.

Brush tops with egg mixture, sprinkle with caraway seeds if desired. Proceed with recipe.

Other Fillings: Empanadas may be dessert also, dried figs, ricotta, cinnamon, sugar, flavoring, pineapple preserve, guava or quince paste, jam, mincemeat, pumpkin or sweet potatoes, cooked, mashed and sweetened.

Sprinkle tops with sugar before baking if desired.

Notes: Turnovers may be cooked in a small saucepan in heated olive oil until golden brown. (The traditional way.)

Cook 2 or 3 at a time (do not crowd) watch carefully that they do not open.

Dough may be cut in different shapes. Circles folded into half moons; squares into triangles or cut two rounds of dough, fill and seal together.

Hope's Chili Colorado

Serves 6

1   **pound pork butt**
1   **teaspoon salt (or to taste)**

In sauce pot cover pork with water, add salt, bring to a boil.

Simmer about 30 minutes, remove from water, cool.

Cut into 1/2 inch cubes. (Save broth for another use.) Place in refrigerator, remove hardened fat.

Sauce

     pork cubes
6   **green onions, chopped**
6   **garlic cloves, minced**
2   **teaspoons red chili powder**
1/4   **cup Marsala Olive Oil**
1/4   **teaspoon cumin**
     salt and pepper to taste

In skillet saute meat, onions and garlic with olive oil. Add cumin and chili powder.

Thicken sauce with 1 cup meat broth (from cooked pork) and 1/4 cup masa mix.

Stir until smooth, simmer about 10 minutes, add salt and pepper.

Berry Breakfast Burritos

Serves 4

4   **flour tortillas (7 to 9 inch)**
1   **cup ricotta, low fat**
2   **cups blueberries or berries of your choice**
1   **teaspoon vanilla or orange extract**
1/4   **teaspoon cardamom or cinnamon**
1/4   **cup confectioners' sugar**
4   **tablespoons pure maple syrup**

> Boost your brainpower with raspberries
>
> The pop-in-your-mouth pretties contain anthocyanins, antioxidants that enhance memory.

In mixing bowl combine all ingredients except syrup.

Spread tortilla equally with berry mixture.

Fold opposite sides of each tortilla over filling, roll from one end to seam side down.

Bake in a 350 degrees oven on a lightly greased baking sheet, 8 to 10 minutes. Serve with syrup.

Sloppy Joes

Serves 4

2	celery stalks, sliced thin
1	onion, chopped
2	bell peppers, sliced or cubed
4	garlic cloves, chopped
1/4	cup Marsala Olive Oil
2 to 3	cups tomatoes, fresh or canned, chopped
	salt, pepper and cayenne to taste
1/2	cup fresh basil, cilantro or parsley, chopped
2	ounces tomato paste
1	pound beef, pork or turkey, lean, ground
4	buns or hard rolls

In large non stick skillet add oil, onion garlic and peppers. Cook covered until crisp tender over medium heat.

Crumble ground meat, add to onion mixture in skillet, cook about 10 minutes.

Add tomatoes, tomato paste, salt, pepper, cayenne and basil. Cook about 10 more minutes or until meat is well done.

Cut buns or hard rolls in half lengthwise. Spoon mixture on one half, cover with second half.

Serve with green salad if desired.

Variation:

1/2	cup olives, sliced
1	cup fresh mushrooms, sliced
1	teaspoon chili or cumin
1	cup dried beans, cooked
1/2	teaspoon paprika or fennel seeds
4	chili peppers, chopped

Sloppy Jose's

Serves 4

1	recipe for Sloppy Joes
1	cup corn, whole kernel
4	slices Velveeta or Monterey Jack cheese
2	cups lettuce, shredded
2	avocados, sliced
4	taco shells, heated

Fill taco shells with lettuce, meat mixture, top with cheese, tomato and avocado slices.

Sloppy Joes mixture may be used as pizza topping.

Taco Salad

Serves 4 to 6

1	cup chayote cooked, sliced
1	cup cherry tomatoes (for garnish)
2	cilantro sprigs (for garnish)
2	green onions, sliced thin
1	cup Cheddar or Monterey Jack cheese, shredded
4	tomatoes, chopped
1	onion, chopped
1	small head lettuce, shredded
1/2	bag tortilla chips (corn) 8 ounces
2	avocados, diced
1	pound chicken, turkey, pork or beef, ground
1	cup dried beans, cooked (or corn)
1	cup jicama, shredded
1	cup olives, sliced
1 or 2	jalapeño, minced
1	carrot, shredded
2	garlic cloves, chopped
	pinch of cumin

In large skillet over medium heat brown meat, onions and garlic in olive oil, cool.

In large salad bowl add remaining ingredients, pour dressing over and toss gently. Garnish with cherry tomatoes and cilantro sprigs.

Dressing

1/3	cup Marsala Olive Fruit Oil (or to taste)
2	garlic cloves (or to taste) minced
	pinch cumin (or chili powder)
1/2	cup fresh cilantro or basil
	pinch of oregano
1	teaspoon paprika
1/3	cup lime, lemon juice or vinegar
1	teaspoon tabasco sauce
1	teaspoon taco seasoning mix

Combine all dressing ingredients in jar of blender, whirl until blended.

Pour into glass covered container, keep refrigerated until ready to serve.

Variation:

1	cup celery sliced thin
1	red bell pepper, minced
1/3	cup sunflower seeds
1	cup pineapple tidbits
1/4	pound elbow pasta, cooked, drained, cooled

Tamale Dough
Makes 12 to 16

2   cups instant masa
1   teaspoon baking powder
1-1/2 cups water or broth
1/2   teaspoon salt or to taste
1/4   cup Marsala Olive Fruit Oil

In mixing bowl combine masa, baking powder and salt, make a well in center add oil and 1-1/4 cups water. Stir adding more water if needed until dough holds together.

Tamales with Pork Filling

1/4   cup Marsala Olive Fruit Oil
1   pound lean pork, ground coarsely
1   onion, chopped
2   cloves garlic
2   bay leaves
       salt and pepper to taste
2   California chiles, cut into strips
2   tomatoes
16   Corn husks
1/4   cup parsley or cilantro, chopped

Remove as much fat from meat as possible. In skillet add oil, meat, onion, garlic, chiles, salt and pepper. Cook until tender. Add tomatoes, bay leaves and parsley. Cook about 20 minutes on low heat. Remove bay leaves.

Soak corn husks for 1 hour in hot water, rinse and dry with paper towels. With corn husk point toward you, place a tablespoon of masa dough on large end. Spread, place a tablespoon of pork filling. Spread with another tablespoon dough to cover filling. Fold sides over covering all. Fold pointed end of corn husk under, with seam outside. Place on rack over water in large pot. Cover with additional husks or foil. Bring water to a boil, lower to simmer. Cover and steam about 1 hour, or until filling pulls away from husks.

Tamales with Cheese and Chile

Follow recipe for tamale with pork. Substitute 8 ounces Monterey Jack cheese cut into 12 to 16 cubes and 4 California chiles roasted, peeled and chopped for meat filling. Proceed with recipe.

Variation:

1-1/2 cups cooked and mashed sweet potatoes

Tamale Pie

Serves 4 to 6

1/4	cup Marsala Olive Fruit Oil
	salt, pepper and red hot pepper flakes to taste
1	pound lean turkey, veal or beef, ground
1	onion, chopped
3	bell peppers, chopped
2	cups fresh or canned tomatoes, chopped
3	tablespoons tomato paste
1-1/2	cups fresh, canned or frozen corn
1	cup fresh mushrooms, sliced
1	cup olives, pitted
1/2	cup fresh basil, parsley or cilantro, chopped
6	garlic cloves, chopped
2	jalapeno peppers, minced
1	teaspoon chili powered (if desired)

Cornmeal Crust

1	cup cornmeal
	salt and pepper to taste
2-1/2	cups broth or water
1-1/2	cups milk, non fat
1/4	cup cream of wheat (or semolina)
1	egg (or 2 egg whites)
1	cup Monterey Jack or Cheddar cheese, shredded
1/2	cup Romano cheese, grated

Over medium heat in large skillet add oil and meat, cook until no longer pink. Add onions, peppers and garlic, cook until tender, about 5 minutes.

Add tomatoes, tomato paste, salt, peppers and basil, cook about 20 minutes.

In saucepan combine cornmeal, cream of wheat, salt, pepper, broth, and milk, cook until thick. Stir in egg whites and grated cheese.

Lightly grease a large baking dish, spoon 1/4 corn mush evenly over bottom. Pour in meat mixture, corn, olives, and mushrooms.

Make a border with remaining cornmeal around edge of baking dish, or spread evenly over top.

Bake at 350 degrees for about 40 minutes. Sprinkle with Monterey Jack cheese, bake 2 or 3 minutes longer. Cover with foil if browning too quickly.

Variation:

1	teaspoon chili powder or cumin
1	cup dried beans or peas, cooked

Substitute chicken or pork, (fat removed), cut into bite size pieces for turkey or 1-1/2 cups water packed tuna.

Tortillas

Makes 12 - 8 inch

2   **cups flour**
1/2   **teaspoon salt**
1/4   **cup Marsala Olive Fruit Oil**
1/2   **cup water, warm**

Combine dry ingredients in mixing bowl. Make well in center, add water and oil. Stir until dough holds together.

Knead until smooth on lightly floured board. Let rest covered about 15 minutes.

Divide dough into 12 pieces. Preheat a griddle or a large heavy skillet over medium heat.

Shape dough into 12 even balls, flatten into round patties. Sprinkle both sides with flour.

On lightly floured board, roll each patty into an 8 inch circle. Place each tortilla on preheated griddle.

Cook until bubbles form on top and underside is golden brown. Turn tortilla, cook until bottom is golden brown.

Press down bubbles with clean kitchen towel. Cover tortillas with dry towel.

Serve immediately or wrap in foil and reheat briefly before serving in a 350 degrees oven for about 10 to 12 minutes.

Best eaten directly from the griddle.

Crab Filling for 6 Tortillas

1/4   **cup Marsala Olive Fruit Oil**
1/2   **cup green onions (white part) sliced**
2   **garlic cloves, minced**
8   **ounces crab, cooked (or canned drained)**
1/2   **cup olives, chopped**
1   **cup grapes, seedless**
2   **tablespoons pine nuts**
4   **tablespoons fresh basil or parsley, chopped**
2   **tablespoons capers**
       salt, pepper and paprika to taste
1   **jalapeno, minced**

Heat oil in skillet, add onions and garlic, cook until crisp tender. Stir in remaining ingredients, cook for 4 to 5 minutes.

Filled Roasted Peppers

Serves 4 to 6

3	bell peppers roasted and peeled
1	7 ounce can tuna, water packed
1/4	cup Marsala or Sciabica olive oil
2	tablespoons lemon juice or to taste
4	olives minced
2	garlic cloves minced
1/4	cup basil, mint, parsley or cilantro chopped
1/2	cup celery finely chopped
1	tomato, plum, chopped small
	salt, pepper and paprika to taste
1/4	cup pinenuts

In mixing bowl combine all ingredients. Halve bell pepper, lay cut side up. Divide tuna mixture evenly between halves.

Roll peppers up, place on serving plate. Garnish with basil, mint or cilantro sprigs. Refrigerate until ready to serve. Drizzle with olive oil.

Variation:

goat cheese with ground almonds, pecans or nuts of your choice, tomatoes chopped, onions caramelized.

Broiled Onions

Serves 6

4	onions cut into 1/2 inch slices across
2	tablespoons Marsala Olive Fruit Oil
1/3	cup lime or lemon juice
	salt and white pepper to taste
1/2	cup Romano or provolone cheese shavings
5-6	basil, parsley or mint sprigs
1	tablespoon capers
2	tablespoons pine nuts

Place onion slices on broiling rack in pan. Brush onion slices with olive oil. Broil 4 inches away from broiler until golden brown.

Turn slices, brush second side with olive oil, broil until golden brown.

Place onions on serving dish, drizzle with juice, sprinkle with capers, pine nuts, salt and pepper, top with cheese shavings. Garnish with basil sprigs.

Walnut Tea Cookies Pg 273   ~   Chocolate Sponge Cake Pg 271
(Cocoa or coffee set, was given to my Mom from her brother around 1914.)

Top left clockwise: Fougasse Pg 171, Whoopie Pies Pg 274, Sweet Tarallini Pg 289, Sugar cookies 282

Big Birthday Cake

Makes 24 to 26 slices

12	eggs room temperature
2	cups sugar
2	cups flour
2	teaspoons baking powder
1/2	teaspoon salt (or to taste)
1/3	cup orange juice or water
1/4	cup Marsala Olive Fruit Oil
2	teaspoons vanilla
1/2	teaspoon almond extract
1/4	teaspoon fiori di Sicilia (or 1 teaspoon orange extract)

In large bowl of mixer add egg whites, beat until foamy. Add 1 cup sugar slowly until whites hold stiff peaks.

In another mixing bowl add flour, remaining sugar, salt and baking powder.

Make well in center, add egg yolks, oil, orange juice and flavorings, stir to blend well.

Pour batter into egg whites, using a rubber spatula, fold gently until blended.

Pour into an ungreased 12 by 3 or 4 inches deep cake pan.

Smooth top, bake in a 350 degrees oven for 40 to 45 minutes or until cake springs back when touched gently on center.

Invert cake in pan on edges of 2 coffee cans, **cool completely**.

Gently run a table knife between cake and pan. Pull bottom easily all around until cake is loosened.

Sprinkle with confectioners' sugar, place large serving cake plate over top and invert.

With serrated knife, cut cake in half making 2 layers. On bottom layer drizzle with liqueur, spread with jam evenly.

Cover with filling, place top layer over, cut side down. Sprinkle top with liqueur, spread jam over evenly.

Frost cake sides and top with whipped cream.

Decorate with chocolate curls or any desired decoration. Dust sides with ground nuts evenly.

Continued

Filling

1	quart whipping cream
1	package vanilla pudding (6 servings size)
1-1/2	cups ricotta, low fat
1/3	cup rum, Galliano, creme de cacao or liqueur of your choice
3/4	cup milk chocolate, chopped small
	raspberry, blackberry or jam of your choice, seedless
3/4	cup confectioners' sugar

Cook pudding according to package directions using 1/4 cup less milk, cool.

In large bowl of mixer whip cream with confectioners' sugar and liqueur.

In mixing bowl mash ricotta, stir in cold pudding, blend, add chocolate.

Fold in 1/4 of the whipped cream in pudding mixture gently. Frost sides and top of cake with remaining whipped cream.

Variation:

lemon or chocolate pudding
drizzle cake layers with maraschino syrup instead of liqueur
pineapple, crushed, drained
strawberries or berries of your choice
peaches, bananas or kiwi
for pink cake or frosting, add a few drops of red food coloring
add 2 or 3 tablespoons cocoa to whipping cream
1/4 to 1/2 teaspoon peppermint extract

There are many combinations, but whatever is used, it always makes a hit.

Have made this cake for years, on birthdays and many special occasions.

My friend Millie who gave me the sponge cake recipe would fill her cake with 3 different flavored puddings.
She would cut the cake to make 4 layers, and spread vanilla pudding on one layer, chocolate on second and lemon on third layer.
The cake was then frosted with sweetened whipped cream and served with strawberries. Cake may be decorated as desired.
Millie also made our three tier (fruit) wedding cake. Years ago fruit cakes for weddings were popular.
Terese likes to decorate her cake with cream, strawberries and blueberries, so it will be red, white and blue, colors of our flag.

Chocolate Cream Puffs
Makes 14 to 16

1/2	cup water
1/4	cup Marsala Olive Oil
3/4	cup flour
1/4	teaspoon salt
1	teaspoon vanilla
2	eggs and 1 egg white
1/3	cup currants or raisins
1/2	cup mini chocolate chips or regular milk chocolate chips

> **Defrazzle your day with a dose of chocolate**
> This sweet staple is high in magnesium, an essential mineral proven to calm nerves and alleviate stress.

Lightly grease cookie sheet. In medium saucepan bring water and olive oil to a boil. Stir in flour and salt all at once.

When mixture forms a ball and leaves the side of the pan, remove from heat. Cool 10 minutes, beat in eggs one at a time. Beating after each addition until mixture is smooth. Stir in vanilla, currants and chocolate chips.

Drop by rounded teaspoon, placing mounds two inches apart on baking sheet.

Bake at 400 degrees for 20 minutes, lower heat to 300 degrees, bake another 18 to 20 minutes or until golden brown.

Traditionally these puffs are deep fried. I like to bake them instead.

Variation:
For savory cream puffs, substitute 3/4 cup shredded cheddar or Roquefort cheese and 1/3 cup pecans chopped small for chocolate. May be made smaller, bake shorter time, until golden.

Eclair Cake
Serves 10 to 12

1	recipe for chocolate cream puffs (omit currants & chips)
1/2	cup milk chocolate, melted

Spread batter into a greased 10 x 15 inch jelly roll pan evenly.

Bake in a 400 degrees oven for 20 to 30 minutes, or until golden brown, cool. Spread top with pudding mixture, drizzle with melted chocolate. To serve cut into squares.

Topping

1	package vanilla pudding (6 serving size)
1	cup ricotta
1	cup whipped cream
1/4	cup mini chocolate chips
2 or 3	tablespoons rum or liqueur of your choice
4	maraschino cherries, chopped

In saucepan cook pudding according to package directions, using 1/4 cup less milk, cool.

In mixing bowl mash ricotta with fork, fold in cold pudding. Add rum, cherries and chips. Fold in whipped cream very gently.

Substitute chocolate curls or 3/4 cup lightly toasted coconut for melted milk chocolate. Serve with sweetened berries if desired.

To make chocolate curls, use a vegetable peeler. Chocolate should be at room temperature.

Free Form Cherry Pie

Serves 6 to 8

1   **recipe for single pie crust**
       substitute 1/3 cup cornmeal or almond flour for white flour
1   **egg white lightly beaten (to brush dough)**

Roll dough out to a 13 inch round

Filling:

1/4   **cup cornstarch or tapioca**
1-1/2   **pounds sweet cherries, pitted (apples or plums cut into wedges)**
1/4   **teaspoon almond extract**
3/4   **cup sugar (or taste)**
       pinch of salt

In mixing bowl stir together cornstarch, cherries, almond extract, sugar and salt. Let stand 15 minutes.

Place rolled out dough on to greased cookie sheet or a 10 inch pyrex pie plate. Brush dough with lightly beaten egg white.

Mound cherry mixture over center of dough round, leaving a 2-1/2 inch border all around.

Fold dough border over up around filling pleating evenly, leaving about 4 inches uncovered in center.

Brush milk over top crust, sprinkle with sugar.

Bake in a 400 degrees oven for 45 to 50 minutes or until crust is golden and fruit mixture is gently bubbling.

Cover pie with foil loosely to prevent over-browning.

Variation for filling:

1-1/4   **cup brown sugar**
       grated peel of 1 orange or 1 lemon
3-1/2   **cups rhubarb cut into 1 inch pieces, cooked until soft**
1-1/2   **cups strawberries or blueberries**
1/3   **cup chocolate chips**
1/2   **teaspoon cinnamon**
1/3   **cup macadamia or hazelnuts toasted, ground**

Brush crust with egg white, sprinkle with nuts. Proceed with recipe as for free form cherry pie.

Serve with vanilla low fat ice cream or frozen yogurt.

Note: Fruits of your choice may be substituted for cherries; apricots, apples, gooseberries, peaches, nectarines, berries etc.

Also nuts of your choice, almonds, pistachio, walnuts etc.

Olive Oil Pie Crust

single crust

1-1/3   cups flour
1/2   teaspoon salt
1   teaspoon baking powder
1/3   cup Marsala Olive Oil
4 to 6 tablespoons ice water, milk or white wine

In mixing bowl, combine flour, salt and baking powder, make well in center.

Pour olive oil and water into same measuring cup (do not stir) add all at once to flour.

With fork, stir lightly until well mixed. Form dough into a ball, flatten slightly.

I use plastic pastry gloves to shape dough.

Add a little more liquid if needed to hold dough together.

Cover; chill in refrigerator for about 30 minutes. Lightly flour surface, roll out dough to about 12 inches in diameter.

Gently place dough into bottom of pie plate, trim about 1/2 inch beyond rim of pan, flute edge.

Pierce bottom and sides with tines of fork to prevent puffing while baking.

Bake in a 350 degrees oven for 8 to 10 minutes or until golden.

Finish pie according to each recipe.

Note:

Pastry may be rolled out between 2 pieces of waxed paper.

This dough may be used for tarts or turnovers also.

Olive Oil Pie Crust

double crust

2   cups flour
1   teaspoon salt
1-3/4   teaspoon baking powder
1/2   cup Marsala Olive Oil
1/4   cup water (a little more if needed to hold dough together)

Follow directions for single crust. Divide dough in half, one a little larger than the other.

Larger rolled out pastry goes in bottom of pie pan.

When using top crust, moisten edge with water, place on top crust. Press both crusts together to seal.

Trim about 1/2 inch beyond rim of pan. Flute edges, bake as recipe directs.

Continued

Orange pastry for single crust:
Substitute orange juice for water, and add grated peel of 1 orange.

Lemon pastry for single crust:
Substitute lemon juice for water and add grated peel of 1 lemon.

Cheese pastry for single crust:
1/4 cup ricotta or 1/3 cup Cheddar cheese, shredded.

Chocolate pastry for single crust:
Add 2 to 3 tablespoons cocoa, 2 tablespoons sugar and 1 teaspoon vanilla.

Cornmeal pastry for single crust: add 1/3 cup cornmeal

Other ingredients for crusts:
poppy seeds or seeds of your choice
ground nuts of your choice
spices and herbs of your choice
coconut
1/4 **cup confectioners' sugar**
2 **tablespoons granulated sugar**

> **Health benefit**
> Outsmart clots with chocolate. This delicious confection contains flavonoids, antioxidants that help keep fatty substances from clogging the bloodstream.

Whole Wheat Pastry
Follow directions for double crust recipe, substitute 1 cup whole wheat pastry flour for white flour.

This pastry goes well for vegetable or meat pies and savory turnovers.

Tart Shells
Single crust pastry will make about 10 shells. Cut dough using a 3 inch cookie cutter.

Carefully fit circles in tart pans or muffin cups.

Pierce bottom and sides with tines of fork to prevent puffing up while baking.

Bake in a 350 degrees oven for 10 to 12 minutes or until golden.

Fill with your favorite filling, bake according to recipe's directions.

Notes: Greasing lightly the rim edge of the pie plate before adding the pie crust will make it easier to cut crust from rim edge of a juicy pie.

Brush bottom crust with a little olive oil or lightly beaten egg white before placing in the filling, it should keep it from getting soggy.

Pie Crust Pastry

Makes 1 single crust

1/4	cup almond flour
1-1/3	cups flour
1/4	teaspoon salt
1/4	cup white wine or milk
1/3	cup Marsala Olive Oil
1	teaspoon baking powder
2	tablespoons sugar
1	egg white (or yolk)

In mixing bowl combine dry ingredients, make well in center. Add remaining ingredients, stir until dough holds together.

Gather dough into a ball, flatten slightly, cover, let rest about 15 minutes.

Roll dough out on lightly floured board or between 2 pieces of waxed paper, to about a 12 inch round.

Ease rolled out dough into a 9 or 10 inch pie plate, trim edges and flute.

Use tines of fork to pinch bottom and sides at 1/2 inch intervals. This helps prevent bubbles from forming in the crust.

Bake in a 400 degrees oven for 10 to 12 minutes or until light golden brown, cool. Fill crust with your favorite filling.

Variation:

1/3	cup pecans or nuts of your choice, ground or finely chopped
1/2	teaspoon cinnamon
1/2	teaspoon nutmeg or cardamom
1	tablespoon sesame seeds or seeds of your choice
	grated peel of 1 orange, lemon or lime
1/3	cup coconut

Substitute 1/2 cup cornmeal or whole wheat flour for white flour.

Savory Pie Crust

Add 1 or 2 of the following:

1/3	cup Cheddar, Romano, provolone (or cheese of your choice) shredded
1/2	teaspoon black pepper
1/2	teaspoon oregano or rosemary
1/4	cup fresh basil, parsley or cilantro, minced
1	teaspoon anise, fennel, poppy or caraway seeds

Ravioli Dolci

Makes 10

Dough

1-1/4	cups flour
1	egg white
1	teaspoon baking powder
1/3	cup sugar
1/2	teaspoon salt
3	tablespoons Marsala Olive Oil
	grated peel of 1 orange or lemon
1	teaspoon vanilla
1/4	teaspoon almond extract

Filling

1-1/4	cups ricotta, low fat
1/4	cup confectioners' sugar
1/4	cup milk chocolate chips
1	tablespoon rum or vanilla
1	tablespoon corn starch
1/4	cup maraschino or candied cherries, chopped
1/4	teaspoon fiori di Sicilia (or 1 teaspoon orange extract)

In mixing bowl add dry ingredients, make well in center. Add remaining ingredients, stir until dough holds together. Add 1 tablespoon of milk if needed.

Gather dough into a ball, cover, let rest about 30 minutes.

Combine filling ingredients in mixing bowl, stir until mixed.

Roll dough out onto a floured board to about 1/4 inch thick. Cut into 4 inch circles with cookie cutter.

Place 1 teaspoon filling a little off center. Moisten edges of rounds with water. Fold over forming a semi circle.

Press edges with tines of fork to seal. Place on lightly greased cookie sheet.

Bake in a 350 degrees oven for about 20 minutes or until golden.

Cool, sprinkle with confectioners' sugar.

Variation for filling:

1/2	cup raisins or currants
1/4	cup walnuts, pine nuts or almonds ground
1	ripe pear, diced small
	grated peel of 1 lemon or orange
2	tablespoons honey
2	tablespoons apricot or fig jam
1/4	cup lemon or orange peel, candied, chopped

Traditionally these ravioli are deep fried.

Sponge Cake

Serves 12

6	eggs separated, room temperature
1	cup flour
1	cup sugar
1/2	teaspoon salt
1	teaspoon baking powder
2	tablespoons Marsala Olive Fruit Oil
1/4	cup orange, lemon juice or water
1	teaspoon vanilla
	grated peel of 1 orange or lemon
1/4	teaspoon "fiori di Sicilia" (or 1 teaspoon orange extract)

In large bowl of mixer add egg whites, beat until foamy.

Add 1/2 cup sugar slowly until whites hold stiff peaks

In another bowl add remaining sugar, yolks, orange juice, olive oil, vanilla, fiori di Sicilia and peel.

Stir, add remaining ingredients, blend until smooth.

Fold in egg whites very gently until well mixed. Do no stir.

Pour into a 10 inch ungreased spring form pan about 4 inches deep, or tube pan.

Bake in a 350 degrees oven for 40 to 50 minutes or until top springs back when pressed gently with finger.

Turn pan upside down to cool, placing edges on 2 coffee cans. If baked in tube pan, place over neck of bottle.

When cool, remove from pan, place on cake plate dusted with confectioners' sugar. Drizzle top with lemon glaze.

Lemon Glaze

1/3	cup lemon juice
2/3	cup sugar
1	teaspoon vanilla

Bring sugar and lemon to a boil. Stir until sugar dissolves, cook 1 minute on simmer, stir in vanilla, cool. Drizzle over top of cake.

A good way to serve sponge cake is to soak it with 1/2 cup condensed milk, 1/2 cup evaporated milk, (low fat) 1/4 cup cream and 1 teaspoon vanilla. Stir together in mixing bowl, pour over cake evenly. Cover with meringue if desired.

Continued next page

Variations:

For spice sponge cake: add 2 teaspoons pumpkin pie spice, substitute brown sugar, packed for white sugar.

For hazelnut sponge cake: add 1/2 cup ground hazelnuts, macadamia or pistachio nuts and 1 tablespoon hazelnut liqueur. Serve with apricot jam.

For almond sponge cake: add 1/2 cup almonds, ground. Variation - 1/2 cup bitter almonds or apricot kernels ground and 1 tablespoon Amaretto liqueur.

For lavender sponge cake: substitute 1 teaspoon (unsprayed) lavender ground, for vanilla. Add 1 cup shredded carrots if desired.

For walnut sponge cake: add 1/4 teaspoon black walnut flavoring and 1/2 cup black walnuts or regular walnuts, ground. Add 1 cup shredded zucchini if desired.

For rose geranium sponge cake: place 4 unsprayed, washed and dried geranium leaves on bottom of cake pan. Pour batter over leaves. Remove after baking.

For poppy seed sponge cake: add 1 or 2 tablespoons poppy seeds and 1 teaspoon pure lemon or maple extract.

For coconut sponge cake: add 3/4 cup coconut, lightly toasted and 1/2 teaspoon pineapple extract.

Cut cake in half making 2 layers. Spread with coconut cream filling. Frost with sweetened whipped cream flavored with 1/2 teaspoon coconut flavoring.

For chocolate sponge cake: add 4 tablespoons cocoa (Dutch) sift with dry ingredients and add 2 extra tablespoons sugar.

Serve with pudding, sweetened whipped cream, top with chocolate curls and fresh raspberries if desired.

May be served cut across, spread bottom layer with strawberry jam. Place top layer, cut side down, over jam, sprinkle with confectioners' sugar.

Note: When using fiori di Sicilia, use 1/4 to 1/2 teaspoon for standard recipes. Too much will cause bitterness, keep refrigerated.

Fiori di Sicilia may be purchased from Italian specialty markets.

Note: Sponge cake makes a good base for fruit shortcake

Strawberry Jam

Makes 2 pints

4   **cups strawberries or fresh figs**
4   **cups sugar**
2   **tablespoons lemon juice**

Place strawberries in saucepan. Add 2 cups sugar. Heat and boil hard 5 minutes, stirring constantly.

Add lemon juice and remaining sugar, continue boiling hard, stirring constantly until syrup is ready to jell or is as thick as desired.

Takes from 2 to 20 minutes, depending on pectin in the fruit.

Fast boiling for a short time helps to keep fresh fruit color and flavor.

Pour in shallow dish, stir occasionally while cooling. Let stand overnight.

Spoon into glasses or jars, cover, keep refrigerated.

(Do not double this recipe.)

To test for jelling:

Dip a clean metal spoon in the boiling jam, hold up edgewise. When 2 heavy drops form and slide together at edge of spoon, the jam is ready to jell.

Try a spoonful on a chilled saucer, too. Chill a few minutes to be sure it jells the way you like it.

Variation:

     peaches and orange peel
     apricots with 1/2 cup crushed pineapple, drained berries,
     plums or a mixture of fruits

With fig jam I cook 2 - 2 inch pieces of vanilla bean in jam and when filling jar, put 1 piece in each.

Protect your heart with peaches

Peaches are rich in dietary fiber, which has been shown to lower levels of cholesterol in the bloodstream. For this reason, a fiber-rich diet can lower your risk of heart disease.

Walnut Tea Cookies

Makes 25 to 30

1	cup flour
1/2	teaspoon salt
1/4	cup Marsala Olive Fruit Oil
1	teaspoon vanilla
1/4	teaspoon almond extract
3/4	cup walnuts, ground
2 to 4	tablespoons orange juice
1/2	cup confectioners sugar
3 to 4	drops fiori di Sicilia (or 1 teaspoon orange extract)

In small mixing bowl combine olive oil, 2 tablespoons orange juice and flavorings.

In another mixing bowl add flour, sugar, salt and nuts.

Stir in oil mixture, mix well. Add remaining orange juice if needed.

Press 1 heaping teaspoon of dough into 2 inch long finger shaped rolls.

Squeeze each roll in palm and fingers of one hand to obtain irregular shape.

Place one inch apart on a greased cookie sheet.

Bake in a 350 degrees oven for 15 to 20 minutes or until golden.

Variation:

1/2	teaspoon pure lemon extract
1/2	teaspoon anise flavoring
	substitute pecans, almonds, hazelnuts or nuts of your choice for walnuts.

Note: Should dough become too soft, the irregular shape will not hold very well.

Recipe may be doubled

Tip: When using fiori di Sicilia, use 1/4 to 1/2 teaspoon in a standard recipe. Too much will cause bitterness.

Keep refrigerated.

> ### Health benefit
> Pecans protect the heart in two ways: Their vitamin E content helps lower LDL cholesterol and pecans' alpha-lonolic acid helps keep heartbeat regular.

Fiori di Sicilia may be purchased from Italian speciality stores.

Olive You!

Whoopie Pies

Makes 10

3/4	cup brown sugar, packed
1	cup flour
1/2	teaspoon baking soda
1/4	teaspoon salt
1/4	cup cocoa (Dutch)
1	egg (or 2 egg whites)
3	tablespoons Marsala or Sciabica olive oil
1	teaspoon vanilla
1/3	cup prepared coffee, orange juice or milk
1/2	cup mini chocolate chips
1/2	teaspoon Danish pastry extract (Watkins)
1	7 ounce jar marshmallow creme

Preheat oven to 350° Sift dry ingredients into mixing bowl. With spoon blend in remaining ingredients, except marshmallow, until smooth. On lightly greased baking sheet, drop by teaspoon making 20 mounds, 2 inches apart. (40 mounds if smaller cookies are desired)

Bake about 12 minutes until puffy and cake tester comes out clean cool on wire rack. When cool spread with 1 teaspoon marshmallow cream on flat side of cookie. Top with another cookie, top side up to make 10 sandwiches.

Note: For mini whoopie pies use a demitasse spoon making about 74 mounds. (The flavor of these cookies are close to oreo cookies.)

Variation:

Fill whoopie pies with low fat vanilla ice cream or any filling desired. Serve with strawberries. May be frozen.

1-6 to 7 ounce box chocolate covered thin mints (about 12 - 1-1/2 inch round mints)

While cookie is still warm, place mint patties on cookie, quickly top with another cookie, top side up. Cool completely.

Note: By filling the whoppie pies with marshmallow cream (egg whites, sweetening and flavor) no need to use typical "shortening based" cream filling. Whoopie pies make a good base for shortcake also.

Health benefit
Studies show people who eat chocolate live longer. The phenols in chocolate prevent clogging of the arteries, a known cause of coronary artery disease.

Apple Pie

Serves 8

	double pie crust pastry
3/4	cup brown sugar (or to taste)
1/4	cup tapioca or corn starch
1	teaspoon cinnamon
2	tablespoons lemon juice
6 to 7	cups apples, sliced (or peaches)

Prepare dough for pastry. Combine apples, tapioca, sugar, lemon juice and cinnamon in mixing bowl.

Let stand about 15 minutes to soften tapioca, stir several times. Preheat oven to 350 degrees. Cut dough into 2 pieces.

On lightly floured surface, roll out one piece into an 11 inch circle. Fit it into a 9-inch pie pan.

Spoon apple mixture into pastry lined pie pan. Roll out second piece, place over filling.

Press edges together and flute as desired. Make several slits on top and sprinkle with sugar evenly.

Cover edge with foil. Bake for 45 to 55 minutes or until crust is deep golden, apples are tender and juices are bubbly. Cool, spread with thin frosting if desired.

Variation:

1/3	cup raisins
1/3	cup cranberries
1	cup blueberries or berries of your choice
1	cup quince, sliced thin
1	cup pears or fruit of your choice
1/3	cup pecans, chopped or nuts of your choice

Note:

Pie may be made with free form pastry crust

> ### Prevent swelling with strawberries
> These sweet berries contain phenol, a phytonutrient that eases inflammation.

Apple and Pumpkin Pie

Serves 8

1	teaspoon five spice
3	cups apples diced small (golden delicious)
3 or 4	cups pumpkin, sweet, diced small
1	teaspoon vanilla powder
3/4	cup brown sugar (or to taste)
1/4	cup pecans, chopped small
1/4	teaspoon salt
2	tablespoons Marsala Olive Oil
2	tablespoons lemon juice
1	egg, lightly beaten with 1 tablespoon water (to brush top)

In large non stick skillet add olive oil, pumpkin, apples and lemon juice. Cook covered on low heat until tender.

Add remaining ingredients, cool.

Follow directions for apple pie. Brush top with egg.

Note:

Many times some apples do not cook tender in the pie but the crust is already cooked. Apples may be softened in a microwaveable bowl for 2 or 3 minutes.

Variation For Crust:

1/3	cup sharp cheddar cheese, shredded
1/4	cup almonds, ground or nuts of your choice
1/4	teaspoon ginger
1/2	teaspoon cinnamon
1/4	teaspoon nutmeg
1/4	teaspoon cloves
1	tablespoon molasses
	pinch of white pepper
1/4	cup coconut

Health benefit

Spicy ginger helps burn fat. Ginger's stimulant properties rev your metabolism to burn fat and calories faster.

Apricot Cobbler

Serves 8 to 10

5 to 6   cups apricots sliced
2 to 3 tablespoons tapioca
1   teaspoon cinnamon
2   tablespoons lemon juice
2/3   cup sugar (or to taste)
          pinch of salt

Topping

1/2   cup brown sugar
1/2   cup rolled oats
1/2   cup flour
1/2   teaspoon cinnamon or nutmeg
1/4   cup Marsala Olive Oil
          pinch of salt

     Blend well in mixing bowl until crumbly. Heat oven to 350 degrees. Lightly grease a 13x9x2 inch baking dish. Combine apricots and remaining ingredients into mixing bowl. Let stand 15 to 20 minutes to soften tapioca. Stir several times.

     Spoon apricot mixture into prepared dish. Bake for 20 minutes. Remove from oven, spread topping over fruit evenly.

     Bake another 10 to 12 minutes or until top is golden and fruit is bubbling.

     Serve warm or cool with sweetened whipped cream, low fat vanilla frozen yogurt or sauce of your choice.

Variation:

        Substitute one cup pineapple, crushed or tidbits for apricots
        apples with raisins or cranberries
        pears with cherries
        quince with apples
        plums and strawberries
        peaches and blueberries
        any fruit of your choice

> **Pop a few berries to prevent heart disease**
> All berries are high in soluble fiber – compounds that help reduce serum cholesterol, which can block your arteries.

Variation for topping:

1/3   cup walnut, ground (or nuts of your choice)
1/3   cup almond flour

Olive You!

Bite Size Gourmet Tidbits

Makes about 110

2	cups flour (preferably cake flour)
1/2	cup Marsala or Sciabica olive oil
1/4	cup water
3/4	teaspoon salt
2	teaspoons baking powder
1	egg
1/2	cup sesame or seeds of your choice

In mixing bowl add dry ingredients, make well in center. In measuring cup add olive oil and water, do not stir.

Pour olive oil and water in all at once. Add egg, stir with fork until dough holds together, knead lightly. Roll into a ball, refrigerate 1 hour.

On lightly floured surface, cut dough into four pieces. Shape into rolls 1-1/2 inch in diameter, Cut each roll into 1/2 inch pieces, roll into balls.

Place on lightly greased baking sheets 1 inch apart, flatten slightly. Moisten pieces with water (using a spray bottle) sprinkle with sesame seeds. Bake in a 350 degrees oven for 12 to 15 minutes or until golden.

Serve as cocktail snacks, with milk, ice coffee, tea or cocoa; croutons in salads or soups, with sweet or dry wine etc.

Chocolate Petite Tidbits

1/3	cup sugar
3	tablespoons molasses
2	tablespoons Marsala or Sciabica orange olive oil
1	egg
1/4	cup cocoa (Dutch)
1/2	teaspoon baking soda
1/4	teaspoon salt
1	cup flour
2	tablespoons milk
1/3	cup mint or white chocolate chips
1	teaspoon vanilla
1/2	teaspoon Danish pastry extract (Watkins)

> **Health benefit**
>
> Molasses is an excellent source of iron. Low iron intake often causes fatigue, especially in women

In mixing bowl add dry ingredients, make well in center. Add remaining ingredients blend, stir in chips, follow directions for gourmet tidbits.

Francesca's Gourmet Tidbits

Makes 125 to 130

3	cups almond flour
1	cup sugar
2	egg whites
1	teaspoon baking powder
1/2	teaspoon lemon oil (or flavoring of your choice)

Beat egg whites until frothy. Add 1/2 cup sugar gradually, beat until stiff peaks hold.

In mixing bowl add remaining sugar, almond flour, baking powder and lemon oil. Fold in beaten egg whites, dough is firm.

When well blended, chill in refrigerator covered for about 30 minutes.

Cut dough into 6 pieces. Shape into rolls about 1/2 inch in diameter. Cut each roll into 1/2 inch pieces, roll into balls.

Place on aluminum (Reynolds release) foil lined cookie sheets, 1/2 inch apart. Flatten slightly.

Bake in a 350 degrees oven for 12 minutes or until very pale golden. Do not over bake.

> ### Almonds keep skin looking young
> Almonds are packed with vitamin E, which not only keeps your heart healthy by maintaining arterial function, but fights free-radical damage to skin, so you look younger longer.

Lime Nut Gourmet Tidbits

Makes 80 to 90

1	teaspoon baking powder
1-1/3	cups flour
1/4	teaspoon salt
1/2	cup confectioners sugar
1/4	cup coconut
1/3	cup pistachio, pecans or nuts of your choice chopped small
1	egg
1/3	cup Marsala or Sciabica lemon olive oil
	grated peel of 1 lime, lemon or orange
1/2	teaspoon Danish pastry extract (Watkins)
1	teaspoon vanilla
	confectioners sugar for coating

Continued

Continued

In mixing bowl add dry ingredients, make well in center. Pour in olive oil, juice, egg and flavorings.

Stir until well blended. Chill dough in refrigerator, cover for about 30 minutes. On lightly floured surface cut dough in half. Roll out each piece to 1/4 inch in diameter.

Cut each roll into 1/2 inch pieces. Roll into little balls, place on cookie sheets lined with (Reynolds release) foil 1/2 inch apart. Flatten each slightly.

Bake in a 350 degrees oven for 12 minutes or until pale golden. Roll in confectioner's sugar while still warm.

To make tidbits, follow recipe for "bite size gourmet tidbits" and combine your favorite cheese, seeds, nuts, flavorings, herbs, dried fruits and vegetables. These tidbits are fun to make, either sweet or savory, both are flavorful.

Variations for dough:
Romano, Gruyere or cheese of your choice, shredded
garlic or onion minced
brown or maple sugar
pecans, cashew or nuts of your choice, finally chopped
jalapeno, habanero or any hot pepper, minced
cinnamon, nutmeg or any spice desired
chocolate, peanut butter, mint, or cappuccino chips
vanilla, raspberry, peach, mint, lime, lemon or flavoring of your choice
cocoa or instant coffee powder
wine, rum, brandy or liqueur desired
molasses or pepper jelly
honey or pure maple syrup
tabasco sauce
coconut
sesame, caraway, poppy or seeds of your choice

Health benefit

Keep your disposition sunny with dried apricots. These naturally sweet treats are high in magnesium, a mineral that helps ease mood swings and fight depression.

Amount of Flavorings For Dough
1/2	cup cheese
1 or 2	teaspoons herbs
1 or 2	tablespoons seeds
1 or 2	teaspoons flavorings
1/2	cup candried or dried fruits or vegetables, chopped small
1	tablespoon jalapeno, minced
1/4 to 1/2	cup sugars
1/3 to 1/2	cup chocolate chips
1 or 2	teaspoons spices
1/3	cup wine, molasses or any liquid, plus 2 to 4 tablespoons flour
1/3	cup cocoa
1/2	cup coconut
	Amounts may be changed to your liking.

Blueberry Strawberry Pudding Cake

2	cups blueberries
2	cups strawberries or raspberries
1/4	cup sugar
1	tablespoon lemon juice
1/4	teaspoon salt
4	eggs
1	cup sugar
1	cup flour
1	teaspoon baking powder
2	tablespoons Marsala olive Oil
1	teaspoon vanilla
	grated peel of 1 orange

Place fruit in bottom of a 9x13 inch greased glass baking dish, sprinkle with 1/4 cup sugar and lemon juice.

Mix and pour remaining ingredients over the fruit evenly.

Bake at 350 degrees for 45 to 50 minutes.

Cool and top with low fat vanilla ice cream or topping of your choice.

Photo by Arturo Acevedo
Our " Rocca Bella Olive Grove" of organically
grown olives. Over 100 years old. They were planted around 1888.

Sugar Cookies

Makes 50 to 60

2	eggs
1/2	cup Sciabica's orange olive oil
2	cups flour
2	teaspoons baking powder
1/2	teaspoon salt
3/4	cup sugar
1	teaspoon vanilla
1/2	teaspoon lemon oil
1/2	cup sugar to roll cookie dough in

Preheat oven to 375 degrees. Grease lightly cookie sheets (or use non stick cooking spray)

In mixing bowl and eggs, olive oil, sugar and flavorings, mix well.

Stir dry ingredients into egg mixture until well blended. Refrigerate covered for about 30 minutes.

Using a melon baller or teaspoon, dip in flour each time, drop dough into shallow bowl with sugar.

Roll dough all around in sugar, flatten slightly, place on prepared baking sheets 2 inches apart.

Bake cookies 10 to 16 minutes or until golden.

Variation:

> Coconut helps jump-start your metabolism
> Coconut is a good source of magnesium, a mineral that works in the thyroid to help regulate metabolism.

1/4	cup poppy seeds
1/3	cup dates, chopped
1/2	cup pecans, almonds or walnuts, finely chopped
1/4	cup molasses
1/4	cup coconut
1	teaspoon cinnamon or spice of your choice

When our dear friend Francesca saw these cookies she said they were perfect to make triffle.

Place cookies in a single layer over bottom of triffle bowl. Spread with raspberry jam, cover with prepared vanilla pudding and pie filling.

Top with sliced bananas, strawberries, peaches or fruit of your choice. Continue layering cookies, jam and pudding, filling bowl to 3/4 full.

Cover with sweetened whipped cream, sprinkle with sliced almonds and chocolate curls. Keep refrigerated until ready to serve.

Variation: sherry or rum, custard, candied fruit, nuts of your choice, grated chocolate, canned chestnut filling, chocolate hazelnut spread

Persimmon Snack Cake

Serves 12

1/2	cup pecans (or nuts of your choice) ground
3/4	cup sugar
1-1/2	cups flour
3/4	teaspoon baking powder
3/4	teaspoon baking soda
1/4	teaspoon salt
1/4	cup Marsala or Sciabica orange olive oil
3	eggs, large
1	teaspoon vanilla
1/2	teaspoon Danish pastry extract (Watkins)
1-1/2	cups persimmon, ripe, firm, diced (Fuyu)
	confectioner's sugar

Streusel

1	teaspoon cinnamon
1/4	cup flour
1/4	cup brown sugar
1/4	teaspoon salt
1/3	cup pecans, ground
2	tablespoons Marsala Olive Oil

Combine streusel ingredients in a small bowl, mix with finger tips until mixture is crumbly and holds together when pinched, set aside.

In another medium mixing bowl add dry ingredients. Make well in center , stir in remaining ingredients until well blended.

Grease a 10 inch baking pan, with removable bottom. Spoon half of batter into pan. Scatter half the fruit over evenly, pressing lightly into batter. Spoon remaining batter over fruit. Sprinkle with streusel evenly.

Bake in a 350 degrees oven for 40 to 50 minutes or until cake tester comes out clean from center. Place cake in it's pan on rack, cool. Sprinkle with confectioner's sugar just before serving.

Variation:

apples, pears, peaches or apricots, diced
cherries pitted, cranberries, raspberries or berries of your choice
bananas, firm, diced
pineapple, crushed, drained
add chocolate chips in streusel if desired

Continued

Note:

A friend gave me this recipe. It called for 1/2 pound animal fat, but I used 1/3 cup olive oil.

The streusel called for 3 tablespoons animal fat, I used 2 tablespoons of olive oil. It is lower in calories, cholesterol and surely just as delicious.

> ### Health benefit
> Cinnamon contains cinnamaldehyde, a volatile oil used by herbalists to combat the fatigue and listlessness that often accompany the flu.

Chocolate Chip Oatmeal Cookies

Makes about 30

1/3	cup Sciabica orange olive oil
1/3	cup brown sugar
1/3	cup sugar
1	egg, large
1	teaspoon vanilla
1/2	teaspoon Danish pastry extract (Watkins)
1	cup flour
3/4	cup quick – cooking oats, uncooked
1/2	cup chocolate chips
1/4	cup currants or raisins
1/4	teaspoon salt
1	teaspoon baking soda
1/4	cup orange juice or milk

Preheat oven to 375 degrees. Spray large cookie sheet with nonstick cooking spray. In mixing bowl mix olive oil, egg, sugars, flavoring and orange juice, stir to blend. Add flour, oats, baking soda and salt, stir until combined. Fold in chocolate chips and currants.

Drop by level tablespoon (or with a 1 inch ice cream scooper) 2 inches apart on to Reynolds aluminum (release) foil lined cookie sheet. Flatten slightly with water moistened tines of fork.

Bake 12 to 14 minutes or until golden brown. Cool on wire rack. Frost as desired.

> ### Health benefit
> Outsmart clots with chocolate. Everybody's favorite sweet contains flavonoids, which stop fatlike substances in the bloodstream.

Pumpkin Spice Bars

Makes 49

2	cups sugar
4	eggs
1/3	cup Marsala Olive Oil
1	can (16 ounces) pumpkin
2	cups flour
2	teaspoons baking powder
2	teaspoons cinnamon
1	teaspoon baking soda
3/4	teaspoon salt
1/2	teaspoon ginger
1/4	teaspoon cloves
1/2	cup raisins or currants
1/2	cup pecans or walnuts, chopped fine

Heat oven to 350 degrees. Grease jelly roll pan, 15-1/2 x 1-1/2 x 2 inch. Beat eggs, sugar, olive oil and pumpkin in mixing bowl.

Stir in dry ingredients. Mix in raisins and nuts. Pour batter into prepared pan\s.

Bake until golden brown, about 25 to 30 minutes, cool. Frost as desired, cut into bars, about 2 x 1-1/2 inches.

Ricotta Chocolate Cake

Serves 12

1	(1 pound 2.5 ounces) chocolate cake mix

Ricotta Filling

1-1/2	cups ricotta, low fat
2	eggs
1/4	cup sugar
1/2	teaspoon Danish pastry extract (Watkins)
1	teaspoon vanilla

In mixing bowl combine eggs, sugar, ricotta and flavorings, blend well.

Grease a 13x9x2 inch baking pan. Beat together cake mix ingredients according to package directions.

(Use only 1/4 cup Marsala Olive Oil instead of the 1/2 cup oil as stated on package) Pour into prepared pan, spoon ricotta mixture over top of cake batter evenly, do not stir.

Bake at 350 degrees for 1 hour and 15 minutes. Cool pan on wire rack, invert onto cake plate. Sprinkle with confectioner's sugar if desired.

Variation:

Stir in 1/4 cup amaretto liqueur or espresso coffee into cake batter.

Chocolate Carrot Cake

Makes 12 to 16 pieces

1	cup flour
3/4	cup sugar
3	tablespoons Marsala Olive Oil
1/4	cup orange juice (or milk)
1/4	cup cocoa (Dutch)
1	teaspoon baking soda
1/2	teaspoon salt
1/2	teaspoon cinnamon
1/4	teaspoon nutmeg
1.4	teaspoon clover
1/4	teaspoon vanilla
2	eggs
2-1/2	cups carrots, shredded
2	ounces coconut
	grated peel of 1 orange

In mixing bowl add dry ingredients. Make well in center.

Add olive oil, juice, vanilla, eggs and peel. Stir until blended.

Fold in coconut and carrots well.

Pour into greased 8 inch square baking pan.

Bake 30 to 35 minutes in a 350 degrees oven. Frost if desired.

Frosting

1/2   cup cappuccino, white, mint or chocolate chips

Remove cake from oven, sprinkle with chips, let stand about 3 to 5 minutes.

When chips have melted, spread top completely.

Variation:

spread with raspberry jam

> ## Health benefit
> Cocoa keeps your heart healthy. Flavonoids in this chocolate product have been shown to reduce the risk of high cholesterol and heart disease.

Potica

Makes 25 to 30 pieces

1	recipe for single olive oil pie crust (pg 266)
1	egg yolk
1/4	cup flour
2	tablespoons sugar
1/2	teaspoon Danish pastry extract (Watkins)

Filling:

1-1/4	cups walnuts or nuts of your choice, ground
1/2	cup raspberry, apricot or jam of your choice
1	teaspoon cinnamon (or to taste)
1	tablespoon Marsala or Sciabica orange olive oil

Make pie dough adding egg yolk, flour, sugar and extract. Cut dough into 2 pieces. Chill covered in refrigerator for about 20 minutes.

On lightly floured surface, roll dough out into an 8 by 10 inch piece.

In mixing bowl combine walnuts, jam, cinnamon and olive oil, blend.

Spread half of filling evenly over rolled out dough leaving 1/2 inch edge around uncovered.

Roll up jelly roll style from longer side. Place on greased baking sheet, seam side down, using a giant 10 x 12 inch aluminum spatula with acrylic handle. (Spatula is also ideal to use for moving pie crust). Repeat with second half of dough and remaining filling.

Bake in a 350 degrees oven for 15 to 20 minutes or until golden. Cool, cut with a serrated knife, into 3/4 inch pieces or desired size.

For savory potica; combine pesto sauce, ground walnuts and Romano cheese, grated.

Variation:

honey
raisins, dates, dried cherries or figs chopped
chocolate chips, coconut or candied chestnuts
poppy seeds or seeds of your choice
cloves, nutmeg or cardamom
rum, espresso powder
biscotti crumbs

Note:

Giant spatula may be purchased at King Arthur Flour call 1-800-827-6836

Glazed Pecans

Makes 2 cups

2   cups pecan halves (or nuts of your choice)
2   tablespoons Marsala Olive Oil
2   tablespoons sugar

Preheat oven to 325 degrees. Lightly oil baking sheet. In mixing bowl toss pecans with olive oil to coat. Mix in sugar, scatter coated pecans on prepared baking sheet.

Bake until pecans are golden brown, stirring occasionally, about 15 minutes. Careful not to over brown. Transfer baking sheet to wire rack, cool completely.

Variation:

1/4   teaspoon cayenne pepper
1/4   teaspoon salt
1/2   teaspoon rosemary (or herb of your choice)
1/2   teaspoon white pepper
1   teaspoon five spice powder
1/2   teaspoon cumin
1   teaspoon cinnamon

Preserved Lemons

6   lemons
6   tablespoons coarse sea salt
4 to 6 bay leaves
       sprigs of rosemary, basil, oregano (or herb of your choice)
1/4   cup cloves, whole
       Marsala Olive Oil

Slice lemons into thick slices (1/4 to 1/2 inch), remove any seeds. Layer in a large non-reactive bowl, sprinkle with sea salt on each layer.

Cover and refrigerate 3 days, tossing slices gently every day. Place in a large wide mouth canning jar, layer the lemon slices with herbs and cloves.

Pour any remaining juice over lemons and cover with oil, seal the jar.

Refrigerate one month before using. Serve with meats, fish or salads.

Variation: 6   tablespoons sugar

Note: Lemons may be cut into wedges

Sweet Tarallini

Makes about 40

1/2	cup Marsala or Sciabica olive oil
1/2	cup vermouth or any sweet wine
1/4	cup sugar
1-3/4 cup to 2 cups flour	
1	tablespoon anise or fennel seeds
1	teaspoon baking powder
1/2	teaspoon salt

Preheat oven to 350 degrees. Line cookie sheet with "Reynolds release" non stick aluminum foil.

In mixing bowl stir olive oil and vermouth together. Add sugar and remaining ingredients, work until dough holds together.

On lightly floured surface knead dough until smooth. It will be soft but not sticky. Cut dough into 40 pieces.

Roll into 4 to 5 inches long and the diameter of a pencil. Form into a ring, press ends together. Place on cookie sheet 1/2 inch apart.

Bake about 20 to 25 minutes or until golden brown, cool, store in airtight tin.

Flavor with orange, lemon or vanilla extract and sprinkle with confectioners sugar if desired.

Savory Tarallini

Makes about 40

1/2	cup Marsala or Sciabica olive oil
1/2	cup vermouth or any sweet wine
1	teaspoon pepper, white
1-3/4 cup to 2 cups flour	
1	teaspoon baking powder
1	teaspoon salt
1/3	cup Romano cheese, grated
1	tablespoon dried tomatoes or olives, minced
1	tablespoon caraway, poppy or anise seeds

Follow directions for sweet taralli.

All Purpose Crepe Batter

Makes 20 to 24

2	cups flour
2-1/4	cups milk
4	eggs
1/4	teaspoon salt
1/4	cup Marsala or Sciabica Olive Oil

With electric mixer or blender combine all ingredients. Beat or blend until smooth for 1 minute. Scrape down sides with rubber spatula and blend another 15 seconds.

Heat a 6 or 7 inch nonstick skillet, brush with olive oil. Pour in 2 tablespoons batter, tilting pan to spread evenly. Cook until golden on both sides. Repeat with remaining batter.

Serve with fruits, jam, ice cream, puddings or filling of your choice.

Savory Whole Wheat Crepes

Makes 20 to 22

4	eggs
1	cup flour
1/2	cup whole wheat flour (or garbanzo flour)
1-1/2	cups milk, non fat
1/2	teaspoon salt
2	tablespoons Marsala or Sciabica Olive Oil
1	tablespoon wheat germ

Follow directions for all purpose crepes.

Serve with grilled meats, fish or vegetables of your choice.

Variation for filling:

ravioli filling
chicken or ham ala king
spinach, cheese, seafood
bean, tamale or taco filling
sloppy Joe filling
caponata
caramelized onions with blue cheese

Continued

Cornmeal Crepes

Makes 12 to 14

3/4	cup flour
1/2	cup cornmeal (or buckwheat)
1/4	teaspoon salt
1-1/4	cups milk, non fat
3	eggs
2	tablespoons Marsala or Sciabica Olive Oil

Follow directions for all purpose crepes, fill with your favorite savory filling.

Chocolate Crepes

Makes 20

4	eggs
1	cup flour
1	cup milk, nonfat
1/2	teaspoon salt
2	tablespoons sugar
3	tablespoons cocoa (Dutch)
1	teaspoon vanilla

Follow directions for all purpose crepes. Fill with sweetened cheese, cream, fruits, jams, pudding etc. Drizzle with honey or pure maple syrup.

Crepe Purses

1	all purpose crepe recipe
2	cups of your favorite filling

Mound 1/4 to 1/3 cup filling in center of each crepe. Gather edges over filling.

Tie purses loosely with blanched strip of leek or scallion.

Place in lightly greased baking dish. Top with tomato gravy, bachamel, seafood, meat sauce or topping of your choice.

Bake in a 350 degrees oven for about 20 minutes.

Continued

Lorraine Crepes

Makes 12

12	crepes, cooked
1	cup Cheddar or Swiss cheese shredded
4	slices Canadian lean bacon, chopped
1	tablespoon corn starch
1/4	teaspoon salt
1/4	teaspoon pepper, white
2	eggs, beaten
1	cup milk, non fat
	pinch of nutmeg

Line 12 greased muffin cups with cooked crepes. Sprinkle evenly with bacon, top with cheese.

Mix corn starch, salt, pepper, nutmeg, eggs and milk, pour over cheese. Bake in a 350 degrees oven for about 15 minutes or until firm. Cool 5 minutes, serve warm.

Note:

For sweet crepes add 2 tablespoons sugar, 1/2 teaspoon cinnamon or nutmeg.

Crepes may be stacked with filling in between; folded over, rolled up, burrito roll, pocket fold etc.

Dessert Crepes

Makes about 16

3	eggs
1	cup milk
2	tablespoons Marsala Olive Oil
3/4	cup flour
2	tablespoons sugar
1/2	teaspoon salt

In jar of blender add all ingredients, blend until smooth.

Heat a 6 or 7 inch non stick skillet, brush with olive oil.

Pour in 2 tablespoons batter, tilting pan to spread. Cook until golden on both sides.

Repeat with remaining batter. Serve with fruits, sauces or your favorite filling.

Blueberry Pie

Serves 8

1	olive oil pastry for 9 inch pie plate
6	cups blueberries
2/3	cup sugar (or to taste)
1/4	cup tapioca or corn starch
2	tablespoons lemon juice
1/2	teaspoon cinnamon, if desired

In mixing bowl combine blueberries and remaining ingredients. Let stand about 15 minutes, toss gently several times to soften tapioca.

Fit pastry into pie plate, fill with blueberry mixture. Roll out remaining dough into a 9 inch circle.

With fluted pastry wheel, cut into 1/2 inch strips (set aside three). Place strips over filling, pressing ends into bottom dough edge.

Roll up three strips, arrange in center. Bake 10 minutes in a 400 degrees oven, reduce heat to 350 degrees, bake about 50 minutes or until filling is bubbly and crust is golden. Cover loosely with foil if browning too quickly.

Lower "bad" cholesterol levels with olive oil.

Research shows that regular consumption of olive oil reduces the amount of bad (LDL) cholesterol in the body.

Peach Shortcake

Makes 8 (12 smaller)

1-1/2	cups flour
1/2	cup corn meal (fine)
1/4	cup brown sugar
1	tablespoon baking powder
1/2	teaspoon salt
1/2	cup Marsala or Sciabica olive oil
1/2 to 2/3	cup milk, non fat
1	egg yolk (or 1 egg white)
1/2	teaspoon lemon or orange oil extract
	grated peel of 1 lemon or orange

Preheat oven to 375 degrees. Lightly grease baking sheet.

In mixing bowl add dry ingredients. Make well in center. Pour in milk and remaining ingredients.

Stir until just evenly moistened. Drop by 1/3 or 1/4 cup full on prepared baking sheet, 1-1/2 inches apart.

Bake for 15 to 18 minutes until deep golden or until cake tester comes out clean, cool.

Using a serrated knife, cut each biscuit in half horizontally.

Place bottom half on plate, spoon peaches and juice onto each biscuit evenly. Spoon on a little cream.

Cover with top half of biscuit, spoon on a few more peaches and a dollop of cream.

Peach Filling

2	pounds peaches, sliced
1/3	cup brown sugar
1	tablespoon lemon or orange juice

Mix in bowl, let stand about 15 minutes, toss gently once or twice.

Cream Topping

1	cup whipping cream
2	tablespoons confectioner's sugar
1	tablespoon brown sugar (or honey)
1	teaspoon vanilla (or 1 tablespoon rum)

Using an electric mixer, beat cream, sugars and vanilla until peaks form.

Limoncello Cooler

1   glass filled with finely crushed ice
3   ounces club soda
1-1/2 ounces limoncello liqueur
      Serve with a straw

Vanilla Cream cooler

2   ounces vanilla ice cream, low fat
1-1/2 ounces frangelico liqueur
1   ounce rum
1   ounce cream liqueur

Combine all ingredients in jar of blender, blend. Pour over glass filled with crushed ice.

> ### Health benefit
> Just one cup of ice cream contains 176 mg of calcium, which is 17% of the RDA for women ages 18-49 and helps regulate blood pressure.

Mango Ginger Colada

1-1/2 ounces ginger liqueur
1-1/2 tablespoons cream of coconut
1   ounce mango juice
5 to 6 ice cubes
1   mango wedge

Combine all ingredients (except mango wedge) in jar of blender; blend.

Process until smooth and frothy. Pour into chilled glass. Garnish with mango wedge (on rim of glass). Serve with straw.

> ### Health benefit
> Stop coughing with mangos. These exotic fruits are a great source of beta-carotene, a nutrient shown to reduce the effects of asthma.

Ginger Lemon Honey Tea

Makes about 2-1/3 cups

2	cups water
10	thin slices gingerroot, fresh
1	lemon sliced
3	tablespoons honey (or to taste)
1/3	cup lemon juice

Bring water, gingerroot and lemon slices to a boil for 1 or 2 minutes.

Remove from heat, steep 10 minutes, strain. Stir in honey and lemon juice.

Mom would make this tea whenever we came down with a cold. Sometimes she added apple peeling, a piece of onion and one or two tablespoons of chamomile.

Poached Quince

2	cups port or any sweet wine
1-1/2	cups sugar (or to taste)
1	cup water
2	bay leaves (remove before serving)
1/4	teaspoon cloves
1/2	teaspoon cinnamon
1/4	teaspoon allspice
	juice of lime or lemon
	grated peel of 1 orange
	6 to 8 cups quince, quartered

In saucepan, combine all the above ingredients, cover. Bring to a boil, lower to simmer for about 2 hours or until syrupy.

Serve warm or cold over cakes, ice cream, rice toast, bread pudding etc.

Sangria Blanco

Serves 8 to 10

1	quart white wine
1	quart club soda
2	cups orange juice
1	orange sliced thin
1	lemon sliced thin
1	lime sliced thin
2	sliced peaches or fruits of your choice
	crushed ice

In large pitcher pour in liquids, add fruits, refrigerate until ready to serve. Pour over crushed ice.

Variation:

cognac
pineapple juice or juice of your choice

Quantities to Serve 100 People

Coffee .... 3 lbs.
Loaf Sugar .... 3 lbs.
Cream .... 3 quarts
Whipping Cream .... 4pts.
Milk .... 6 gallons
Fruit Cocktail .... 2-1/2 gallons
Fruit Juice .... 4 no. 10 cans (26 lbs.)
Tomato Juice .... 4 no. 10 cans (26 lbs.)
Soup .... 5 gallons
Oysters .... 18 quarts
Weiners .... 25 lbs.
Meat Loaf .... 24 lbs.
Ham .... 40 lbs
Beef .... 40 lbs.
Roast Pork .... 40 lbs.
Hamburger .... 30-36 lbs.
Scalloped Potatoes .... 5 gallons
Vegetables .... 4 no.10 cans (26 lbs.)
Baked Beans .... 5 gallons
Beets .... 30 lbs.
Cauliflower .... 18 lbs.
Cabbage for Slaw .... 20 lbs.
Carrots .... 33 lbs.
Rolls 200
Potatoes .... 40 lbs.
Potato Salad .... 12 quarts
Fruit Salad .... 20 quarts
Vegetable Salad .... 20 quarts
Lettuce .... 20 heads
Salad Dressing .... 3 quarts
Pies 18
Cakes 8
Ice Cream .... 4 gallons
Cheese .... 3 lbs.
Olives .... 1-3/4 lbs.
Pickles .... 2 quarts
Nuts .... 3 lbs. sorted
Spaghetti .... 5 gallons
Tea .... 1/3 pound and 6 gallons water
Bread .... 200 slices or 12 - 1 pound loaves
Turkey or Chicken .... 50 to 70 pounds
Lemonade .... 40 to 60 lemons & 6 gallons water
Watermelon .... 150 pounds

To serve 50 people, divide by 2. To serve 25 people, divide by 4.

Measurements & Substitutions

Measurements

a pinch	1/8 teaspoon or less
3 teaspoons	1 tablespoon
4 tablespoons	1/4 cup
8 tablespoons	1/2 cup
12 tablespoons	3/4 cup
16 tablespoons	1 cup
2 cups	1 pint
4 cups	1 quart
4 quarts	1 gallon
8 quarts	1 peck
4 pecks	1 bushel
16 ounces	1 pound
32 ounces	1 quart
8 ounces liquid	1 cup
1 ounce liquid	2 tablespoons

For liquid and dry measurements use standard measuring spoons and cups. All measurements are level.

Substitutions

Ingredient	Quantity	Substitute
self-rising flour	1 cup	1 cup all-purpose flour, 1/2 tsp. salt, and 1 tsp. baking powder
cornstarch	1 tablespoon	2 T. flour or 2 tsp. quick-cooking tapioca
baking powder	1 teaspoon	1/4 tsp. baking soda plus 1/2 tsp. cream of tartar
powdered sugar	1 cup	1 c. granulated sugar plus 1 tsp. cornstarch
brown sugar	1/2 cup	2 T. molasses in 1/2 c. granulated sugar
sour milk	1 cup	1 T. lemon juice or vinegar plus sweet milk to make 1 c. (let stand 5 minutes)
whole milk	1 cup	1/2 c. evaporated milk plus 1/2 c. water
cracker crumbs	3/4 cup	1 c. bread crumbs
chocolate	1 square (1oz.)	3 or 4 T. cocoa plus 1 T. olive oil
fresh herbs	1 tablespoon	1 tsp. dried herbs
fresh onion	1 small	1 T. instant minced onion, rehydrated
dry mustard	1 teaspoon	1 T. prepared mustard
tomato juice	1 cup	1/2 c. tomato sauce plus 1/2 c. water
catsup or chili sauce	1 cup	1 c. tomato sauce plus 1/2 c. sugar and 2 T. vinegar (for use in cooking)

Index